IMAGES
of Rail

LARAMIE RAILROADS

On the Cover: The M-10004 was the first of four trains in a series. They were nicknamed "the Chevy" for the prominent grill. The photograph shows train No. 102, the eastbound train for the *City of San Francisco* line. Train No. 101 followed the same route west. (Photograph by R.H. Kindig; A.J. Wolff Collection.)

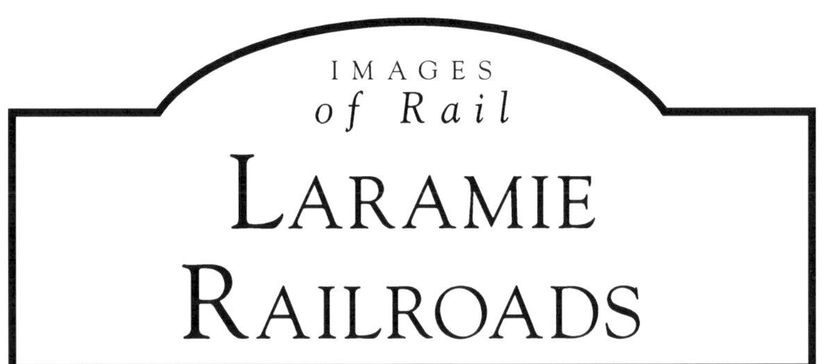

Lawrence Ostresh and Jerry Hansen

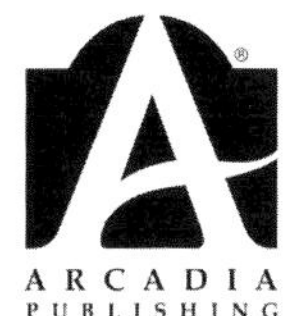

ISBN 978-1-4671-3083-7

Published by Arcadia Publishing
Charleston, South Carolina

Printed in the United States of America

Library of Congress Control Number: 2014934337

For all general information, please contact Arcadia Publishing:
Telephone 843-853-2070
Fax 843-853-0044
E-mail sales@arcadiapublishing.com
For customer service and orders:
Toll-Free 1-888-313-2665

Visit us on the Internet at www.arcadiapublishing.com

This book is dedicated to the railroaders and families of railroaders who helped build and grow the town of Laramie, Wyoming.

Contents

ACKNOWLEDGMENTS

The authors would like to thank all of the people and organizations who were generous enough to donate photographs, and the stories behind them, from various collections. We would particularly like to thank our two biggest contributors, James L. Ehernberger and A.J. Wolff. We would also like to thank the staff of the Laramie Plains Museum. Thanks also to Ann Brande, from Ludwig Photography, who not only allowed us access to her great-great-grandfather's collection but also offered us her technical expertise and the use of her photographic facilities. Finally, we would like to thank Erik Ostresh, who helped assemble much of this book.

The following photograph collections appear as abbreviations and in shortened form in courtesy lines: Jerry Hansen Collection (JHC); James L. Ehernberger Collection (JLEC); A.J. Wolff Collection (AJWC); Laramie Plains Museum Collection (LPM); and Beinecke Rare Book and Manuscript Library, Yale University (Beinecke). Where the name of the photographer or artist is not listed, the identity has not been determined.

INTRODUCTION

I grew up in Laramie, Wyoming, the son of a University of Wyoming geography professor and dedicated railfan. When my father, Lawrence Ostresh Jr., requested my help in what turned out to be his last book, I was honored in the way most sons are when their fathers enlist their help on an important project. However, I did not anticipate how engaging the story of Laramie's railroading past would be. I knew my hometown only as a quaint college town.

Laramie is locally known for its historic Western downtown and its university, with juxtaposed rough and smooth sandstone architecture. The residential neighborhoods are shaded and protected from the sun and the winds by tall spruce and cottonwood trees that have been there "forever." Of course, rationally, I knew that there was more to my home than that. Someone had laid the foundations of that historic downtown. Someone had quarried the stone that built the University of Wyoming. And someone had planted the seeds for those trees that shaded our summers and quieted the winter winds. And then there were the town relics, reminders that all progress has a price. Foundations and stone walls to buildings long abandoned still stood when I was young. A giant smokestack, still one of the tallest structures in town, went nowhere. Finally, most vivid of all from my childhood memories, a derelict steam locomotive sat quietly, rusting away in our local LaBonte Park.

As I began helping my father write this book, I soon discovered the truth of those relics. There was a story behind each one. And for each story behind a local ruin, there are half a dozen more stories that had only pictures as proof. With each new story came a new appreciation for my hometown. Laramie had not always been a college town. In fact, I learned that it was not until the 1950s and 1960s that the university rose to become the primary economic engine of the town. It shared those honors with the Union Pacific Railroad. The further back in time I went, the less significant the university was and the more prominent the railroad became. Tracing the town all the way back to its beginnings reveals that Laramie was indeed a railroad town.

The Laramie Valley had been known to trappers since the early decades of the 19th century. Indeed, the city took the name of one of the first mountain men in the area, Jaques LaRamie. That being the case, the first official interest in the area came at the height of Manifest Destiny, when a survey was sent through the area to look for potential routes for railroads. The real show began in 1868, when the Transcontinental Railroad finally arrived. From that moment, the story of Laramie blossomed.

Because of Laramie's geographical location, it became one of the two most important cities along the Union Pacific portion of the original Transcontinental Railroad. A natural feature between the future cities of Laramie and Cheyenne, called the "Gangplank," allowed access from the plains of the Great Basin into the Rocky Mountains. Laramie's location as the first major stop after locomotives made the climb into the Rockies slated it for several key railroad industries that would become the early backbone of the local economy.

The early rail industries continued to flourish throughout the latter half of the 1800s and into the early 1900s. In this era, prior to modern fire codes, labor laws, and safety standards, Laramie's industrial progress came at a high price. Fires and explosions abounded during this time, and the eventual demise of many of these industries was directly linked to industrial accidents. One of Laramie's biggest industries, the rolling mill, had burned several times until, finally, an explosion caused a fire that completely destroyed the building. Heavy industry was not the only victim of these calamities. In an era of steam locomotives, embers from the engines were a constant threat to buildings and houses near the tracks. The Thornburg Hotel, a building that acted as both the first hotel and the first train depot, was destroyed by fire in 1917. In addition to industrial accidents, weather, as any local resident can attest, has been a continual challenge. In particular, the blizzards of 1888, 1917, and 1948 were each powerful enough not only to stop traffic along the mainline but also to alter Union Pacific policies and operating procedures.

The final contributing characters to the story of Laramie's railroading past were the local train lines, two of which headed away from the Union Pacific mainline and ventured into the county and beyond. The first, a small line only about eight miles in length, ventured out to local gypsum quarries to ferry raw materials to the cement plant. The other headed all the way up the local "Snowy Range" mountains to a coal seam. Along the way, it serviced a few local timber communities. This line changed names and owners many times over the years, but it is most commonly referred to as the Coalmont branch, the title conferred on it by the Union Pacific during its possession of the line.

It is from the Coalmont branch that Laramie acquired my own personal favorite relic: a little steam locomotive that once sat sadly rusting away. That engine was the 535, built over 100 years ago to lead timber trains in Oregon. It was purchased and used along the Coalmont branch by the Laramie North Park & Western Railroad and then by the Union Pacific Railroad (UP). The 535 was, in a way, the real-life "Little Engine that Could," as it hauled mixed freight and passenger trains up and down the mountains. Later in its operational life, the UP put it to use as a switcher engine in the rail yards. It was finally retired and placed on display.

In recent years, the Historic Laramie Railroad Depot Association, with my father as one of the driving forces, has gone to great lengths to rescue and repair the 535. It has now been moved and placed on display next to Laramie's depot, along with a restored caboose, crew bunk car, and a wedge snowplow. No longer a derelict relic that I recall from my childhood, it now sits as a proud reminder of the history of Laramie and the railroads that built the town.

—Erik Ostresh

One

1868

Transcontinental Railroad and the Beginning of Laramie City

On July 1, 1862, Pres. Abraham Lincoln signed the Pacific Railway Act. This law created the Union Pacific Railroad and authorized government loans and land grants to aid in the construction of the nation's first transcontinental railroad, which would connect Omaha, Nebraska, to Sacramento, California. As the Union Pacific raced west across prairies, mountains, and basins in 1867 and 1868, the Territory of Wyoming and many of its southern towns and cities were founded, including Laramie. In 1869, the Union Pacific met the Central Pacific at Promontory Summit, Utah, and the Transcontinental Railroad was complete. This is the story of the railroads of Laramie, a fabled place along the Union Pacific's overland route.

The Laramie Valley had been known by trappers and fur traders from the early 1800s. The first mention of it in reference to a possible railroad was when Capt. Howard Stansbury led one of the first surveying expeditions to Utah between 1849 and 1851. Along his route, he stumbled upon the Laramie Valley and shared a rather cordial campsite with a local Indian chief whose name, when translated into English, was Buffalo Dung. Years later, Gen. Grenville Dodge discovered a natural causeway between the Great Plains and the Rocky Mountains. This causeway, nicknamed the "Gangplank" and situated between the future cities of Laramie and Cheyenne, made the settlements of those two cities necessary for the completion of the Transcontinental Railroad.

Laramie began as one of the most violent of the "Hell on Wheels" tent cities. Steve Long, the city's first marshal, recruited a small band of corrupt deputies who then began to rob, waylay, and sometimes murder their way into settlers' money and land holdings. N.K. Boswell, a frustrated landowner turned county sheriff, helped organize a vigilance committee, which eventually lynched Long and his associates. With the election of Boswell as sheriff, Laramie quickly settled down to become the relatively quiet town that it remains today.

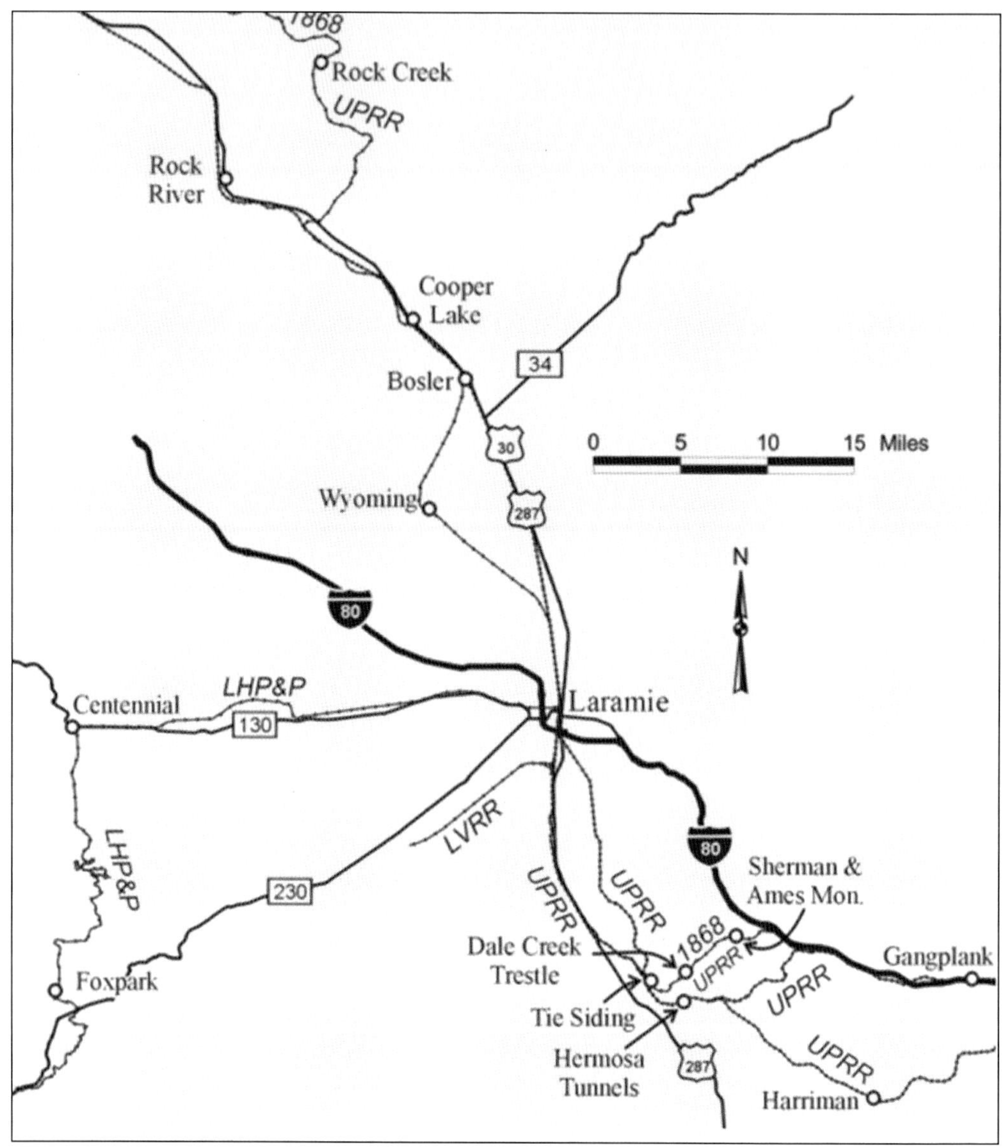

This map shows the major railroad lines throughout Albany County over the years. Most of the major roads in the county would follow close to the routes selected by various railroad surveyors in the 19th and early 20th centuries. (Map by Lawrence Ostresh Jr., Lawrence Ostresh Jr. Collection.)

Gen. Grenville Dodge was a railroad surveyor turned Civil War general who resigned his commission to become the chief engineer of the Union Pacific Railroad. On September 21, 1865, he discovered a key geologic structure that provided an easy route for the Transcontinental Railroad from the Great Plains across the Rocky Mountains. (Photograph by Matthew Brady; US National Archives.)

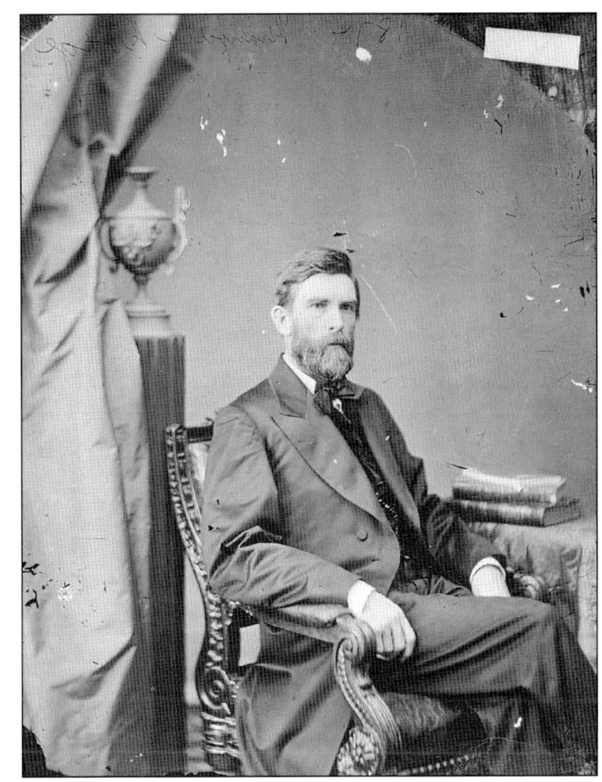

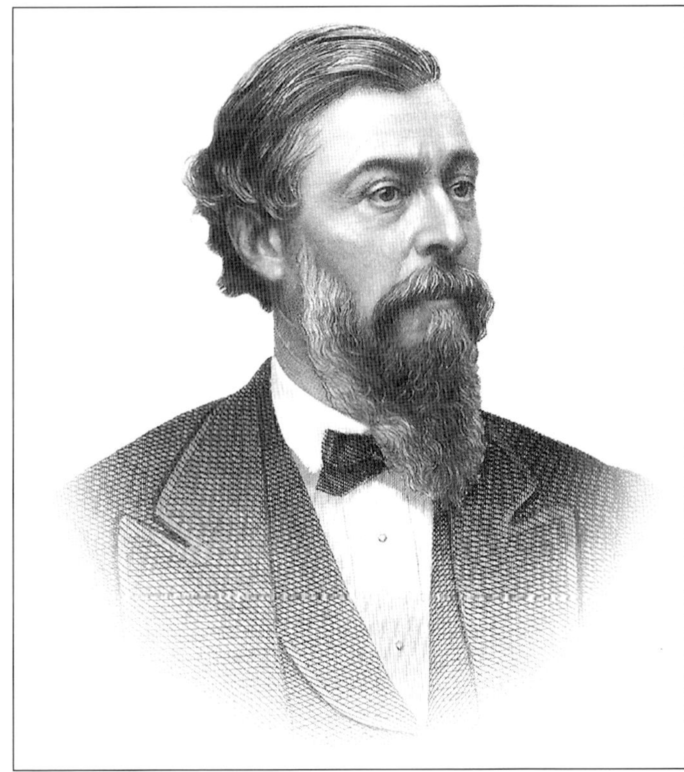

Dr. Thomas Clark Durant was a medical doctor turned railroad promoter and financier. The vice president of the Union Pacific during its construction years, he often clashed with Dodge as he attempted to change Dodge's planned route for the railroad. Durant is shown here sometime between 1865 and 1870. (Engraving by Robert O'Brien, based on a photograph by Matthew Brady; US National Archives.)

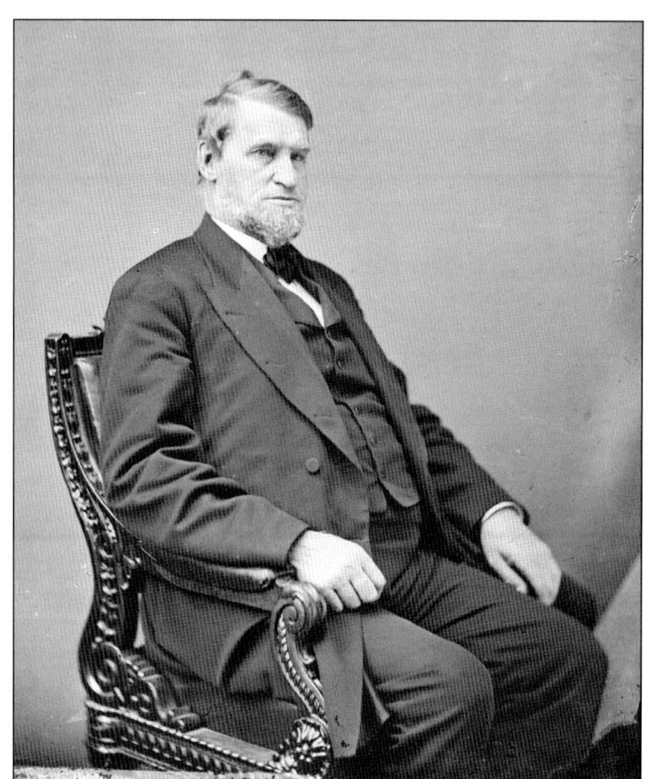

Congressman Oakes Ames was a member of the US House of Representatives from Massachusetts's 2nd District. In 1865, Pres. Abraham Lincoln requested he take a leading role in the Union Pacific Railroad, the construction of which had stalled. Ames, seen here around 1872, is honored as one of the leading personalities behind the construction of the Transcontinental Railroad, although he was later embroiled in the Credit Mobilier Scandal. (Photograph by Matthew Brady; US National Archives.)

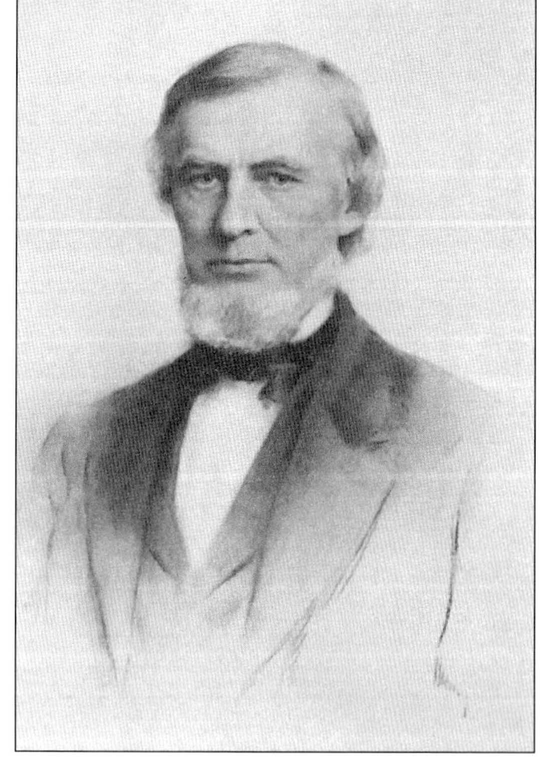

Oakes Ames's brother Oliver Ames, a bright, skillful manager and meticulous bookkeeper, was the president of the Union Pacific Railroad from 1866 to 1871, its major construction years. Along with his brother, Oliver, seen here around 1869, is commemorated on the Ames Monument (see page 32). (Anna Lee Ames Frolich Collection.)

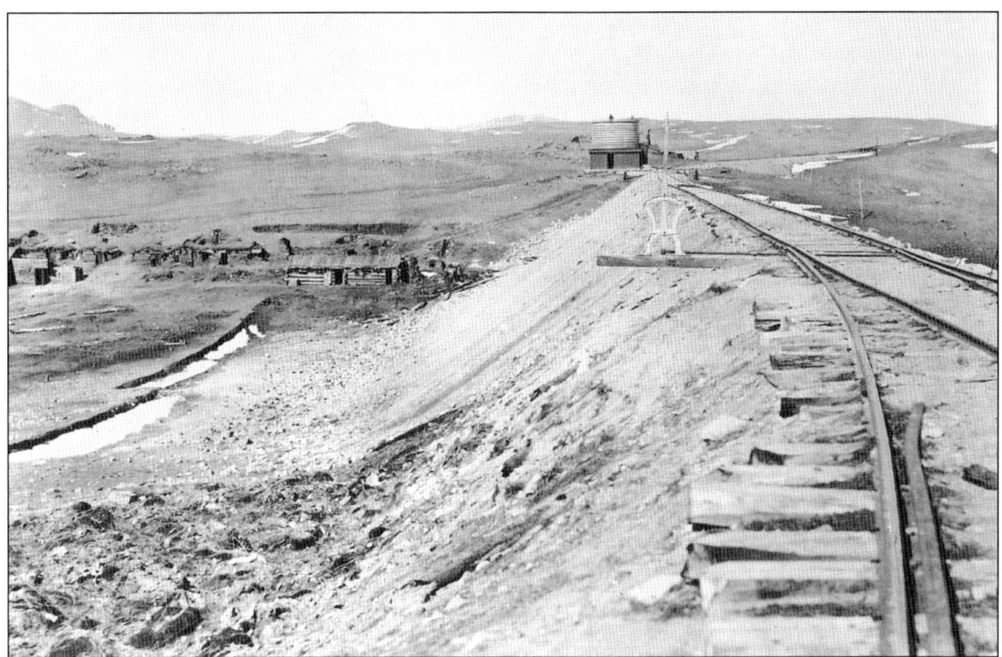

The "Gangplank" was the key geologic feature that General Dodge discovered in 1865. At this location, the Great Plains rise and the Rocky Mountains descend, meeting at the same elevation and providing an easy passage into the mountains. In this west-facing image from 1868, the plains are behind the photographer, and the Rockies present a relatively flat surface ahead. (Photograph by A.J. Russell; JLEC.)

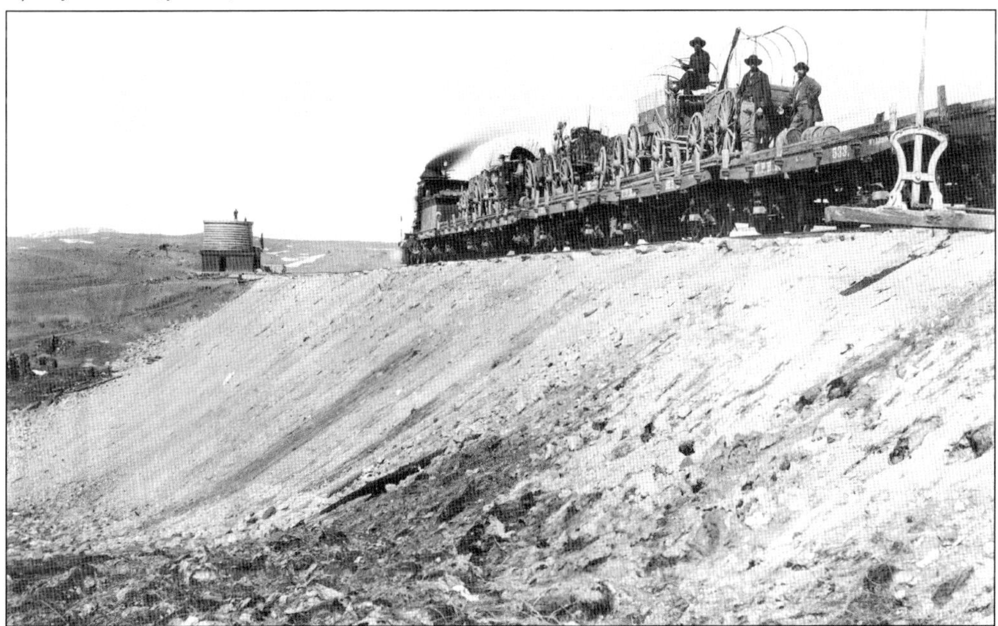

The route over the Gangplank was not without its difficulties. The large fill shown here had to be constructed just west of the point of contact of the plains and mountains. The fill still exists today at the Harriman exit (342) on Interstate 80 and looks very much as it does in this 1868 photograph. (Photograph by A.J. Russell; Beinecke.)

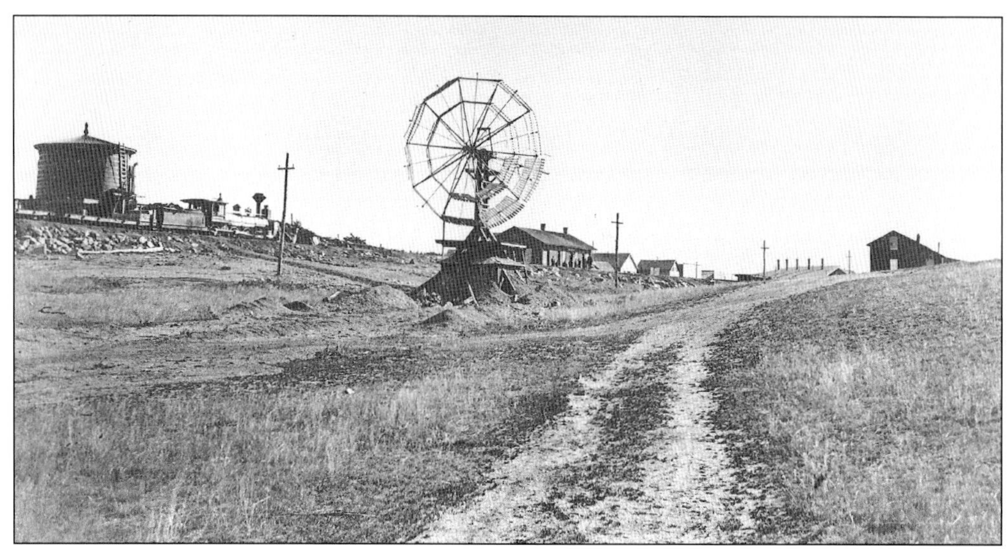

The town of Sherman, Wyoming, was built at the highest point of the Transcontinental Railroad (8,247 feet). The railroad route crosses over the Laramie Mountains and is known as "Sherman Hill." Steep grades over the hill required helper engines during the time of steam locomotion. The windmill pumps water for the tank (left) in this 1870 photograph. (Photograph by W.H. Jackson; JLEC.)

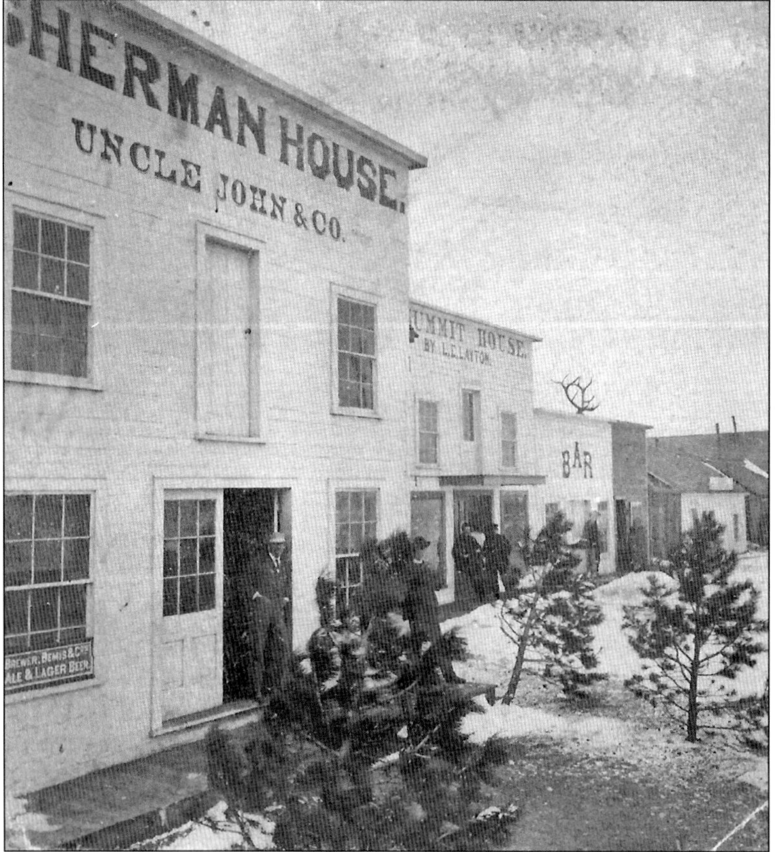

Sherman was located midway between Cheyenne and Laramie. Though small, the town was critical for tending to the locomotives as they made the difficult climb up the Rocky Mountains. In its most prosperous era, Sherman had a water tower, a five-stall roundhouse and turntable, a tannery, a sawmill, several bars and eating houses, and about 200 residents. This photograph was taken around 1870. (JLEC.)

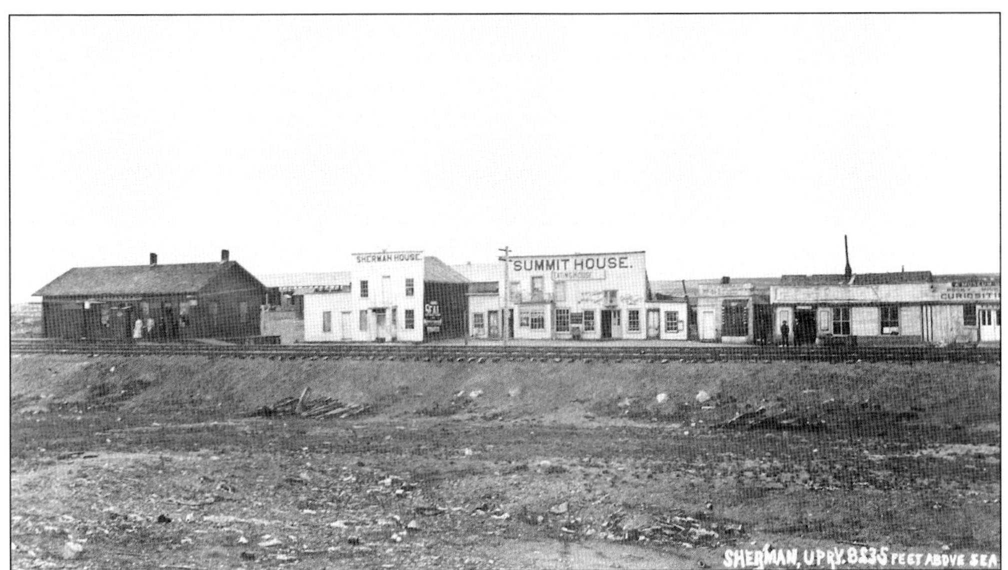

The Sherman train station is seen at left around 1870. The Sherman House and the Summit House, two eating establishments, are seen at center. Meals were not regularly served on trains until the 1880s; in the early years, passengers disembarked at stations for their sustenance. (Photograph by C.R. Savage; JLEC.)

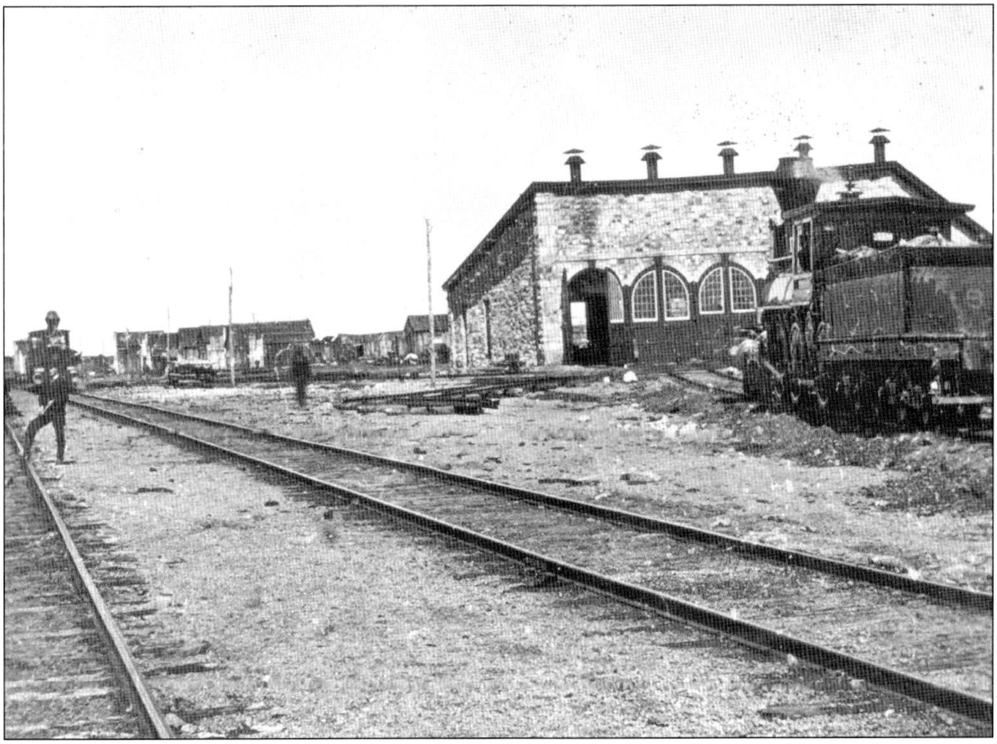

The five-stall Sherman roundhouse can be seen here as a locomotive heads for its berth in 1869. Today, Sherman is a ghost town, and no structures remain. However, the foundation for the roundhouse is still plainly visible (it can be found on Google maps), as is the turntable pit. (Photograph by A.C. Hull; US Geological Survey Collection.)

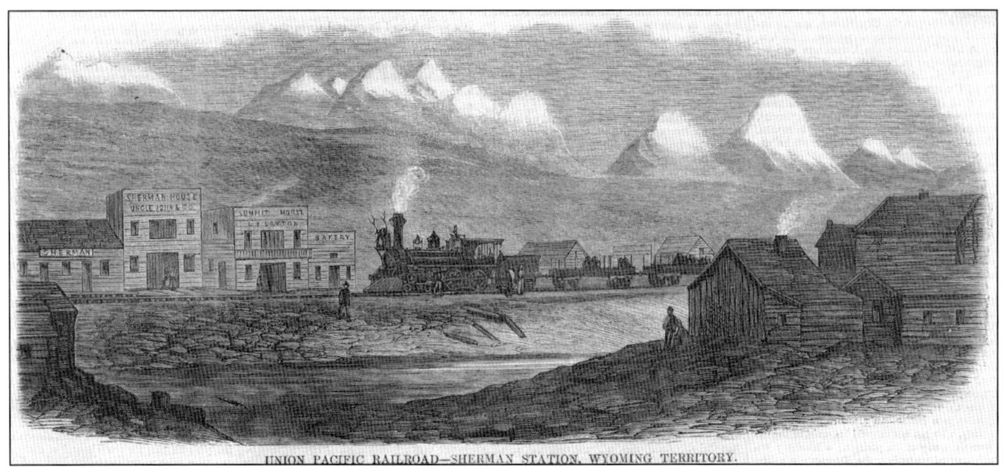

UNION PACIFIC RAILROAD—SHERMAN STATION, WYOMING TERRITORY.

This sketch of the town of Sherman appeared in *Harper's Weekly* in 1869. The mountains in the background (Pole Mountain, Turtle Rock, and Vedauwoo) have been highly exaggerated. Note the set of antlers strapped to the front of the locomotive. This was apparently a common way to decorate an engine in the 1860s and 1870s (see page 30). (Beinecke.)

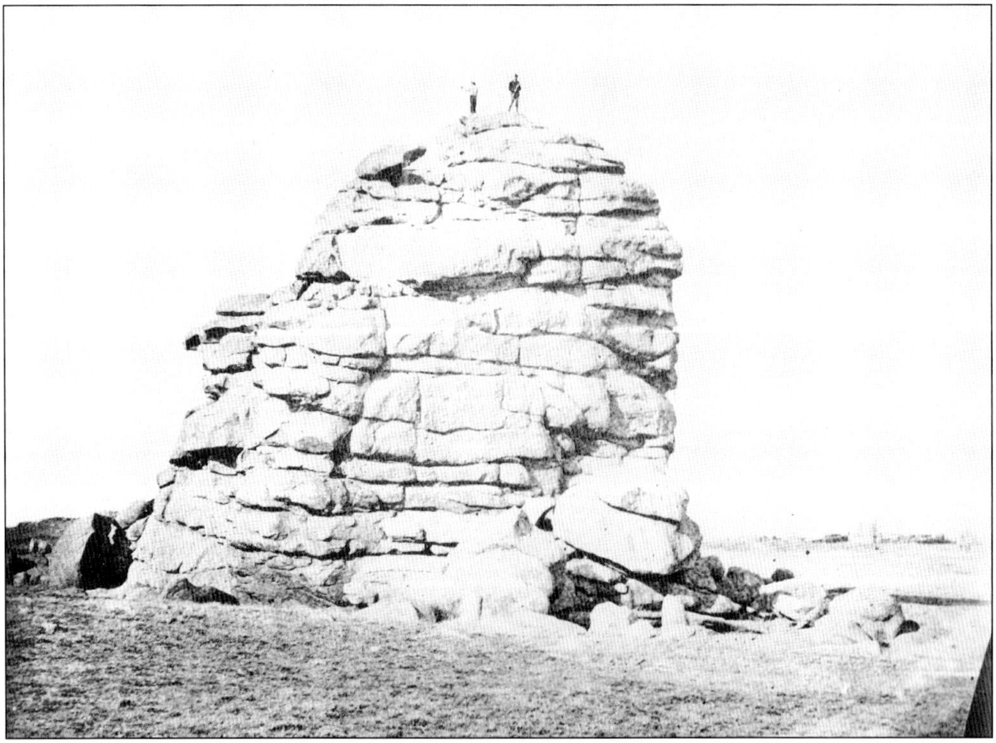

Reeds Rock was an outcropping a half-mile west of Sherman. A few years after this 1868 photograph was taken, it would become the major source of stone for Ames Monument (see pages 32 and 33). It was named for Samuel Reed, engineer of construction and superintendent of operations for the Union Pacific during the construction years. (Photograph by A.J. Russell; Beinecke.)

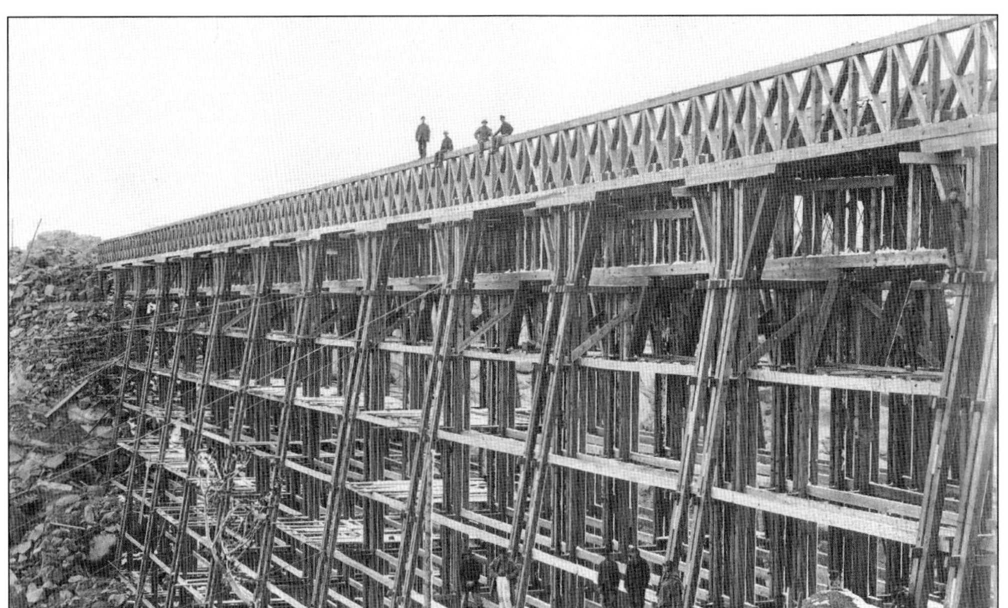

If discovering the Gangplank was the lucky break that made the Laramie-to-Cheyenne route along the Transcontinental Railroad possible, then the Dale Creek Trestle became the biggest technological hurdle. This photograph shows the original bridge during construction in March 1868. Many of these early photographs show daredevils perched precariously on the bridge. (Photograph by A.J. Russell; Beinecke.)

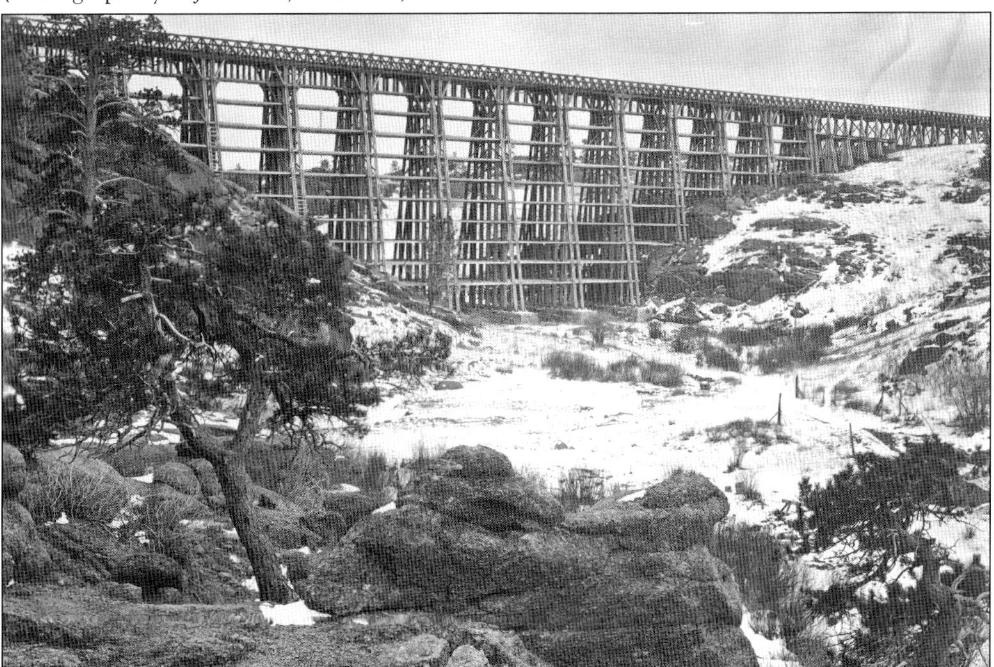

This photograph shows the Dale Creek Trestle after its completion in April 1868. At 708 feet long and 125 feet high, it was the biggest bridge along the original Transcontinental Railroad. It was built by L.B. Boomer Bridge Works of Chicago, Illinois, for $200,000. (Photograph by A.J. Russell; Beinecke.)

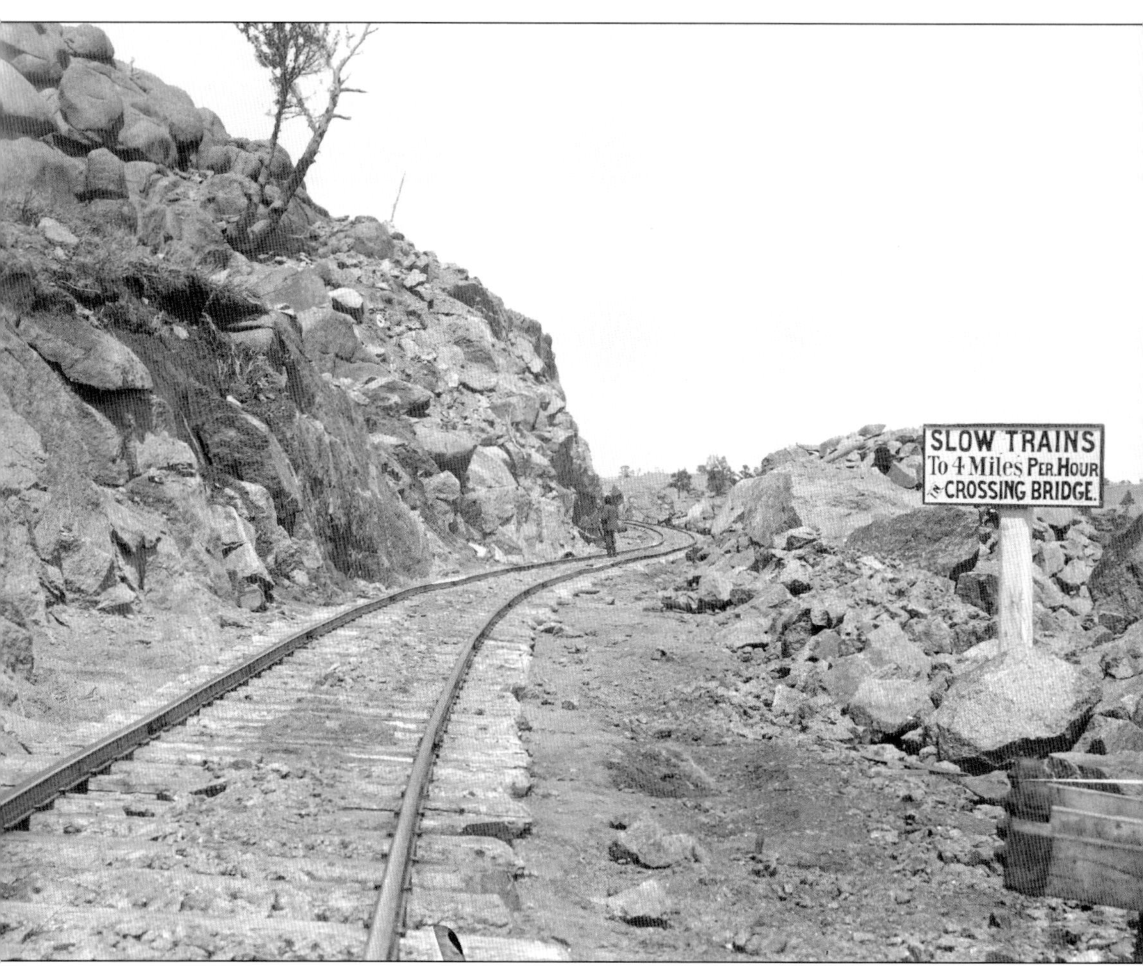

This 1868 photograph shows the western approach to the Dale Creek Trestle. Winds racing up Dale Creek Canyon swayed the bridge, forcing trains to slow dramatically. Guards called "bridge tenders" were stationed at both sides of the trestle to halt trains entirely if the winds were too strong. (Photograph by A.J. Russell; Beinecke.)

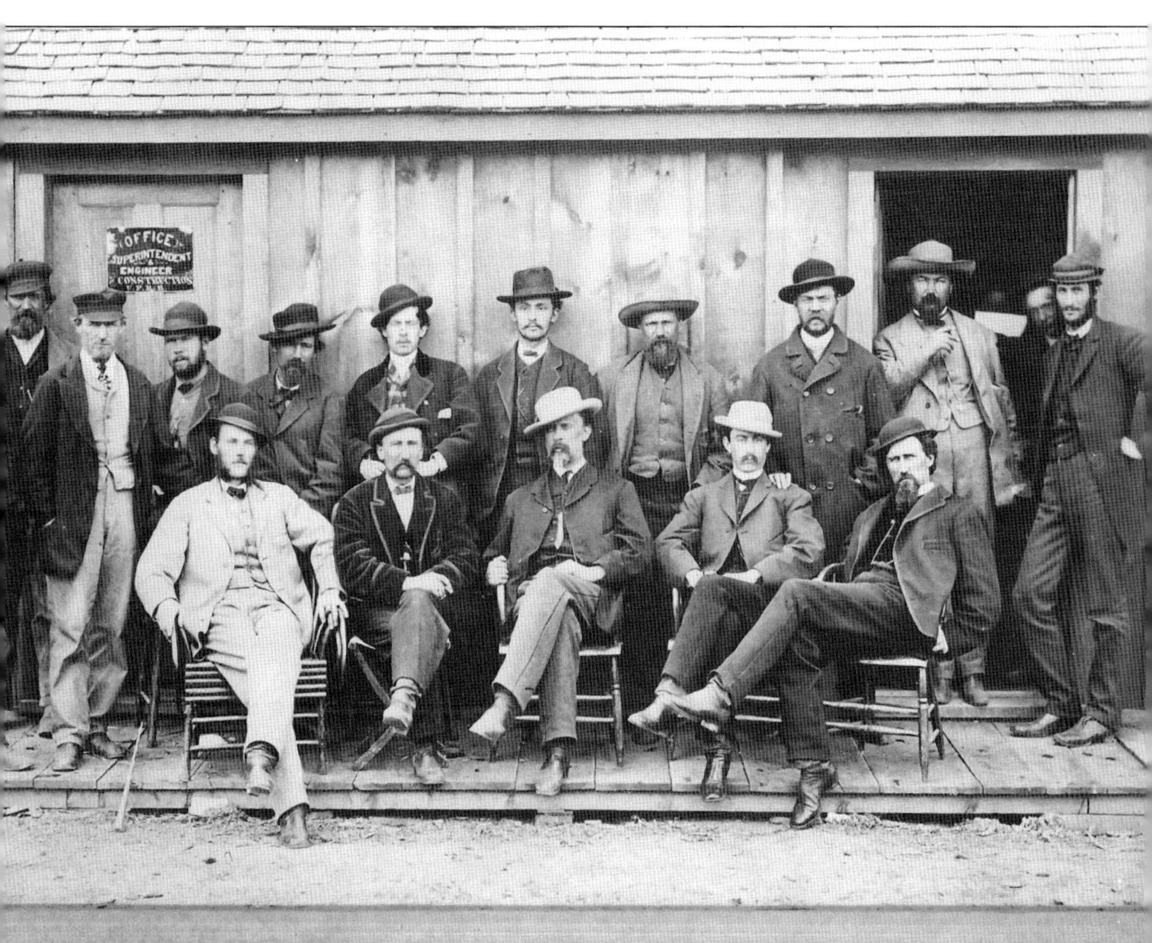

In early 1868, Laramie was the construction headquarters for the Union Pacific Railroad. The men in this photograph were the key management personnel during the Transcontinental Railroad's march across Albany County. Shown here are, from left to right, (seated) Mr. Benedict (engineering department), unidentified, A.A. Bean (master of transportation), W.P. Kennedy (paymaster), and A.P. Wood (engineer on shop construction); (standing) two unidentified, O.C. Smith (assistant paymaster), two unidentified, Charles Bean (secretary to A.A. Bean), three unidentified, Mr. Reynolds (Reynolds & McDowell Contractors), and two unidentified. (Photograph by A.J. Russell; JLEC.)

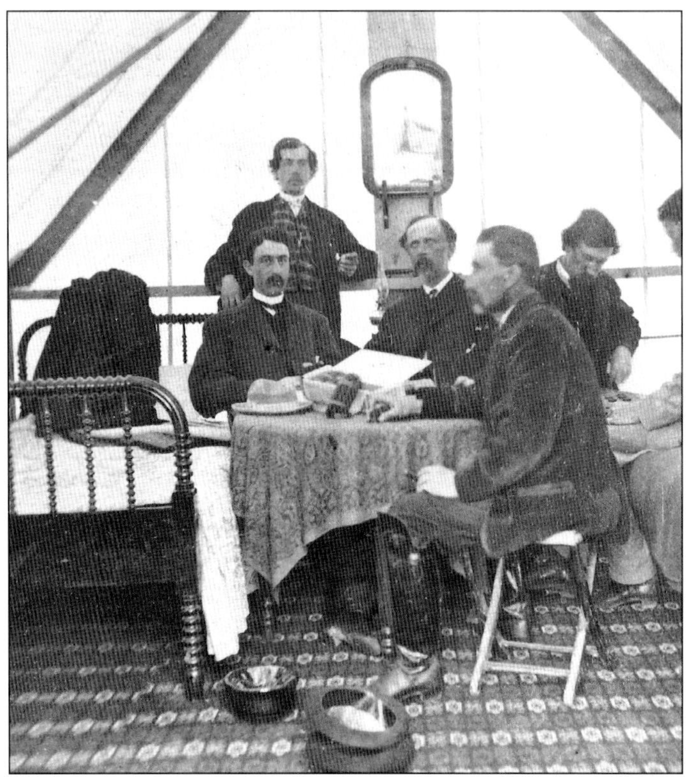

Though only made of canvas and poles, the paymaster's tent was perhaps the most important structure for the early railroad workers. Most workers were paid between $1 and $3 per day, which was far more than the average wage elsewhere in the United States. Paymaster W.P. Kennedy is seated on the left in this 1868 photograph. (Photograph by A.J. Russell; JLEC.)

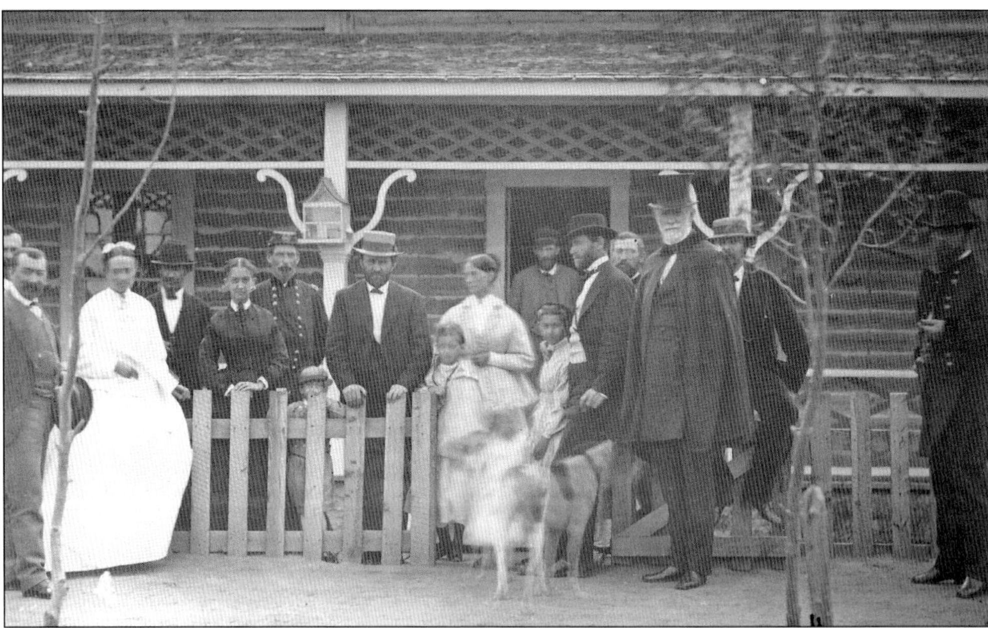

As the Union Pacific pressed on through 1868, Thomas Durant continued to interfere with the route planned by Grenville Dodge. The tension between the two became so great that presidential candidate Ulysses S. Grant (behind the dog) wound up mediating the dispute during a visit to Laramie. The good of the railroad and Dodge's indispensability decided the dispute in his favor. (Photograph by A.J. Russell; JLEC.)

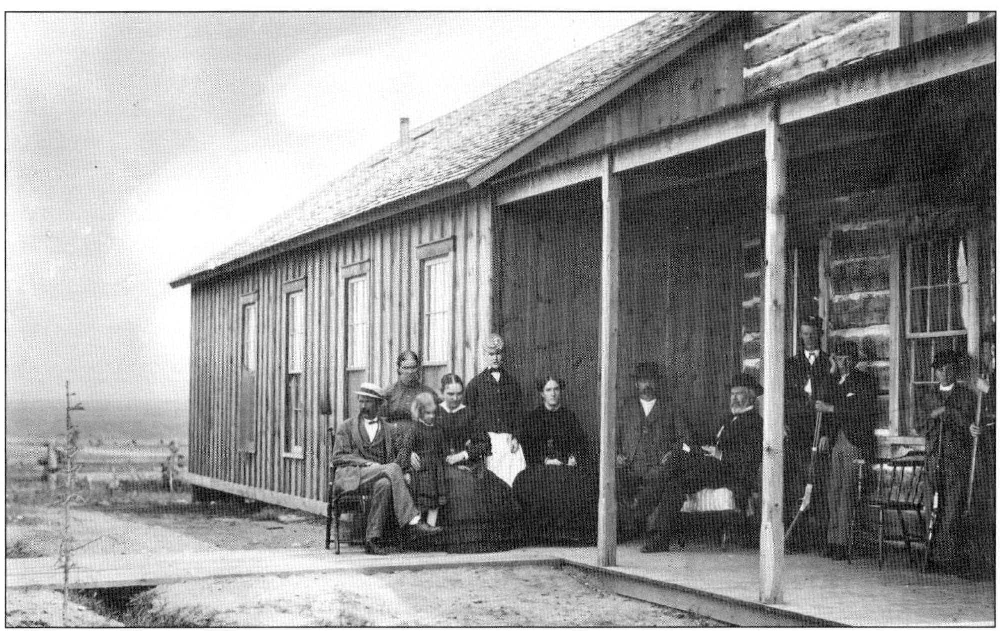

The Transcontinental Railroad was financed in large part by government subsidy bonds, which, in the mountains west of Cheyenne, amounted to $48,000 per mile. This 1868 photograph shows government railroad commissioners at Laramie with their families. The commissioners had to periodically inspect the line for conformity with the agreed-upon construction standards. Money from the bonds was contingent on their approval. (Photograph by A.J. Russell; JLEC.)

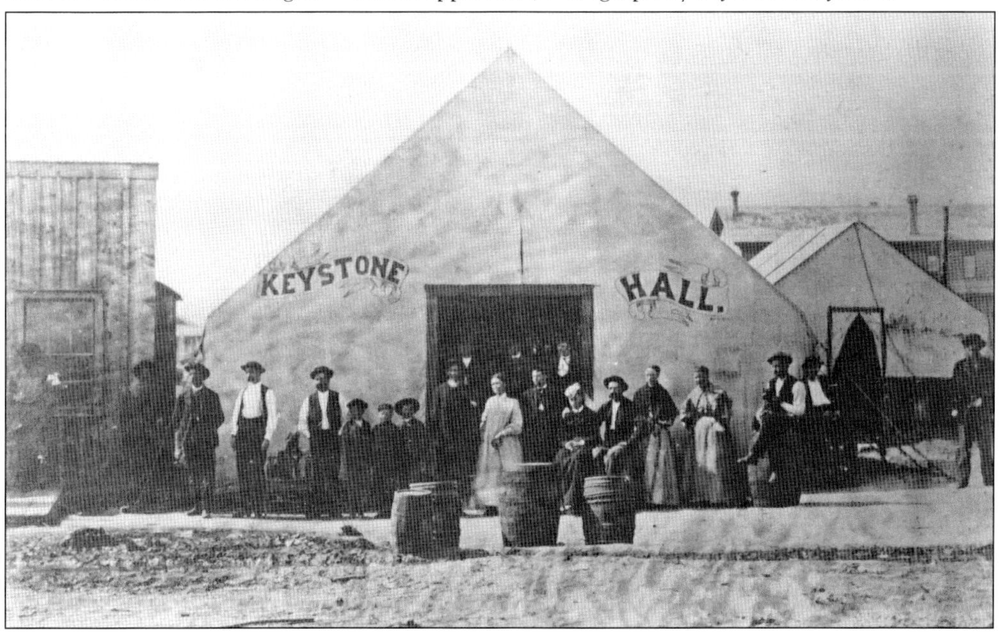

Laramie began as a "Hell on Wheels" railroad tent city. This was a short, but violent, phase in the city's life, and the same was true for many similar tent cities along the Transcontinental Railroad. The Keystone Dance Hall, seen here in 1868, entertained many a railroad worker in Laramie before moving farther down the line. A longer-lasting structure is the Union Pacific Hotel, visible in the distance at right. (Photograph by A.C. Hull; LPM.)

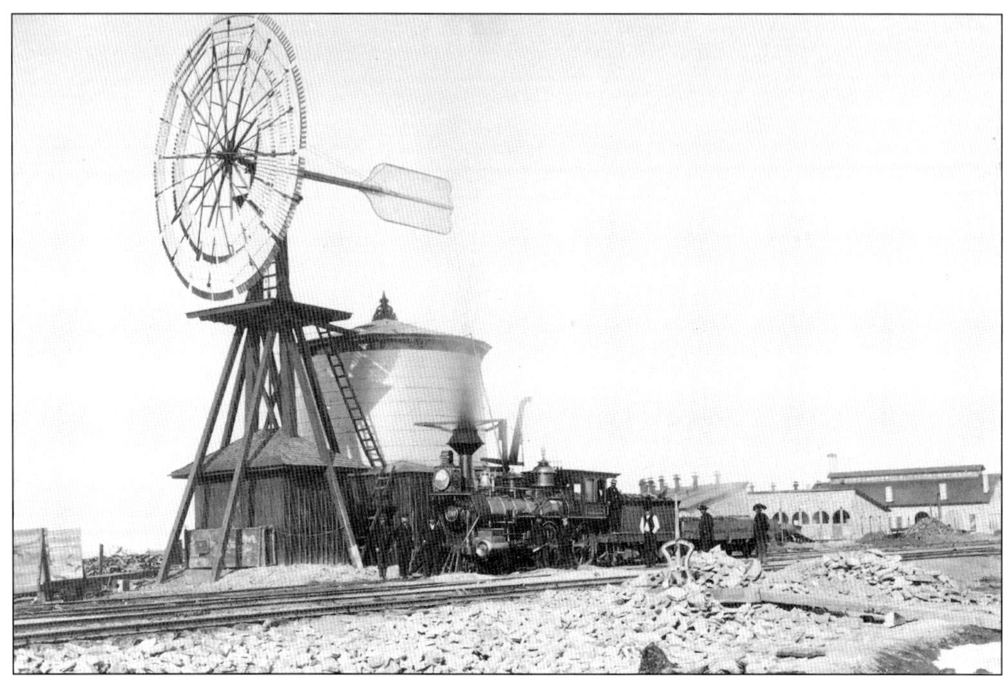

Seen here in 1868, Laramie's huge windmill, over 60 feet high, was located about where Sheridan Street is today, about 100 feet west of the present-day Union Pacific main line. It was used to pump water into the attached tank. The roundhouse and machine shop are in the background at right. Locomotives of the day required water every 14 miles and a machine shop every 100 miles. (Photograph by A.J. Russell; Beinecke.)

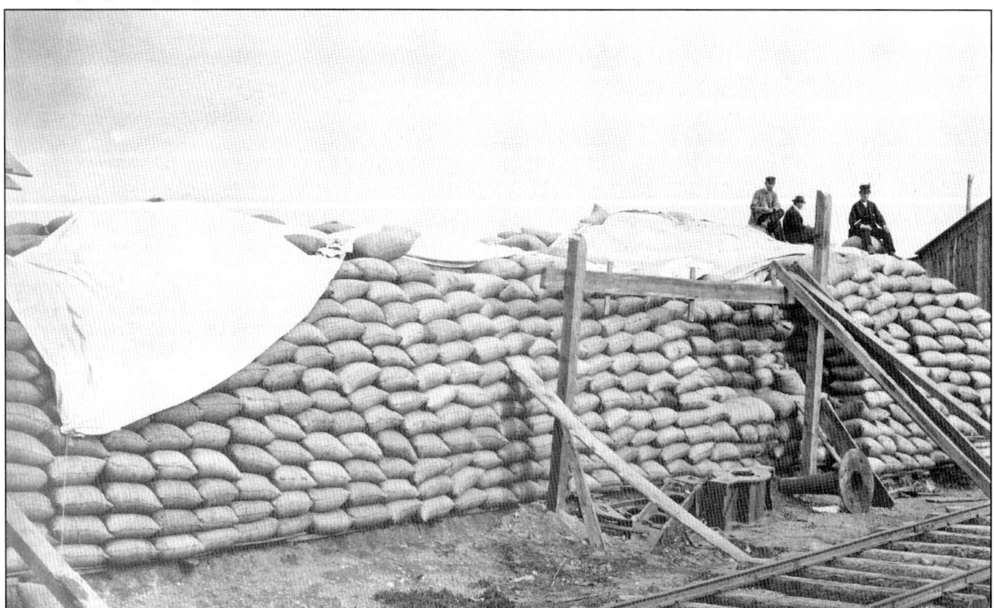

Supplying food for the thousands of railroad workers was much like feeding an army. The grain sacks stored here will be transported down the line to make bread and biscuits for the men building the Union Pacific portion of the Transcontinental Railroad. This photograph was taken in 1868. (Photograph by A.J. Russell; Beinecke.)

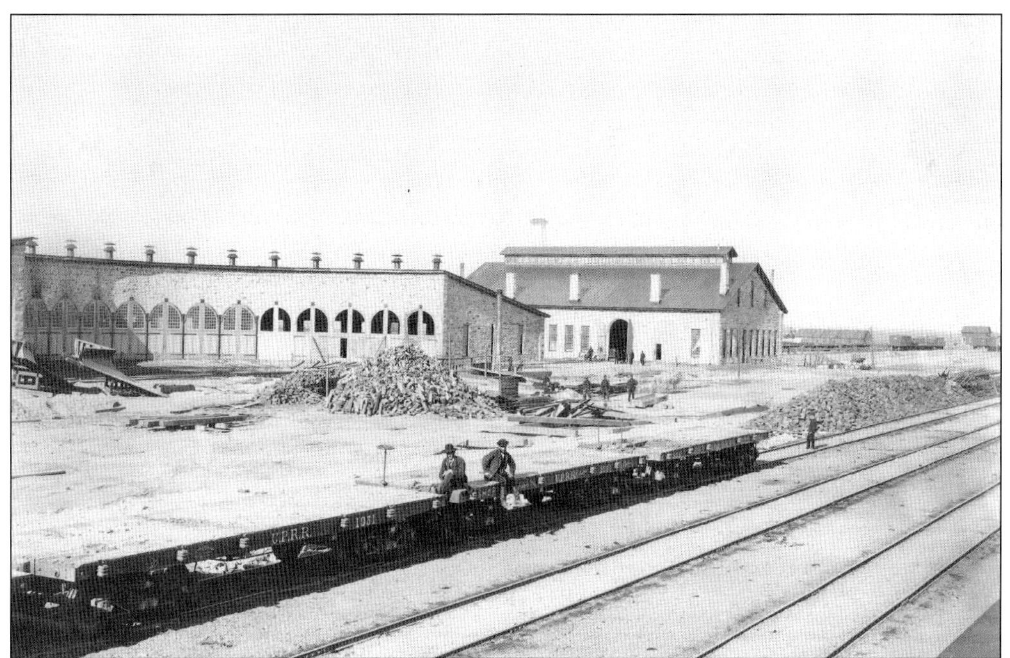

The roundhouse and machine shops, seen here in 1868, were the first two critical facilities to arrive in Laramie. Located at the western base of Sherman Hill and with plentiful water from the Laramie River, Laramie was a logical location for both of these structures, and the city became a major stop on the Union Pacific "Overland Route." (Photograph by A.J. Russell; Beinecke.)

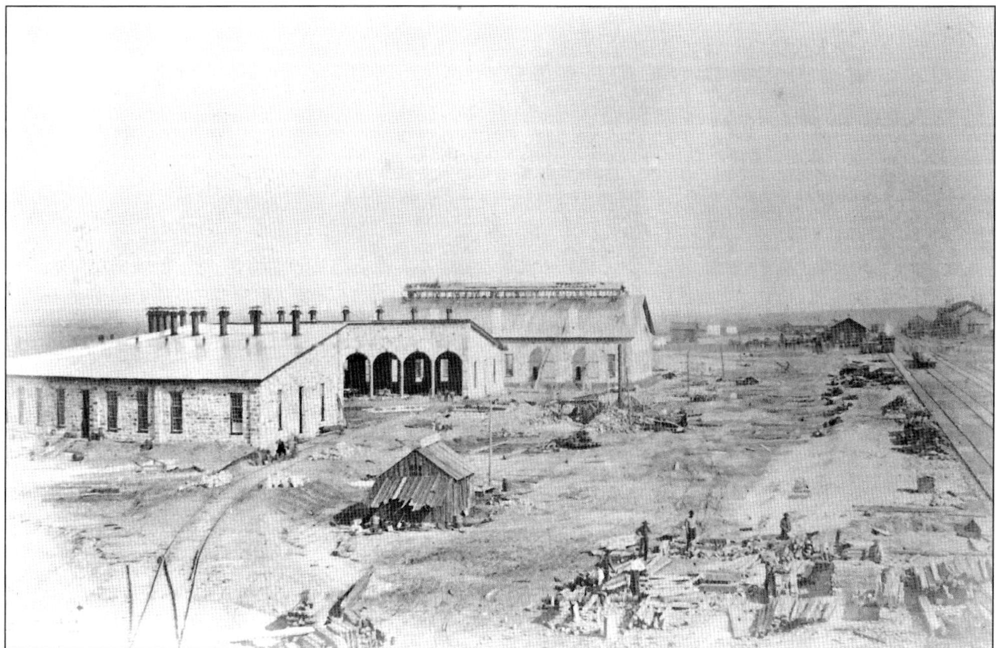

This 1868 photograph shows the Laramie roundhouse and machine shops under construction. The roundhouse was located due west of the present-day Laramie railroad depot at First and Kearney Streets. The machine shops were one block north, aligned with present-day Custer Street. The tall building in the right background is the Union Pacific Hotel. (Photograph by A.C. Hull; JLEC.)

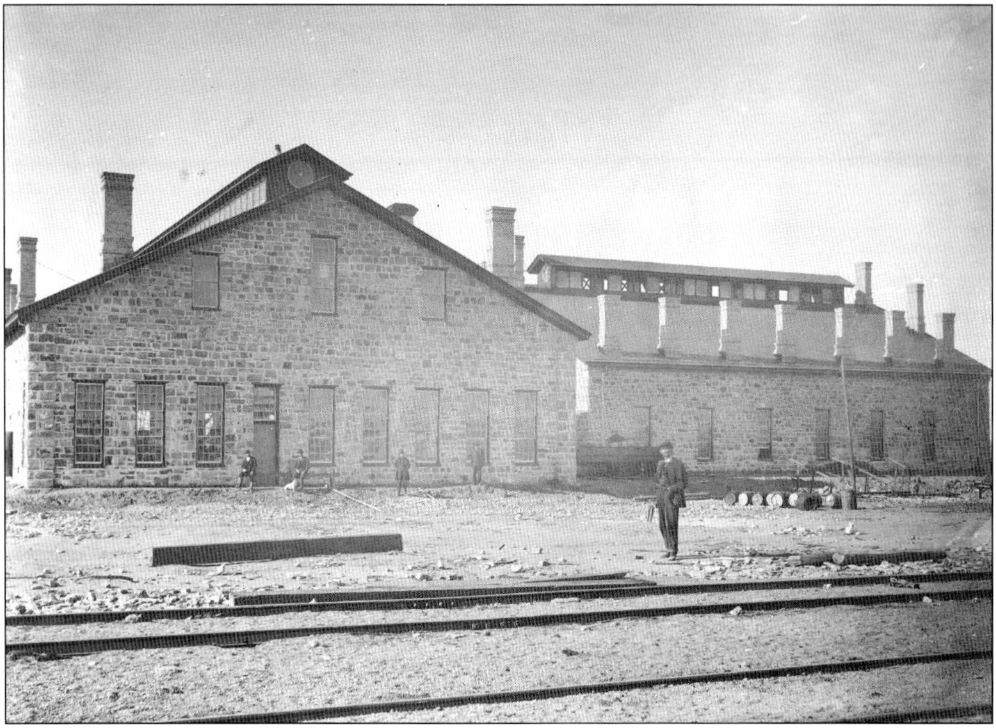

The machine shop (left) and the power plant (right) are seen here in 1868. The main purpose of the power plant was to generate steam, which was then piped to stationary steam engines for mechanical power in the machine shop and roundhouse. The steam also provided heat for the various railroad buildings. (Photograph by A.J. Russell; Beinecke.)

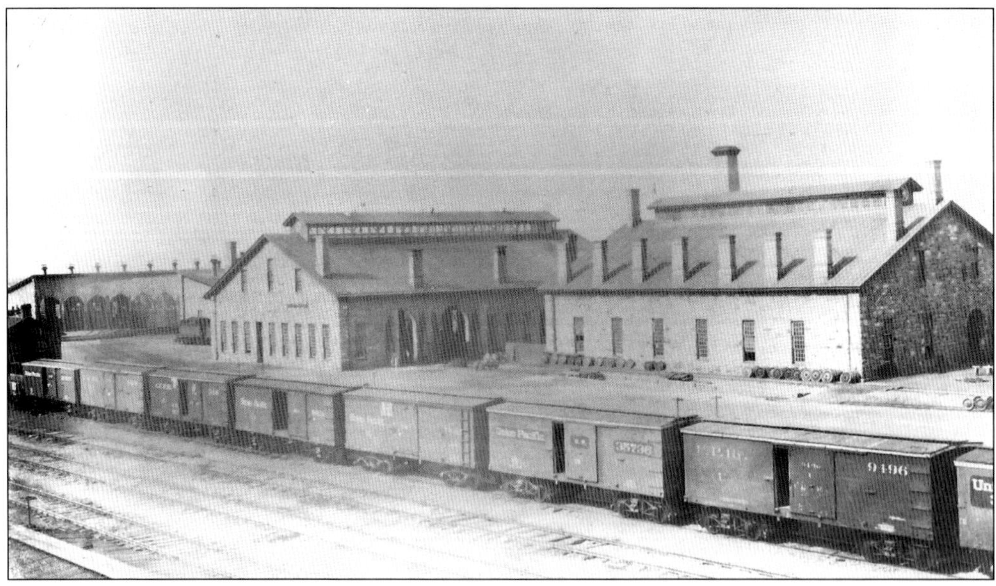

Shown in this 1868 photograph are the Laramie roundhouse (left), the machine shop (center), and the powerhouse. The wheels leaning against the powerhouse are locomotive drivers. The boxcars in the foreground are 28 feet long and have arch bar trucks, which was standard for the day. (Wyoming State Archives; JLEC.)

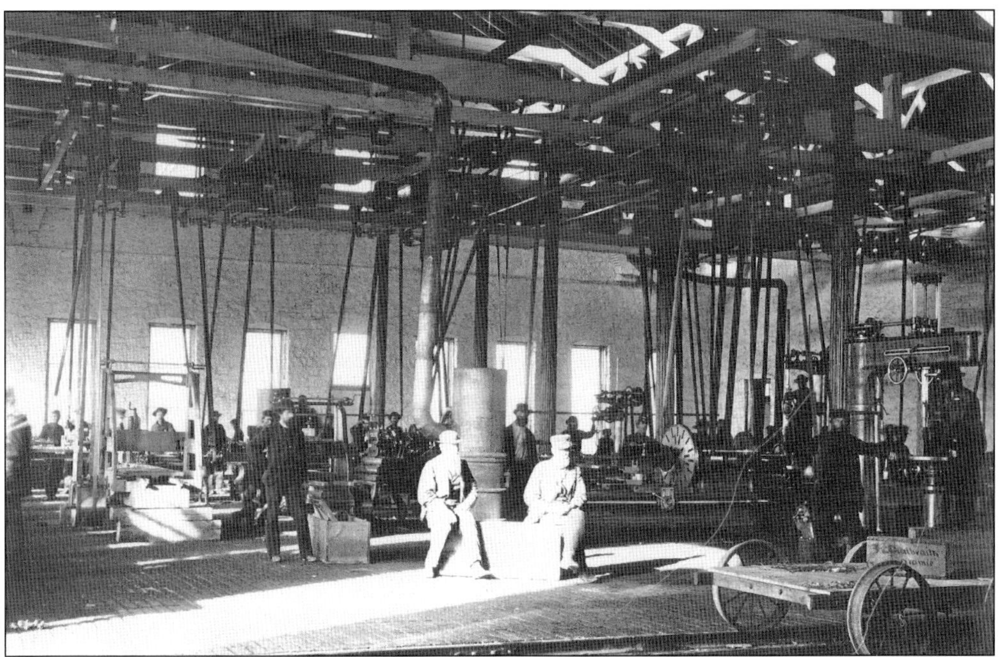

This is an interior view of the machine shop in 1868. Belts connect pulleys in the ceiling to transmit power to a variety of lathes, presses, and other metal-shaping machines at ground level. The pulleys are interconnected and are ultimately driven by steam generated in the powerhouse. (Photograph by A.J. Russell; Beinecke.)

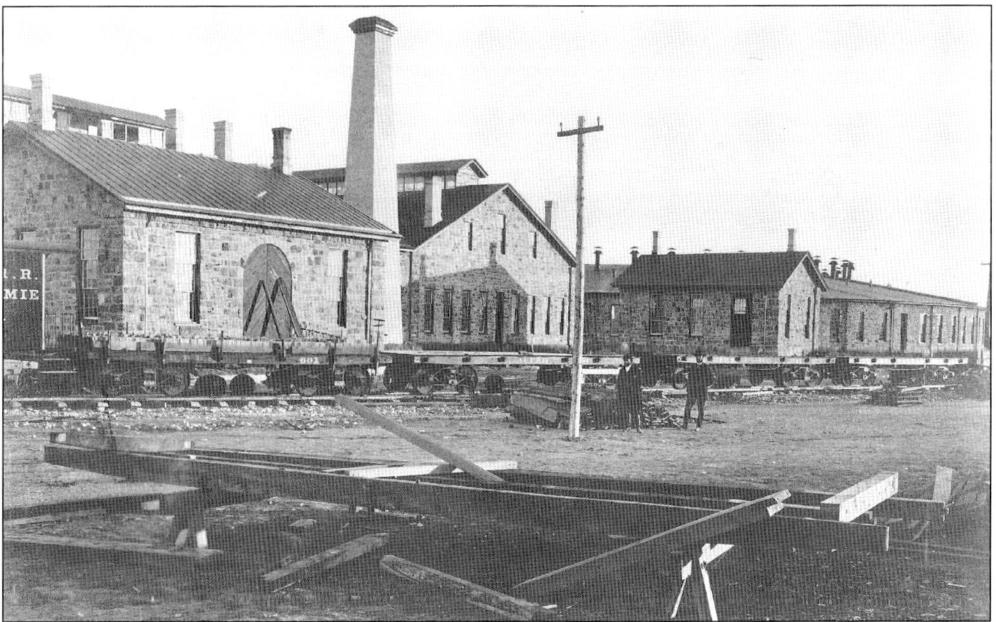

This image shows the west side of several railroad maintenance structures in 1868. Oil storage buildings are at left and right of center. The roof of the powerhouse peeks above the storage building on the left. The machine shop is in the center, and at far right is the roundhouse. The rock used to construct these buildings came from a quarry near present-day Rock River. (Photograph by A.J. Russell; JLEC.)

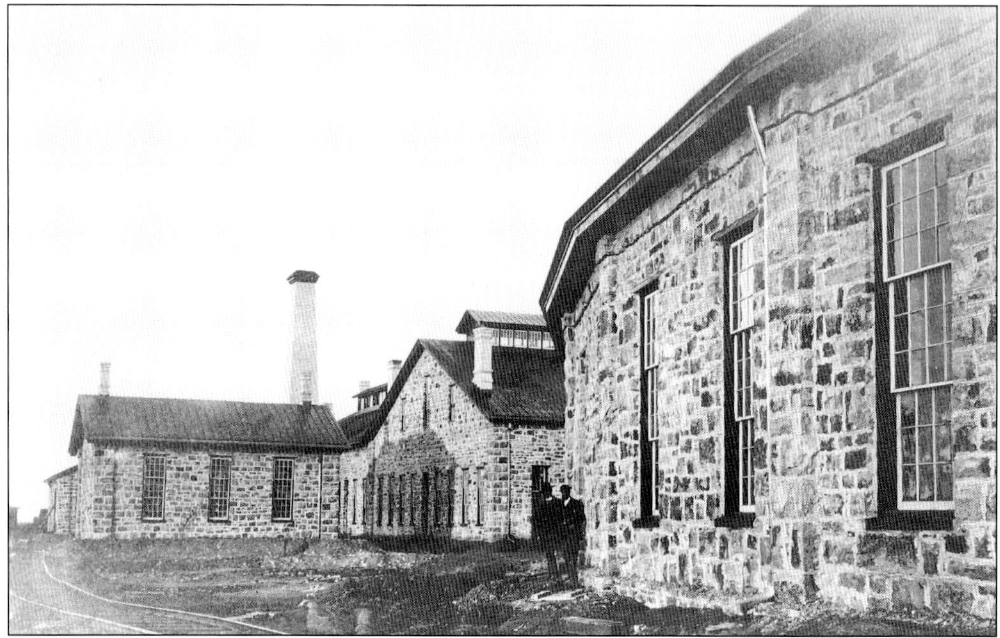

This photograph, also from 1868, shows the west side of the Laramie railroad complex from another angle. The roundhouse is at right, and the machine shop is at center. The large smoke stack left of center is for the power plant, while the plant itself is just visible between the stack and the machine shop. Oil storage houses are on the left. (Photograph by A.J. Russell; JLEC.)

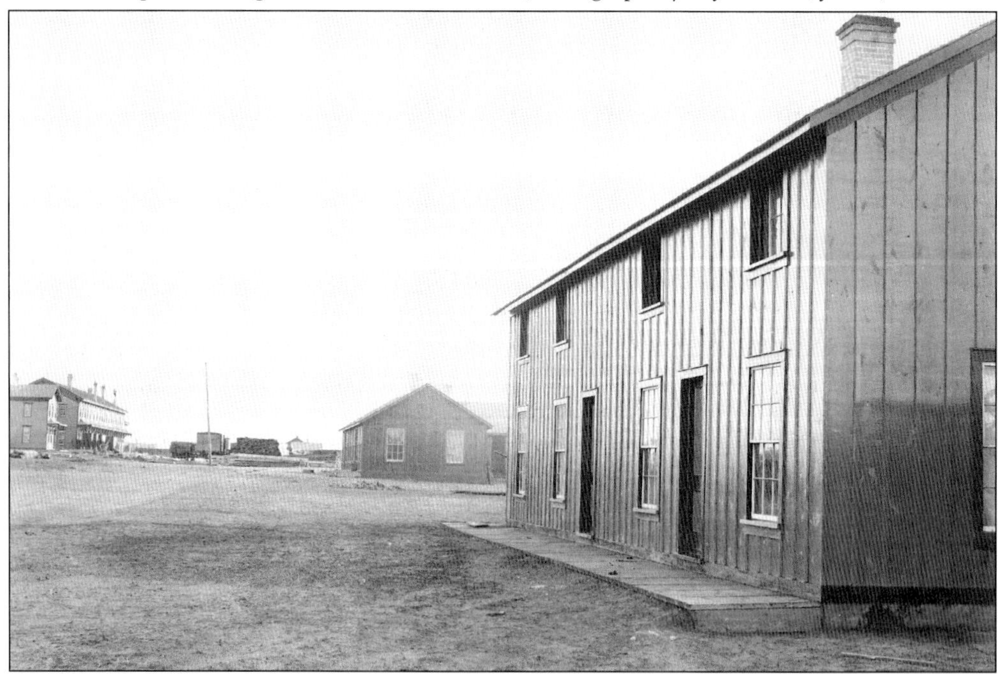

The Union Pacific Hospital (right), one of the first medical facilities in Laramie, was located in the railroad yards west of Fremont Street. The building beyond it, at center, provided an office and residences for the hospital personnel. The Union Pacific Hotel is visible to the left (southeast) in this 1868 view. (Photograph by A.J. Russell; Beinecke.)

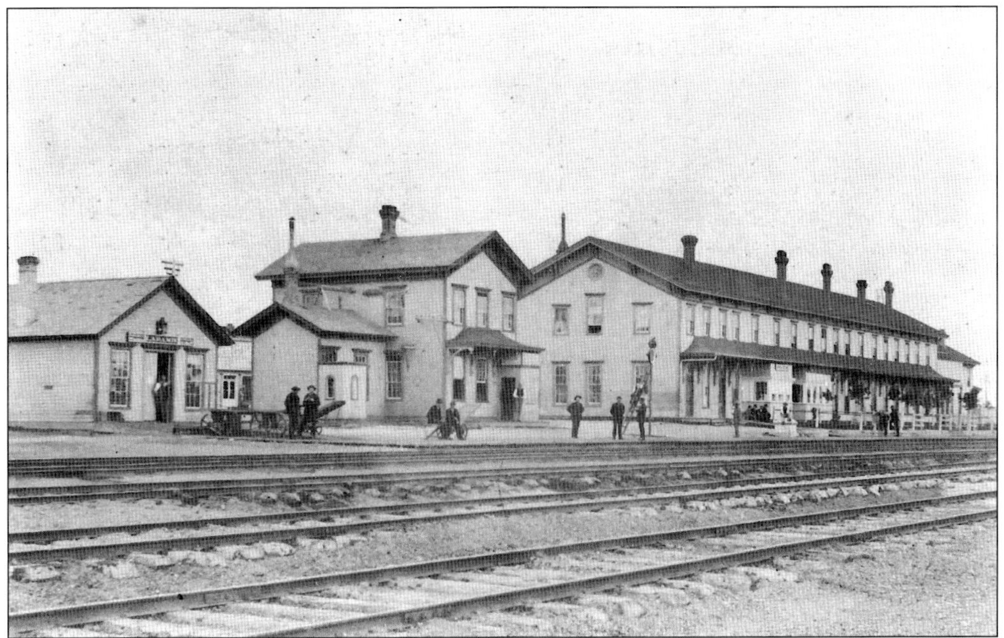

Laramie's first railroad station is the small building to the left in this 1868 photograph. The ticket office was inside, but the large waiting areas commonly associated with railroad depots would be an innovation for the future. The superintendant's office is to the right of the station, and the Union Pacific Hotel is the long building at far right. By 1885, the station was part of the hotel. (Photograph by A.J. Russell; JLEC.)

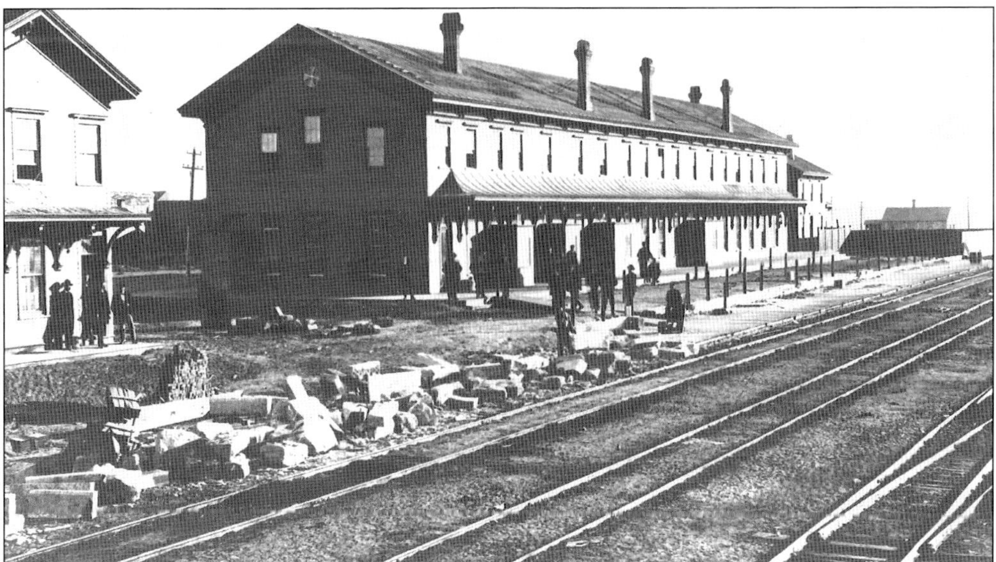

The Union Pacific Hotel, seen here in 1868, served passengers breakfast and supper in its dining room and lunch in a separate area. The hotel was located west of First Street, and it aligned with Ivinson Avenue. The modern-day railroad tracks run on top of the site of the hotel. (Photograph by A.J. Russell; JLEC.)

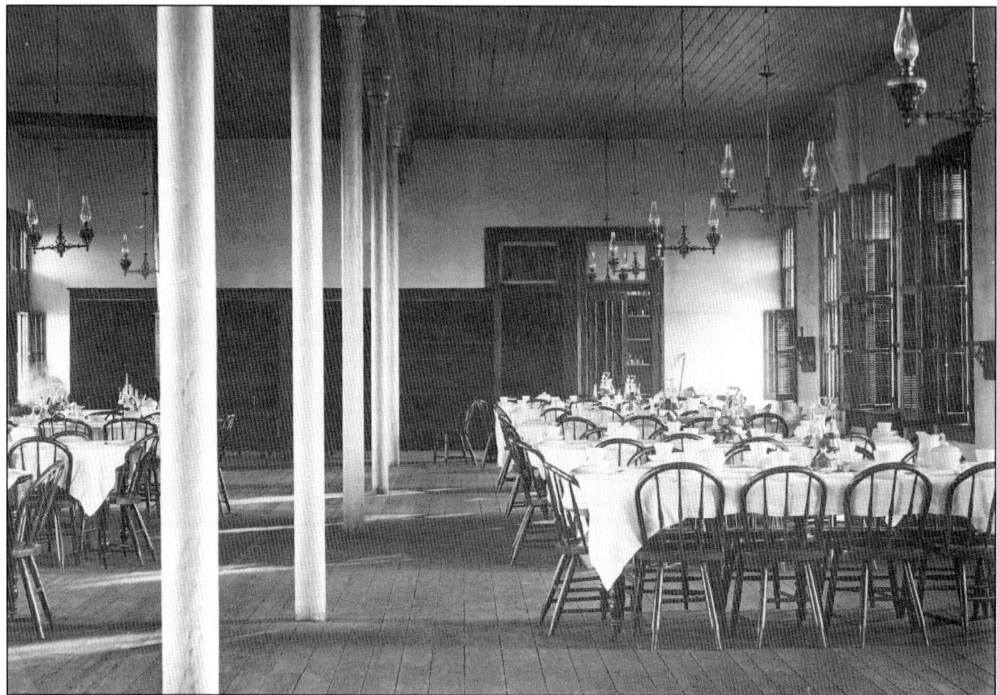

White linen tablecloths, fine china, and napkins tucked into water glasses indicate elegant dining at its best in the Union Pacific Hotel, seen here in 1868. Trains made 30-minute stops here three times a day to revitalize their passengers in the days before railroad dining cars. Imitation marble columns support the ceiling, and natural lighting is maximized. (Photograph by A.J. Russell; Beinecke.)

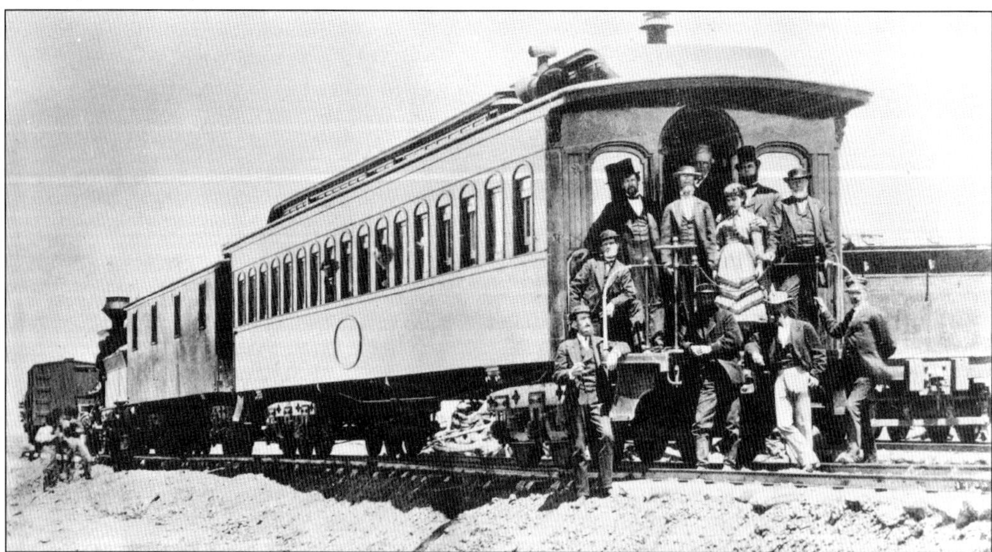

An inspection party arrives at Rock Creek, 42 miles north of Laramie, in 1868. In the party is Cornelius Bushnell, a Union Pacific director for whom the town of Bushnell, Nebraska, is named. In addition to subsidy bonds, the US government also provided land grants to help finance the Transcontinental Railroad. These grants were contingent upon proper construction, as determined by the inspection parties. (Photograph by A.J. Russell; LPM.)

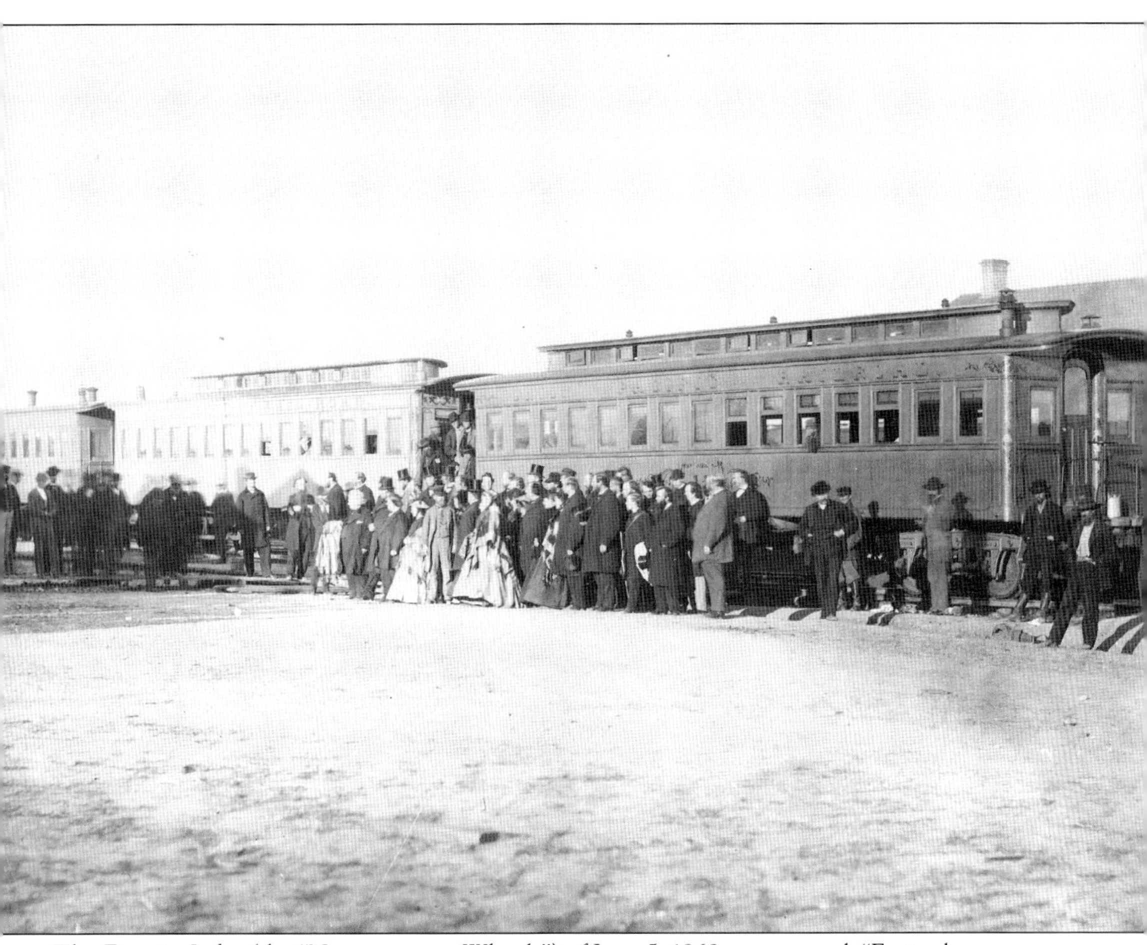

The *Frontier Index* (the "Newspaper on Wheels") of June 5, 1868, announced, "Forty clergymen, fresh from the Northern Methodist Chicago Conference, arrived in [Laramie] last evening by the mail train. . . . A number of the party walked around town after night and peeped into the dance halls, gambling halls and other sporting institutions. The result of the inspection was a desire to convert the wicked ones." (Photograph by A.J. Russell; Beinecke.)

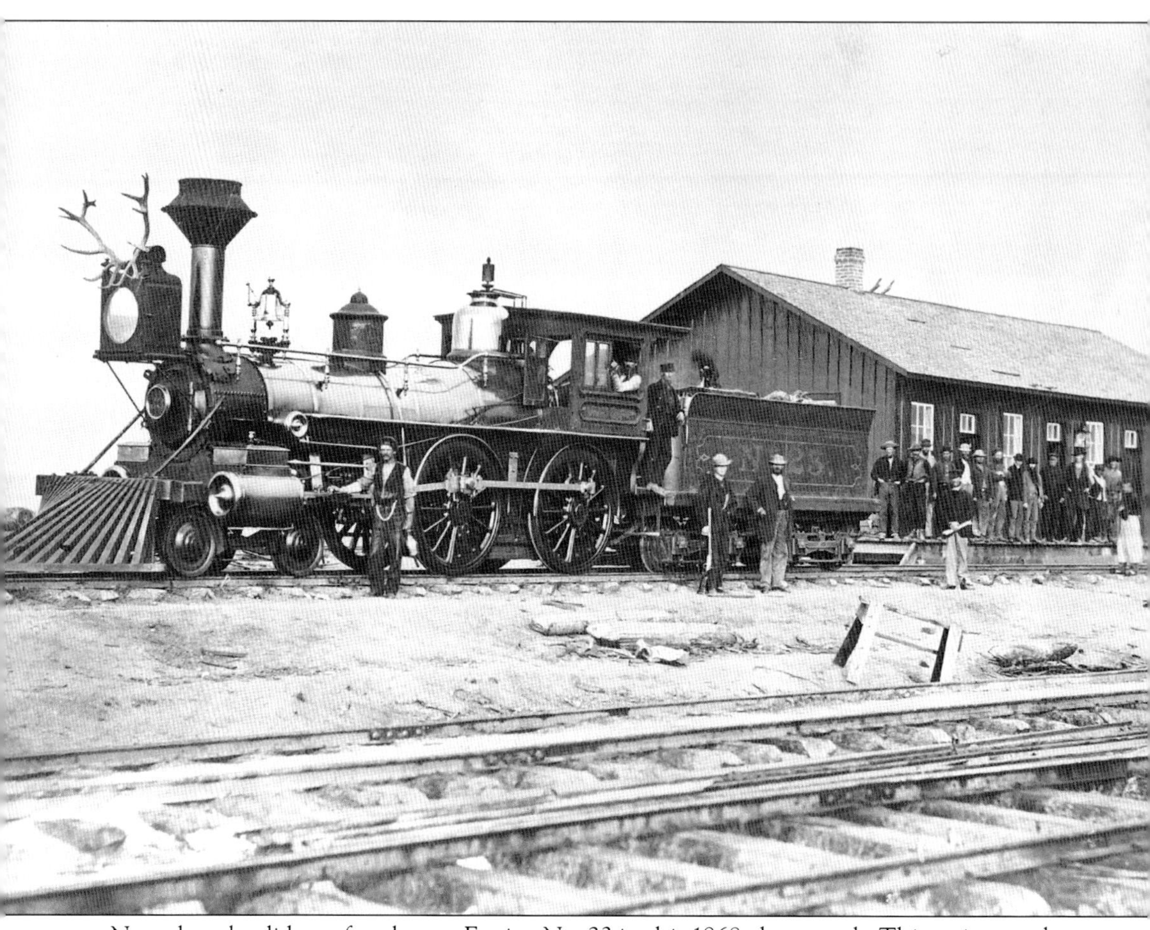

Note the splendid set of antlers on Engine No. 23 in this 1868 photograph. This train crew knew how to make an impression! This photograph was taken 15 miles north of Laramie, at a station with the lyrical name Wyoming, Wyoming. The engine is a 4-4-0 American—the numbers indicate that the engine has four wheels in the front "pilot" truck, four powered drivers, and no trailing truck. (Photograph by A.J. Russell; JLEC.)

Two

1870–1900

Laramie Industries in the Early Years

Laramie's first and most powerful economic engine was the Union Pacific Railroad and the industries that sprouted up to support it. In 1868, the most critical industries had already been built and placed in operation. The roundhouse, engine turntable, and machine shop were all critical facilities to support and maintain steam locomotive engines that arrived in Laramie. The climb from the Great Plains into the Rockies demanded a lot from the early steam-powered locomotives, and the need for such facilities in the cities just before and after that climb helped to spur early growth in Laramie and Cheyenne.

By the early 1870s, many more supporting industries had arrived. Perhaps the most important were the rolling mills that went to work primarily smelting down worn-out track to create new track. A tie plant arrived as well that shaped and treated rail ties with creosote before they went out on the line. The relationship between the railroads and early agriculture was also apparent with the Laramie stockyards. By the late 1800s, local gypsum quarries supported plaster mills and cement factories. To this day, Laramie still has an operating cement factory.

In all respects, Laramie was a working-class town in its early years, so much so that, at one point, it was labeled the "Pittsburgh of the West." In 1886, a new industry came to the town. The University of Wyoming was created, and its very first building, "Old Main," was erected using a sandstone-block construction. Though its name was certainly not original for a founding building of a university, its architectural design did go on to influence much of the building designs at the university and in the city. The university's economic contribution to early Laramie may have been insignificant next to the booming working-class industries at the time, but the school would eventually dominate the town and transform it into the largely white-collar college town it is today.

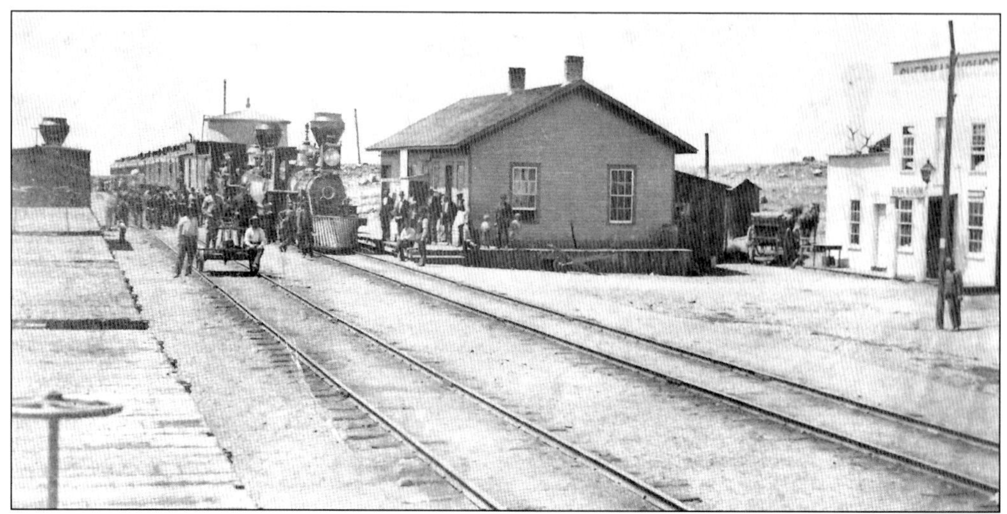

A pair of locomotives arrive at Sherman from Laramie in this 1874 photograph. They are pulling a train of passenger cars. The passengers have disembarked, perhaps for meals at nearby eateries. In order to achieve the climb to the Rockies, two engines were often used. Men pose on a handcart on the middle track, and a westbound train of empty flatcars is on the left. (JLEC.)

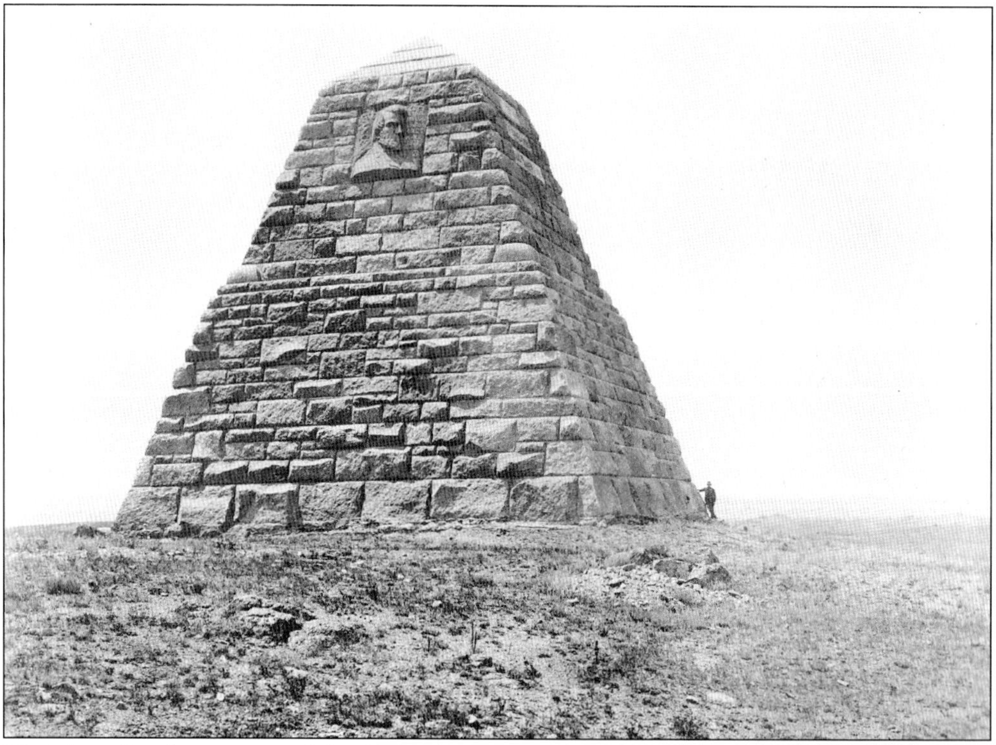

The Union Pacific constructed the 60-foot-high granite Ames Monument near Sherman between 1880 and 1882 for a cost of $65,000. The monument, seen here in 1905, commemorates the contributions of brothers Oakes and Oliver Ames to the building of the Transcontinental Railroad. Architect Henry Hobson Richardson designed the monument, and sculptor Augustus Saint-Gaudens created the sandstone medallions of Oakes and Oliver Ames. (Photograph by J.E. Stimson; JLEC.)

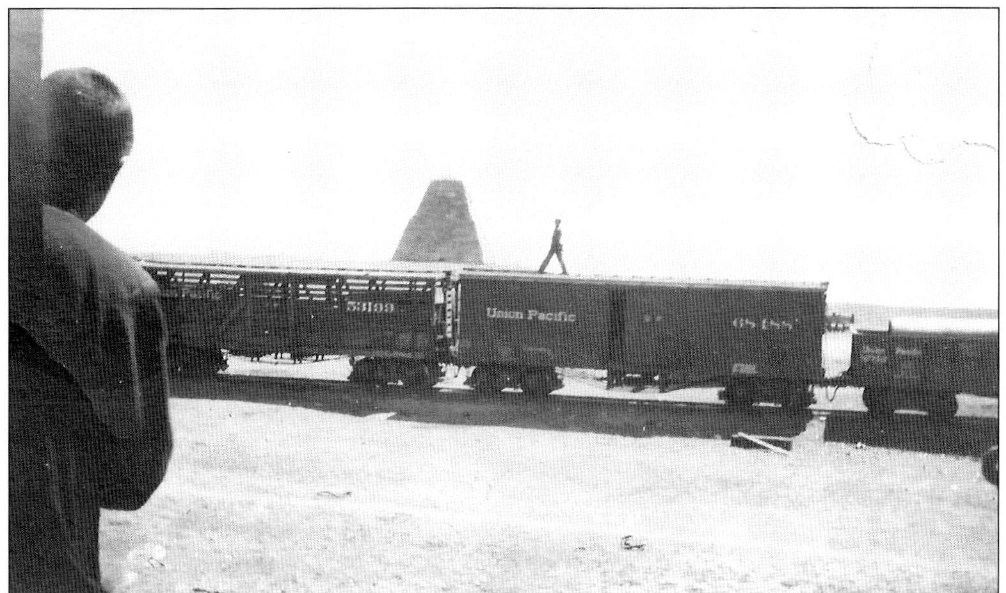

This photograph of the Ames Monument as a train rolls past was taken near the turn of the century. Stock car No. 53199 is on the left, boxcar No. 68188 is in the center, and a gondola car is on the right. A brakeman strides across the roof walk to set the cars' hand brakes in preparation for the trip down to Laramie. (JLEC.)

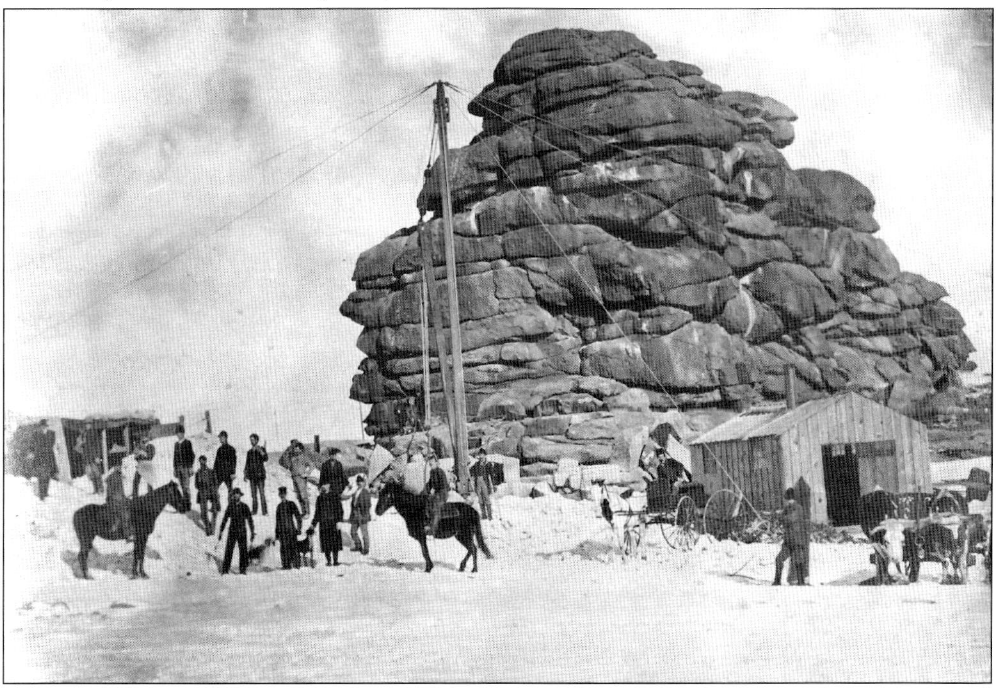

Reeds Rock, half a mile west of Sherman, provided stone for the construction of the nearby Ames Monument. The tall spar is a stiff-leg derrick used to load the blocks of granite, some weighing up to five tons, onto stout wagons pulled by oxen. Reeds Rock is composed of light pink granite, similar to the rock formations of nearby Vedauwoo Glen in the Medicine Bow National Forest. This photograph was taken sometime between 1878 and 1880. (JLEC.)

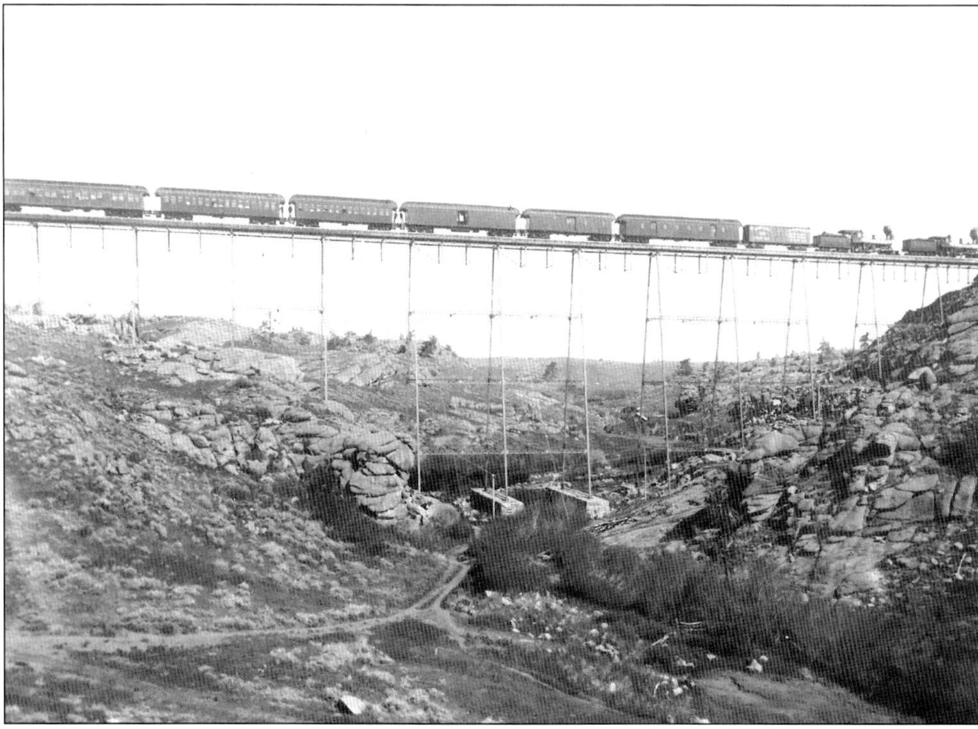

In this 1884 photograph, two locomotives cross Dale Creek Trestle as they pull a passenger train up "Sherman Hill," the railroad name for the Laramie Mountains between Laramie and Cheyenne. This, the second of three versions of the bridge, was built in 1876. Its iron-beam construction contrasts radically from the wood beams of the original. Appropriately enough, its nickname was "the spider web." (JLEC.)

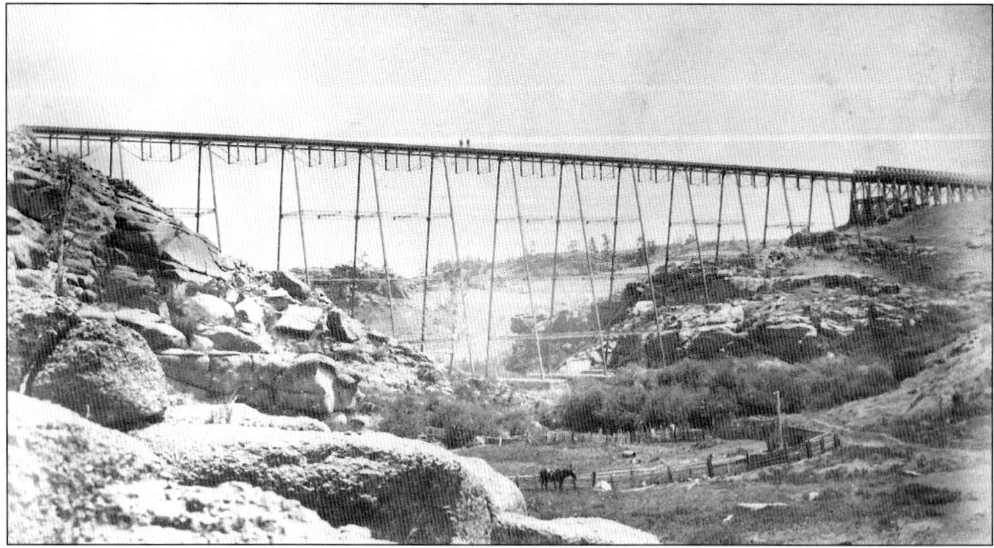

This 1880 photograph of "the spider web" faces south, with the west end of the bridge on the right. The wooden trestle on the right is all that remains of the original 1868 bridge. This trestle continued into the third version of the bridge but burned in 1890. It was replaced by a long fill and dressed-sandstone abutment. (JLEC.)

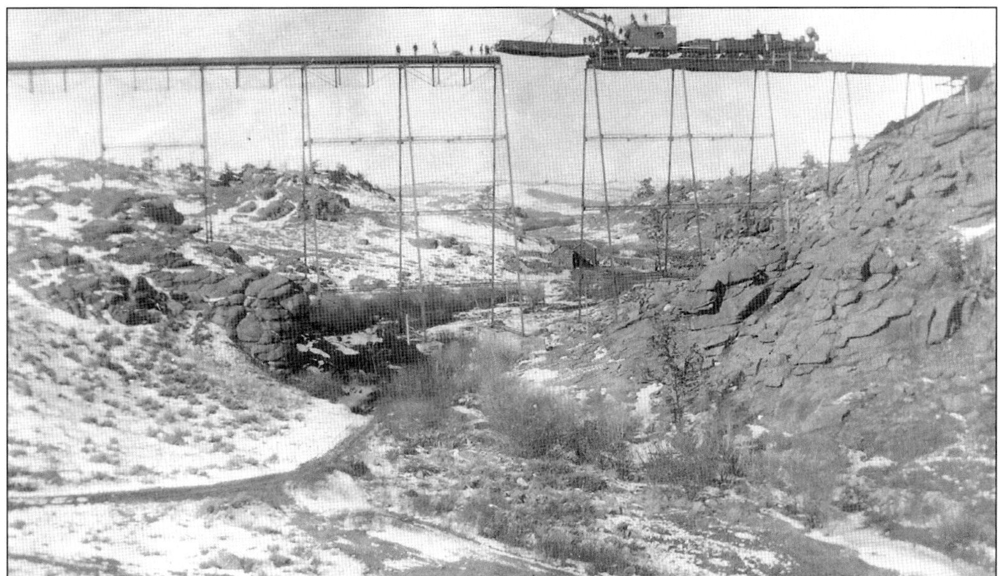

A steam-operated derrick replaces an old iron truss (left) with a new steel girder (right) as the third version of the Dale Creek Trestle is constructed in 1885. Passenger and freight service continued without interruption during the replacement, the derrick being moved to a siding about a mile to the east (right) while revenue trains passed. (Photograph by SM Hartwell & Son; JLEC.)

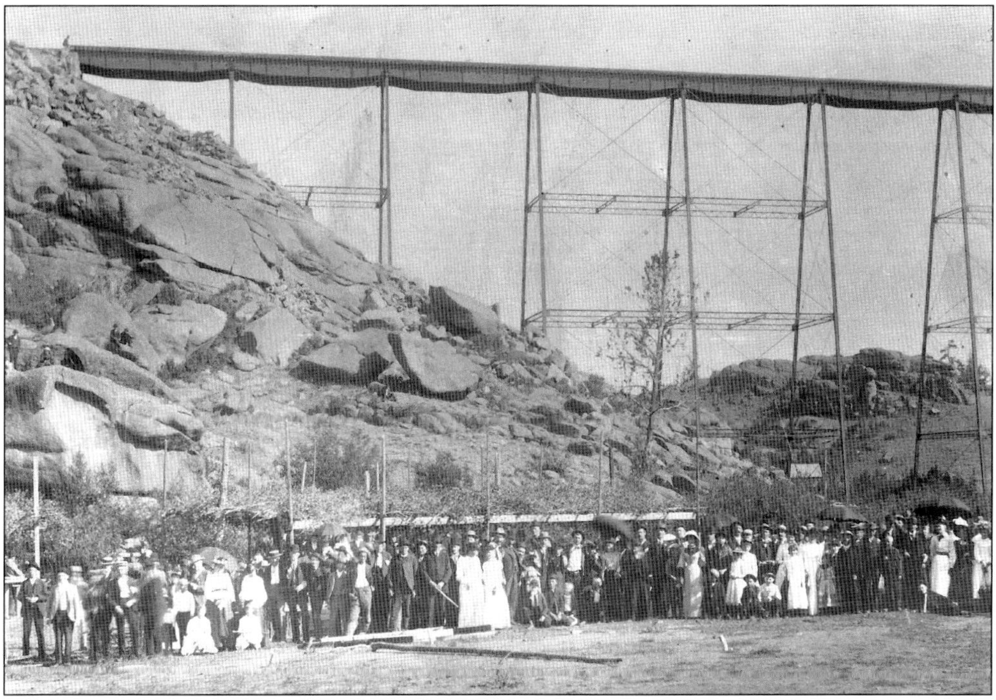

Picnickers from Albany County enjoy a sunny outing in 1895 at the base of the third version of Dale Creek Trestle. The Union Pacific regularly ran excursion trains of such revelers to the trestle from Cheyenne and Laramie throughout the summers. This version of the bridge used the iron beams of the second version for vertical piers, but the spidery trusses were replaced with more substantial steel girders. (JHC.)

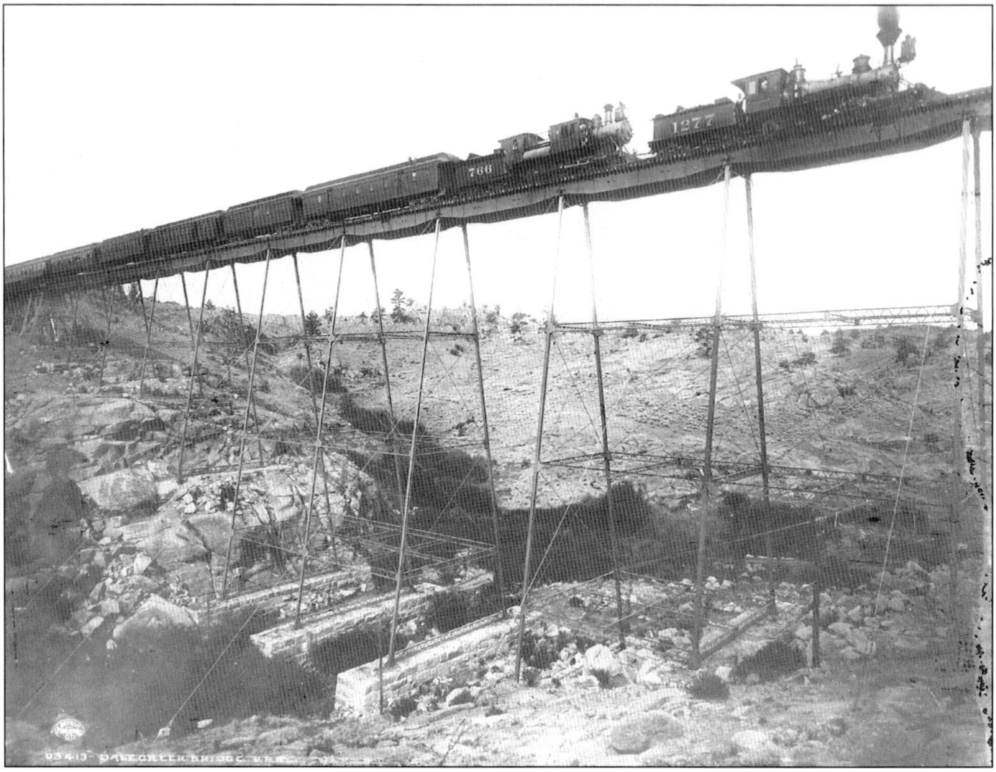

A double-headed passenger train crosses Dale Creek Trestle around 1890. The rear locomotive is called a "camelback." Most camelbacks had only one cab, but Union Pacific engines had two, one for the engineer (center) the other for the fireman (rear). The lead engine is a Consolidation class. Heavier and more powerful engines such as this were increasingly common on railroads in the latter years of the 19th century. (Photograph by W.H. Jackson; JLEC.)

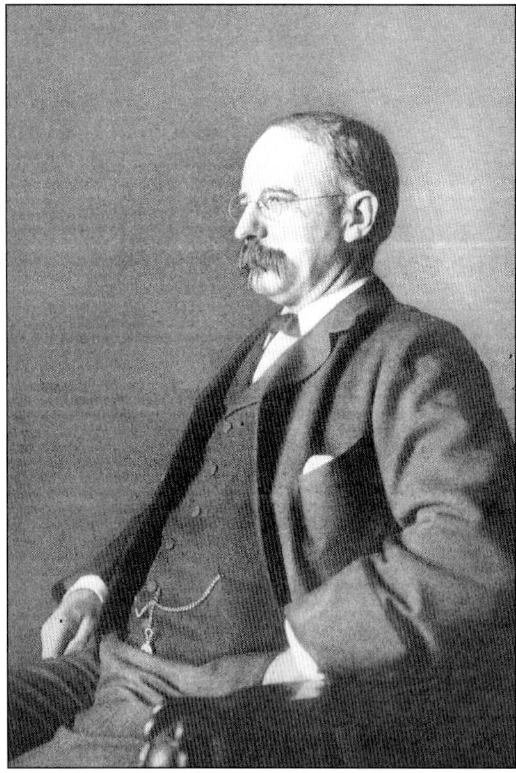

In 1893, the Union Pacific went bankrupt. It was purchased by an investment group headed by Edward Henry Harriman (seen here around 1899), who already had a controlling interest in many other railroads. From the late 1890s through 1909, Harriman improved the Union Pacific in many ways, including shortening the line across Wyoming by about 32 miles. (Clarence Darrow Digital Collection, University of Minnesota Law Library.)

The Dale Creek Trestle was in service in one form or another from 1868 until 1901. Under Harriman's stewardship, the line over Sherman Hill was rerouted three miles south, and the town of Sherman and the Dale Creek Trestle were abandoned. This is a c. 1901 photograph of the dismantling of the bridge. The piers were reused for a Union Pacific bridge in Kansas. (Photograph by J.E. Stimson; JHC.)

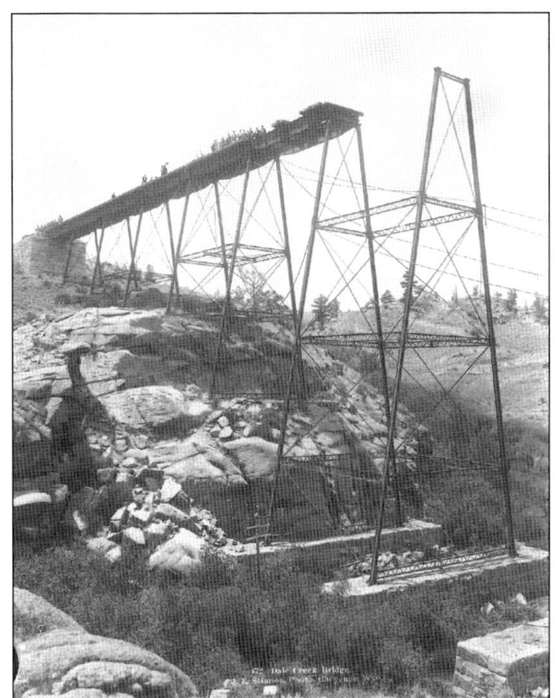

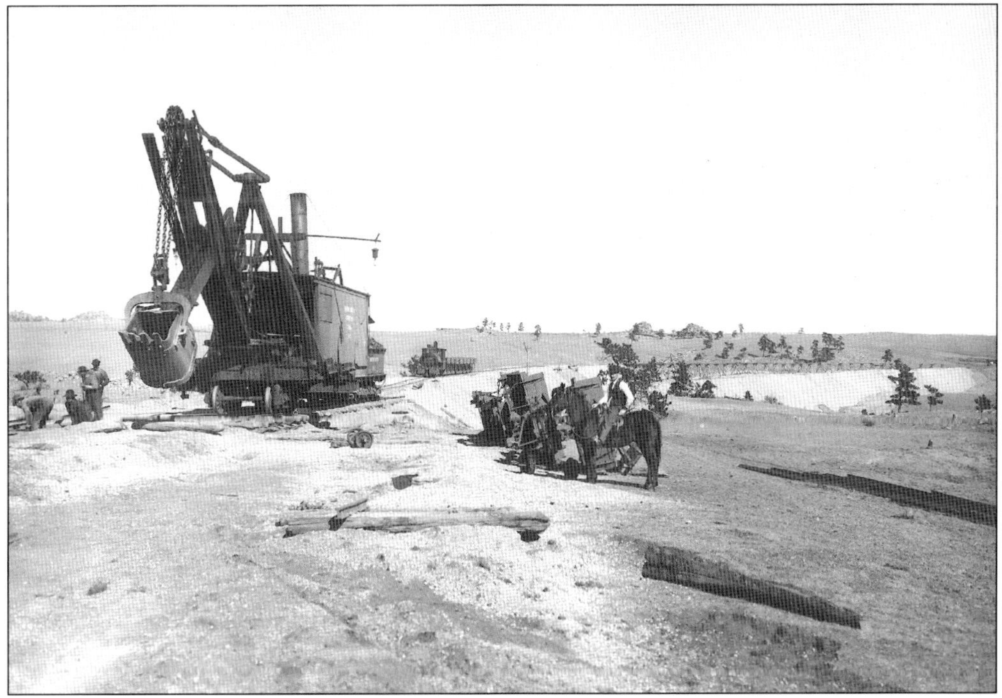

The new 1901 main line departed from the original route just west of Buford, with a broad, sweeping curve built on a fill on Southerland's Ranch. This curve is highly visible today, because it is just south of Interstate 80 near the Buford exit. The steam shovel in this 1901 photograph is standard gauge, while the "dinky" engine and cars behind it are narrow gauge. (Photograph by J.E. Stimson; JLEC.)

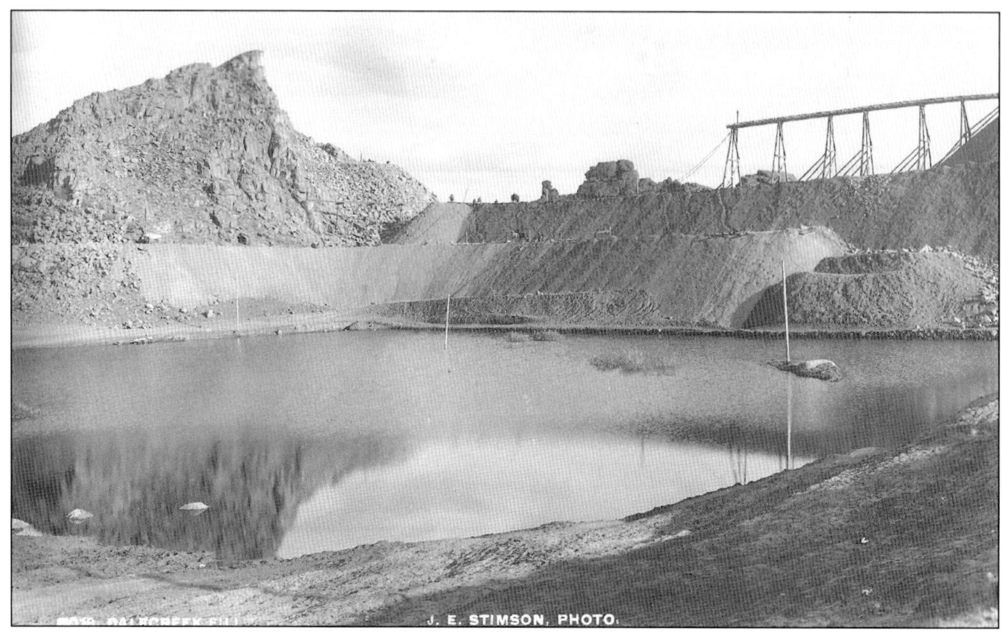

The new main line was about three miles south of the original. While it was no shorter than its predecessor, the main line's summit was 234 feet lower. This advantage accommodated longer, heavier, and faster trains. However, the new line entailed the construction of several long, high fills, such as the one shown here in 1901, and a 1,800-foot tunnel. (Photograph by J.E. Stimson; Wyoming State Archives.)

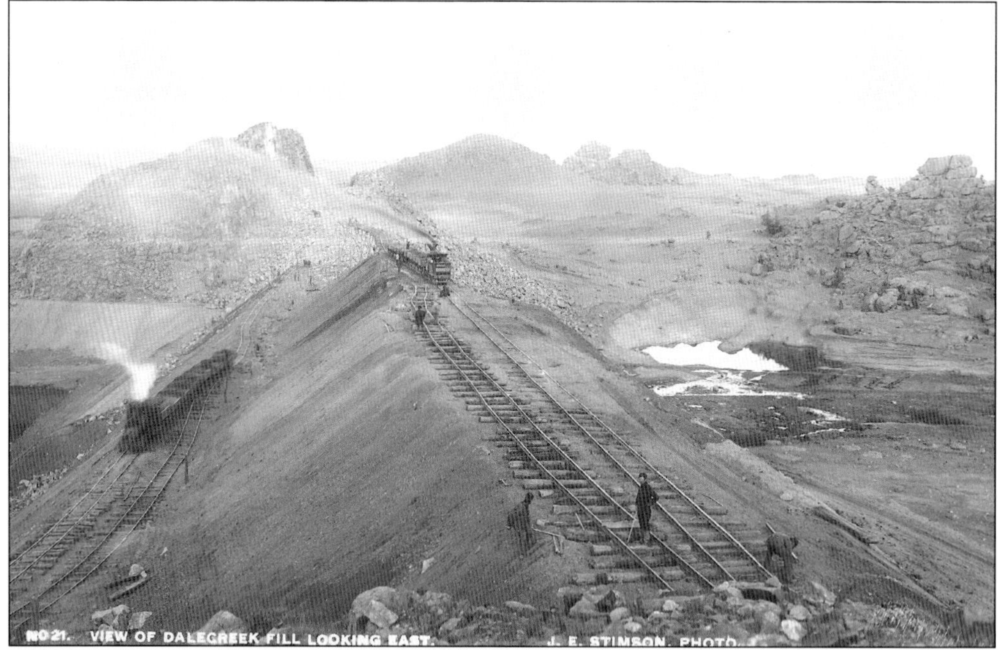

The "Big Fill" nears completion in 1901. It is over a mile long and more than 100 feet high near its center. The hillock on the left is near the center of the fill. The tracks in the photograph are temporary narrow-gauge ones used for construction only. The engines are dinkies, and the cars are side dumps. (Photograph by J.E. Stimson; Wyoming State Archives.)

Hermosa Tunnel, at 1,800 feet, is the longest tunnel on the Overland Route of the Union Pacific between Omaha and Ogden. When completed in 1901, it had a single bore; a second was finished in 1917. This is the portal of the west side in 1901. A shack for the section crew is to the left of the track. (Photograph by J.E. Stimson; Wyoming State Archives.)

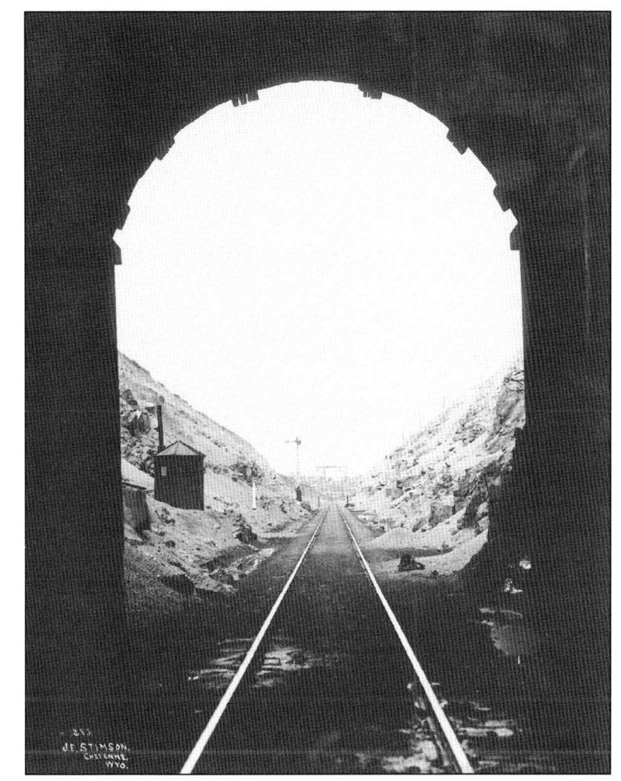

Mechanized track-laying is seen here around 1901. A conveyor to the left of the tall machine carries ties to the front of the track, where men set them in place (far left). Rails are carried forward by conveyors on both sides of the machine and are spiked in place on the ties (center). Once the rails are spiked, the machine advances, and the process is repeated. (Photograph by J.E. Stimson; JLEC.)

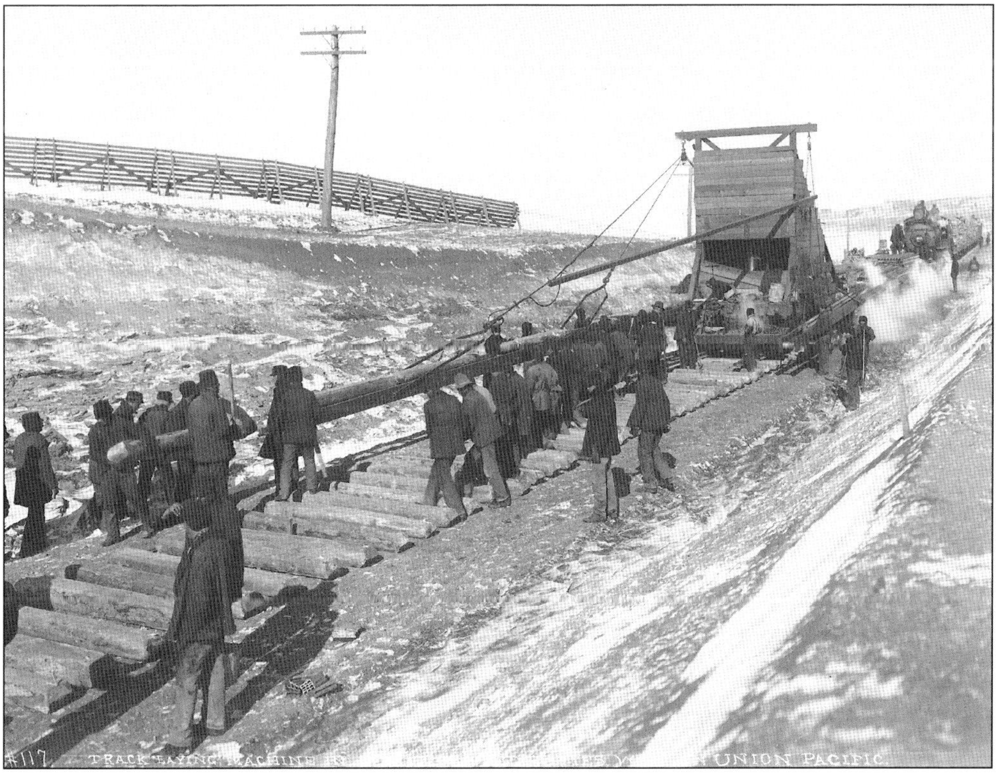

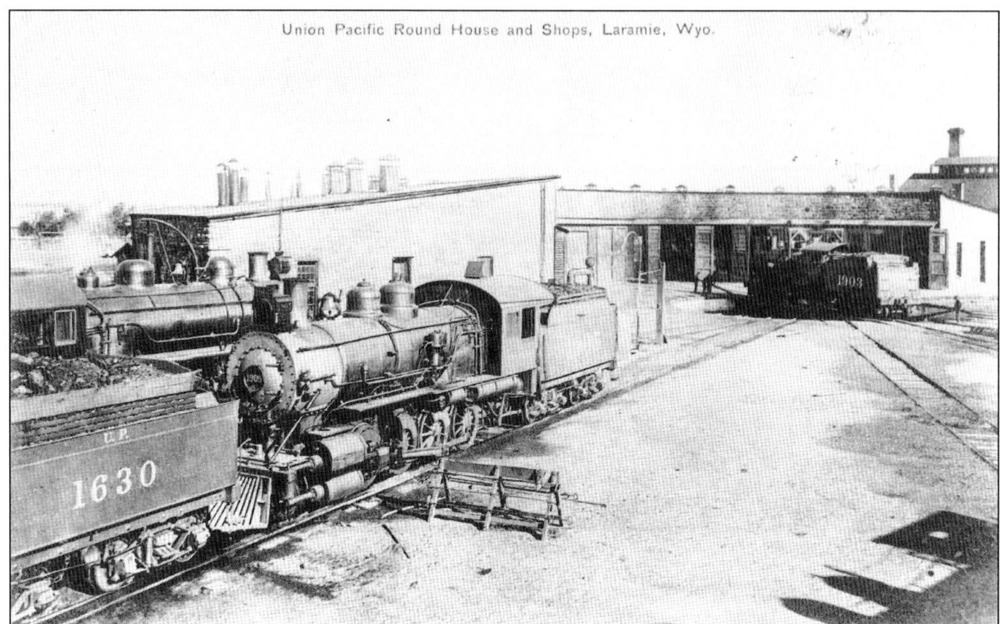

The Union Pacific roundhouse and shops were very busy in the 1890s. Shown here at the turn of the century, engines No. 1905 and No. 1630 are leaving the turntable, while an unidentified engine waits. Engine No. 1903 is taking a spin on it. Engine 1905 is a 2-8-0 Consolidation engine, meaning the leading pilot truck has two wheels, there are eight powered drivers, and there is no trailing truck. (JHC.)

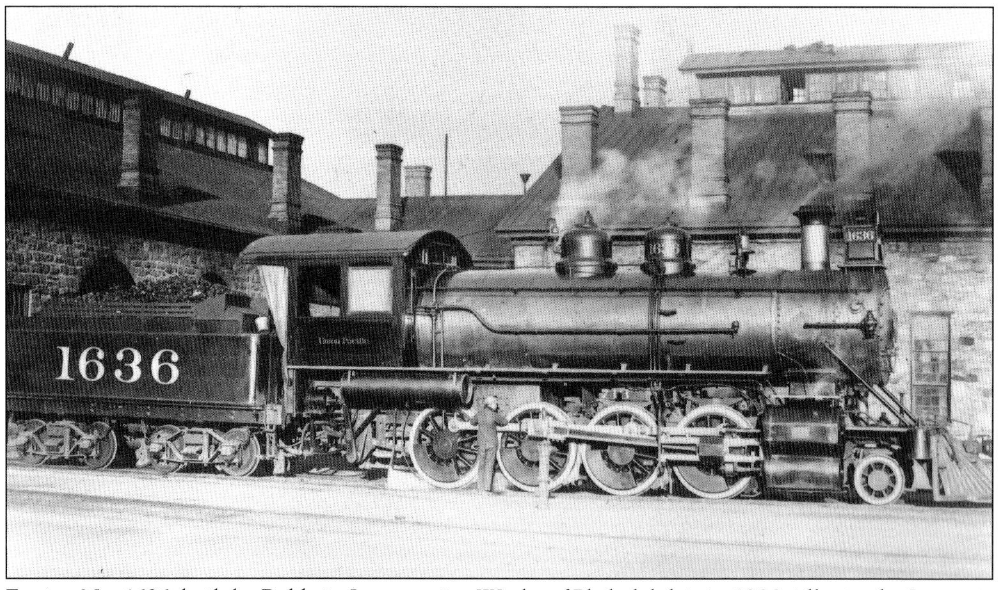

Engine No. 1636, built by Baldwin Locomotive Works of Philadelphia in 1900, idles in the Laramie railroad yards. It is a 2-8-0 Consolidation engine. The cylinders are "compound," meaning that the steam was used twice, first going to the lower, smaller, high-pressure cylinders, and then to the upper, larger, low-pressure cylinders before being exhausted through the stack. (Photograph by M.F. Jukes; JLEC.)

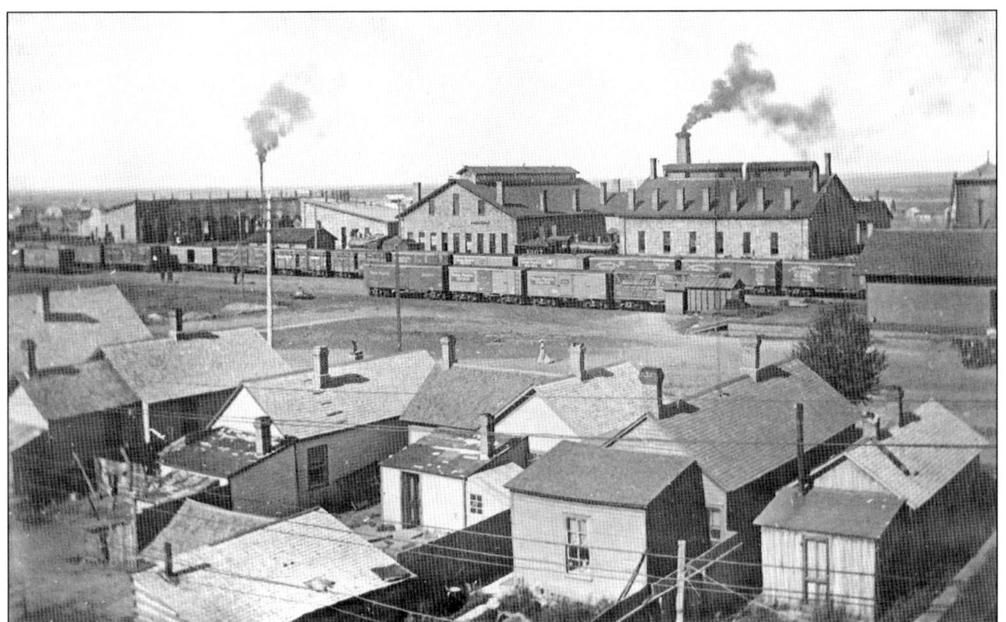

This 1897 view of Laramie's railroad complex shows not only the roundhouse, shops, and power plant but also some of the early trackside houses. These shotgun-style homes were common at the time, and many of them still survive, although not at this location. The view is to the west, from about Second and Garfield Streets. (American Heritage Center.)

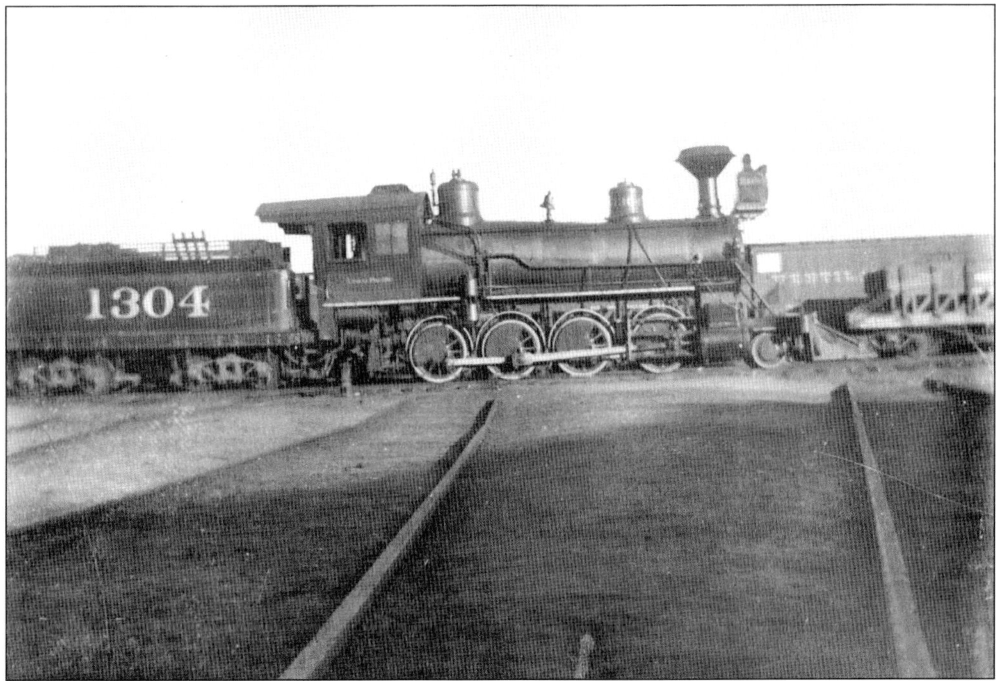

Engine No. 1304 was built in 1886 by Baldwin Locomotive Works of Philadelphia. Originally, it was a camelback locomotive with a Wooten firebox, but in 1894, it was converted to a standard cab and firebox. The photograph was taken in the Laramie yards sometime after 1894. The purpose of the tracks in the foreground is unknown, but perhaps they were used to store wheels. (LPM.)

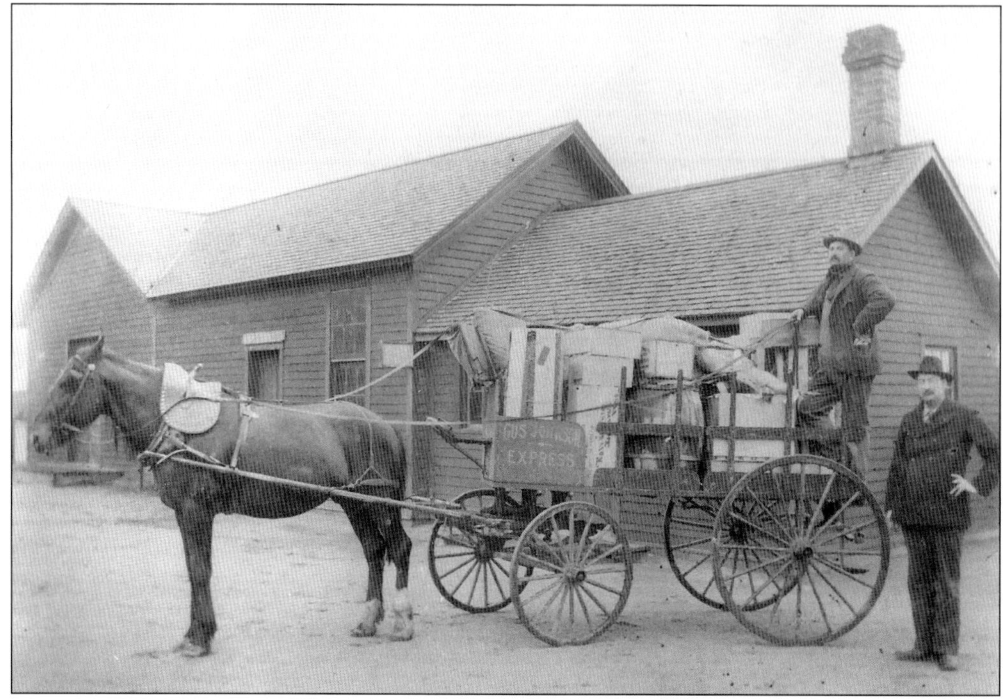

The Union Pacific express baggage office is in the background of this c. 1896 photograph. The horse, wagon, and men are from the Gus Johnson Express Service, which had a contract with the Union Pacific to deliver express freight. Such private delivery services were common before the creation of the Railway Express Agency (REA), a monopoly created by the federal government in 1917. (Wyoming State Archives.)

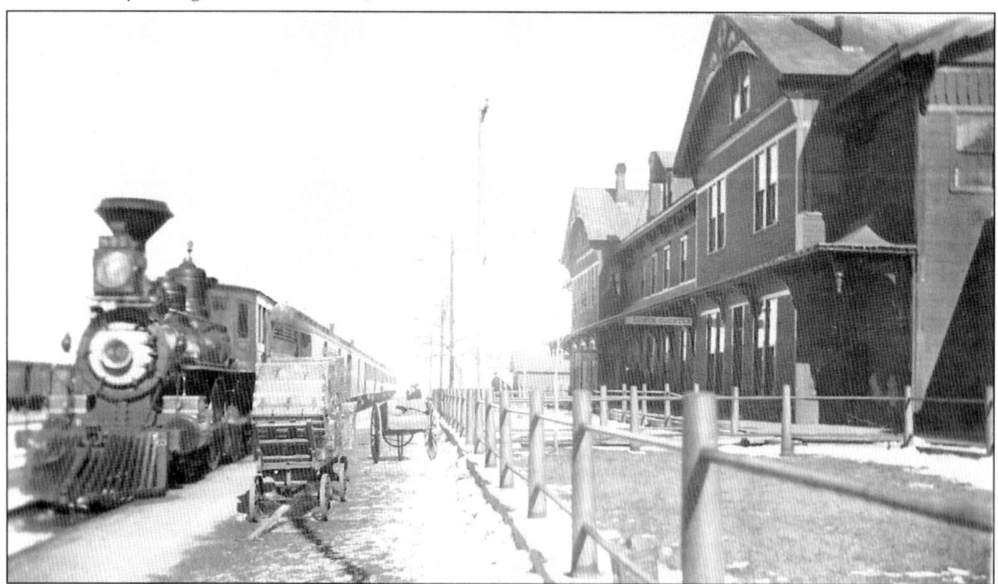

An eastbound passenger train arrives at the Union Pacific Hotel and depot around 1894. The hotel was named Thornburgh Hotel on November 21, 1879, in honor of Maj. Thomas Thornburgh, who died in one of the last Indian battles in America, on September 29, 1879. Note the light-painted trim on the station. (Wyoming State Archives.)

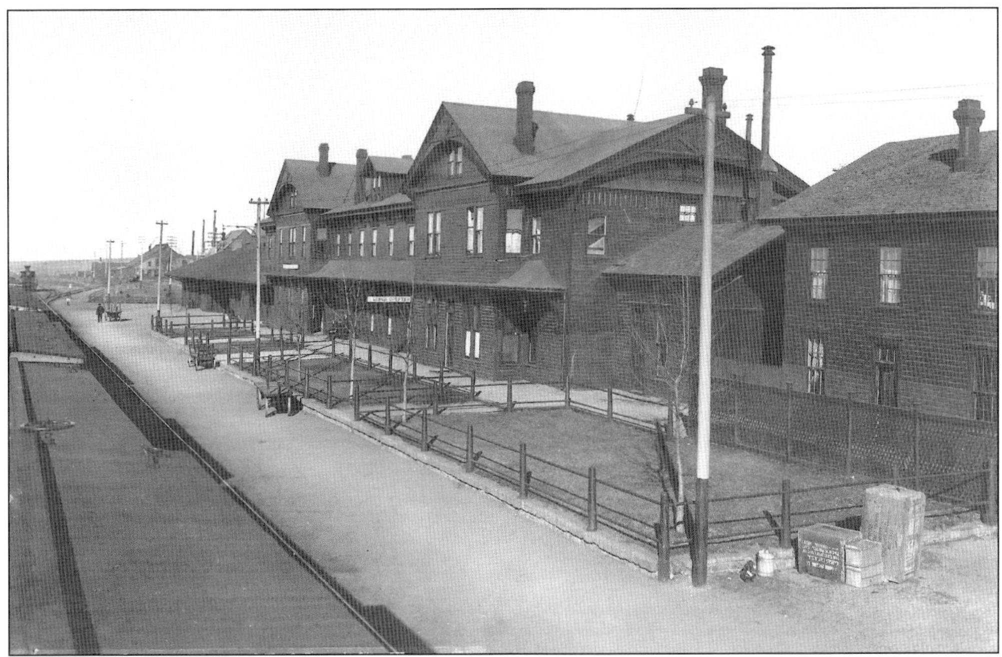

The Thornburgh Hotel is photographed from the top of a train car at the turn of the century. Fire was an ever-present danger, due to the hotel's proximity to the tracks. Burning embers from the steam locomotives often leapt to the building, but fires were quickly put out. Note the hotel's paint scheme compared to the photograph on the previous page. The building was painted red in April 1896. (Photograph by J.E. Stimson; Wyoming State Archives.)

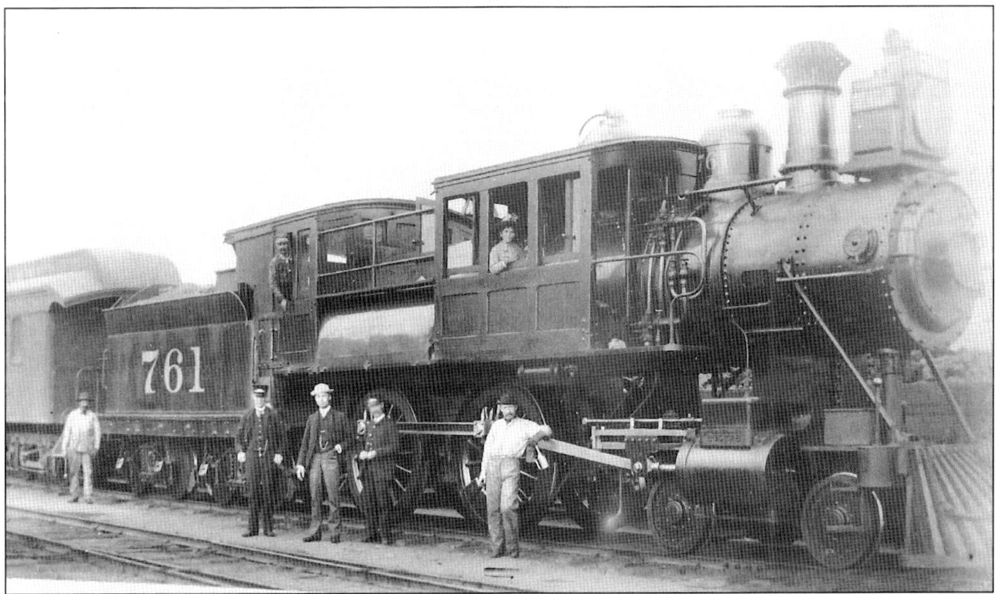

Engine No. 761, built by Rogers in 1887, has camelback cabs for both the engineer and the fireman. The engine has an extra-large Wooten firebox that was able to burn low-grade coal, and this firebox forced the camelback cab arrangement. The Union Pacific had 10 similar camelbacks from 1887 to 1891 or 1892, when they were rebuilt with standard fireboxes and cabs. This photograph was taken in 1890. (JLEC.)

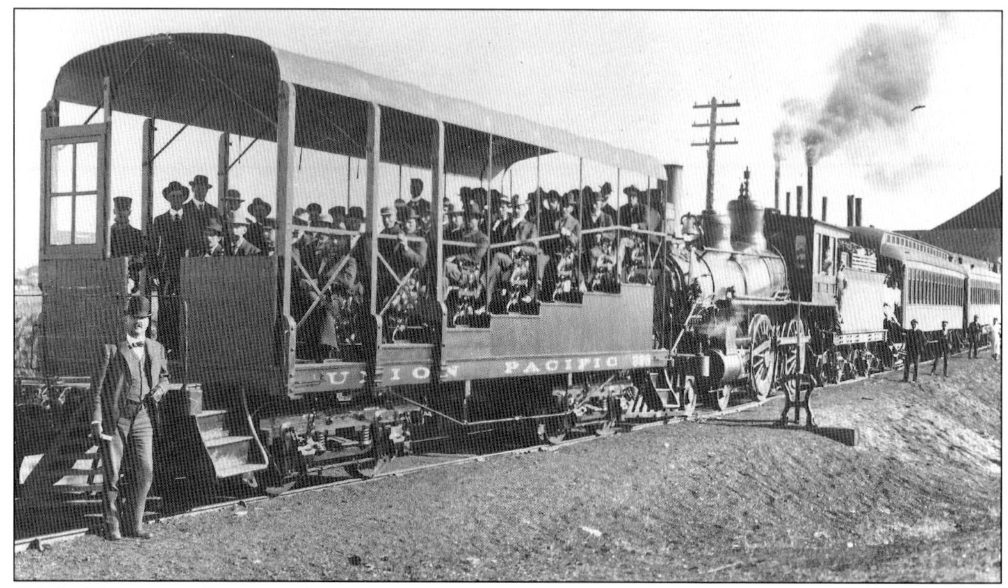

Of the Union Pacific's 80 miles of mainline track in Albany County, 72 miles were realigned and shortened from 1899 to 1901 under Harriman's tutelage. This is more miles than in any other county on the entire system. An inspection car filled with railroad officials, such as the one seen here around 1901, was a common site during the reconstruction. (JLEC.)

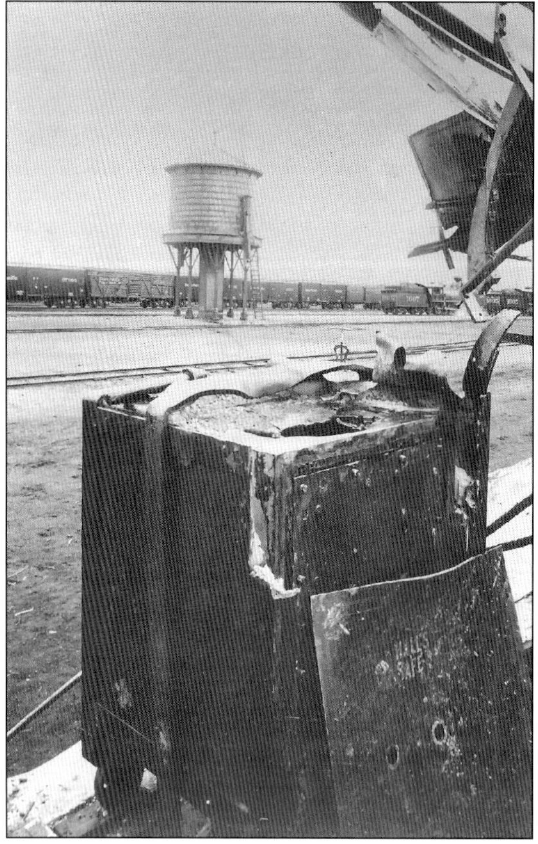

On June 2, 1899, some of Butch Cassidy's "Wild Bunch," but probably not Cassidy himself, carried out their most infamous train heist near Wilcox, Wyoming. Following the heist, the blown-up baggage car and safe were brought to Laramie. This photograph shows the hole blown in the top of the safe. Safes made by Hall's Safe & Co. were commonly used by the Union Pacific Railroad. (Western History Research Center, University of Wyoming.)

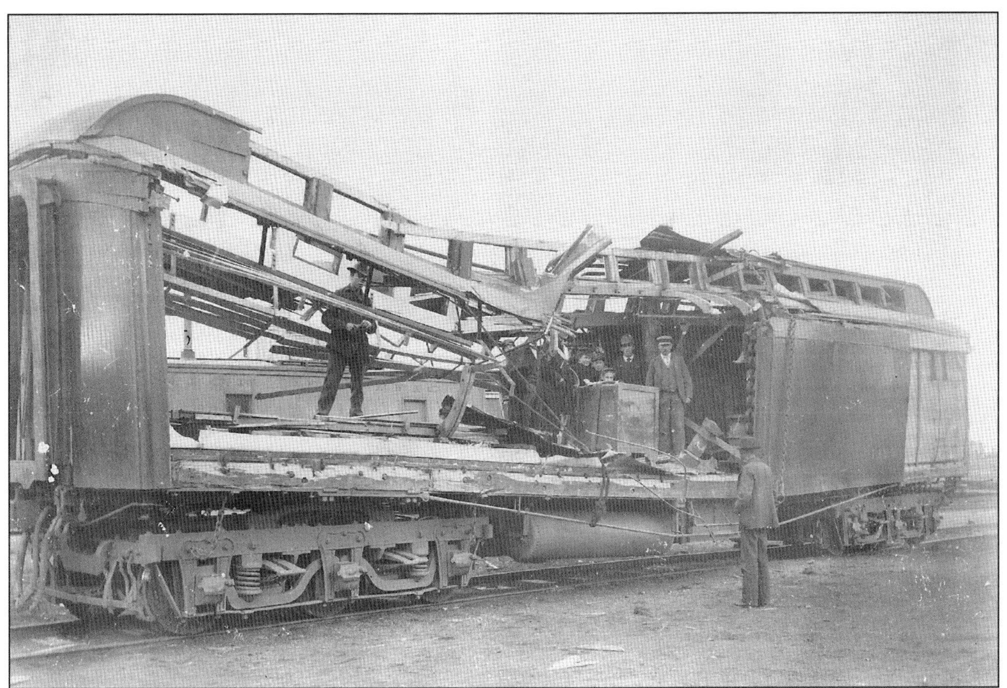

When express-car agent Charles Woodcock refused to supply the bandits with the combination to the safe, they blew it open with dynamite. They used too much, and the explosion not only opened the safe, it also blew out the sides and roof of the car. The car, seen here in 1899, was towed to Laramie from Wilcox and became a town curiosity. (JLEC.)

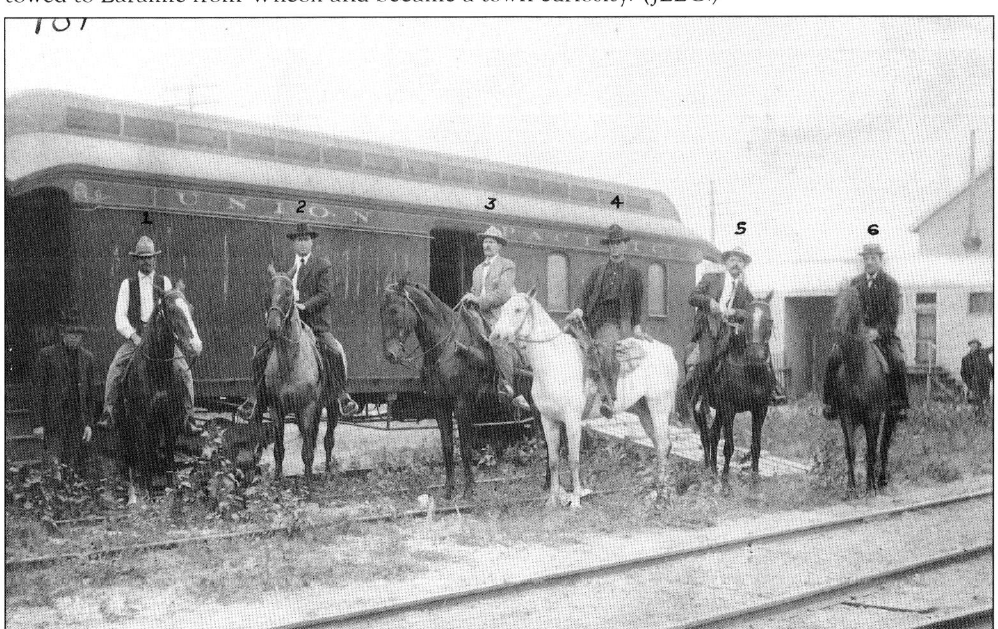

This is part of the posse assigned to track down the thieves after the Wilcox train robbery. Shown here on horseback are, from left to right, George Hiatt, T.T. Kelliher, Joe Lefors, H. Davis, Si Funk, and Jeff Carr. Within 24 hours of the holdup, a posse of nearly 100 men was chasing the thieves, who escaped with more than $30,000 in bank notes and jewelry. (JLEC.)

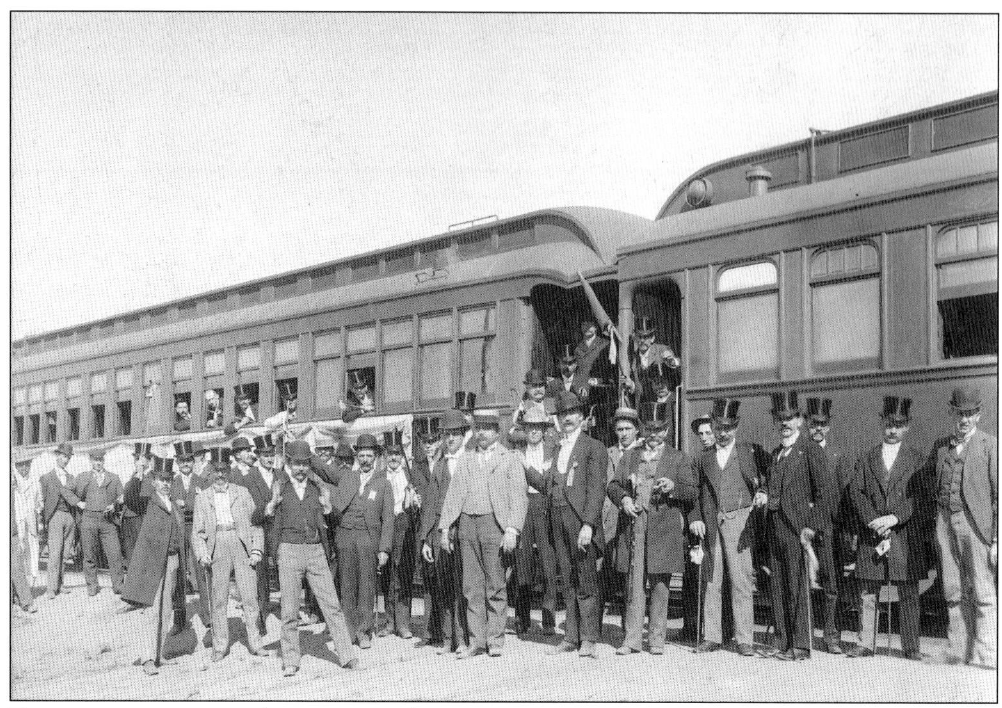

Train outings were popular events at the turn of the century. Here, a convention of men from the Elks lodge boards a train for one such event sometime between 1901 and 1906. Note the popularity of top hats among the members. (LPM.)

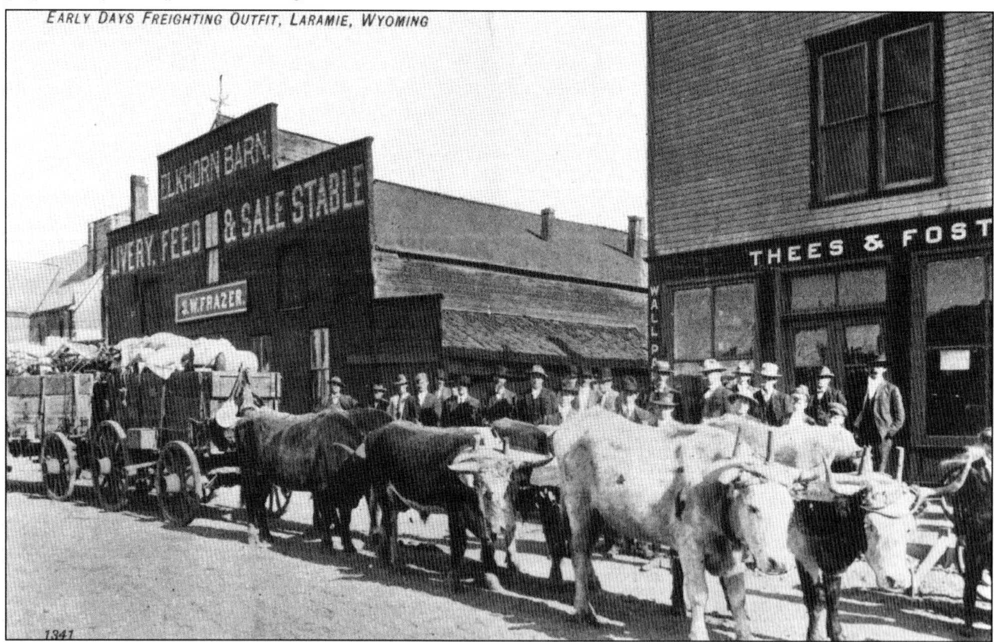

A teamster guides his oxen and freight wagons through town around 1901. Prior to the construction of the Transcontinental Railroad, the ox-driven wagon train was the primary means of moving freight throughout the West. It still remained an important freight hauler for local deliveries until the advent of the automobile. (LPM.)

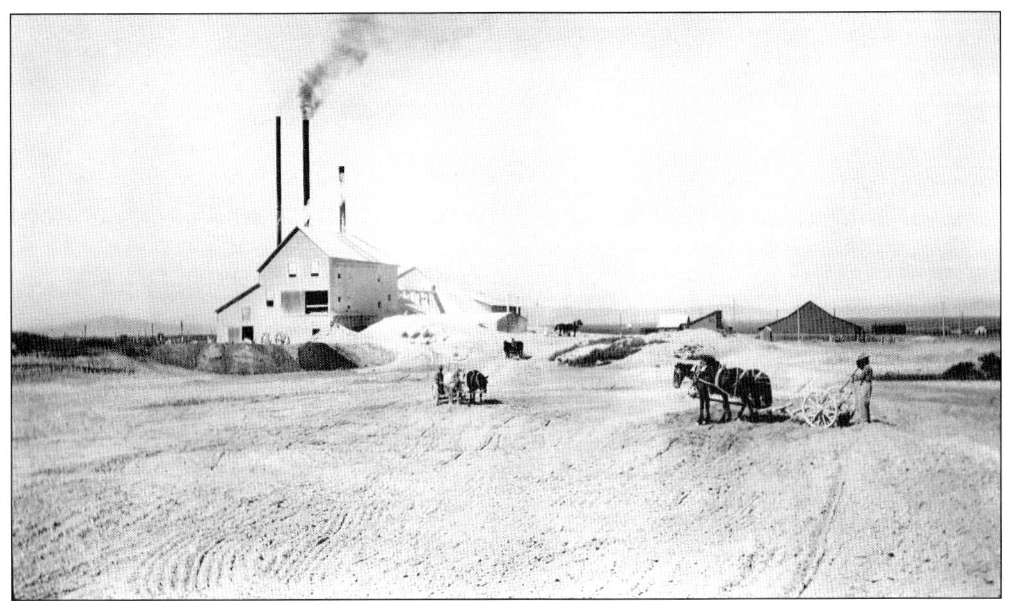

Because of the availability of gypsum deposits near Laramie, a plaster plant was a natural addition to the town. This photograph, taken sometime between 1894 and 1900, shows the Standard Plaster Mill. Built in 1894, the plant was turned into the Acme Cement Plant in 1896. (Photograph by E.F. Burchard; US Geological Survey Collection.)

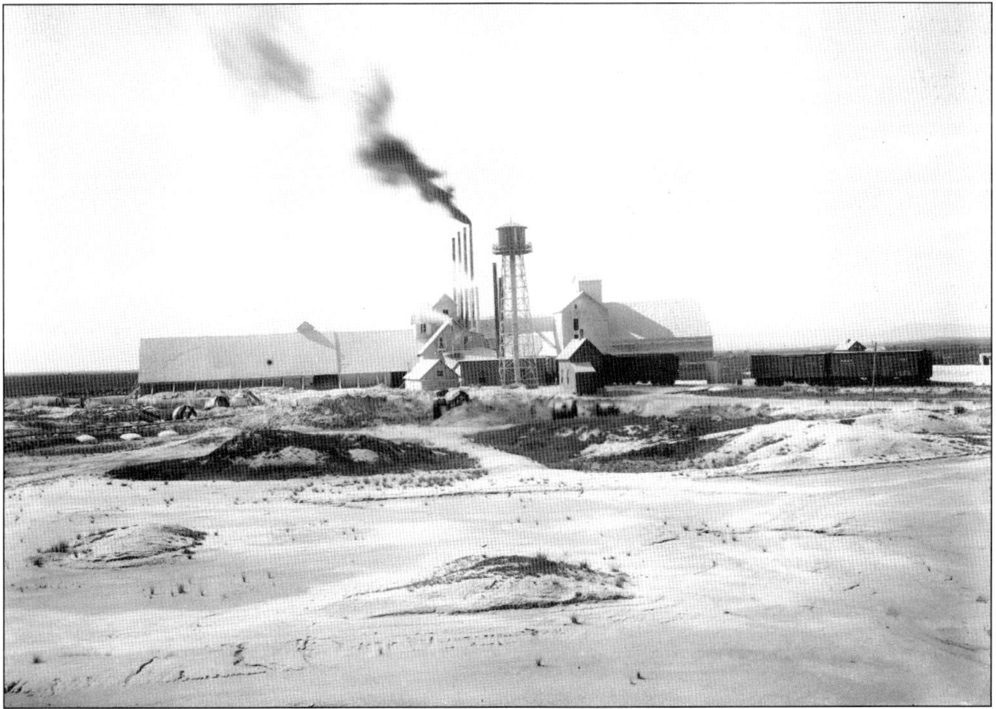

This is another view of the Standard Plaster Mill. Seen from this angle are the railroad boxcars used to transport the finished product from the plant. The factory, seen here sometime between 1894 and 1900, was located near the present-day I-80 exit 313 (South Third Street) and used gypsum from nearby quarries as its major material. (LPM.)

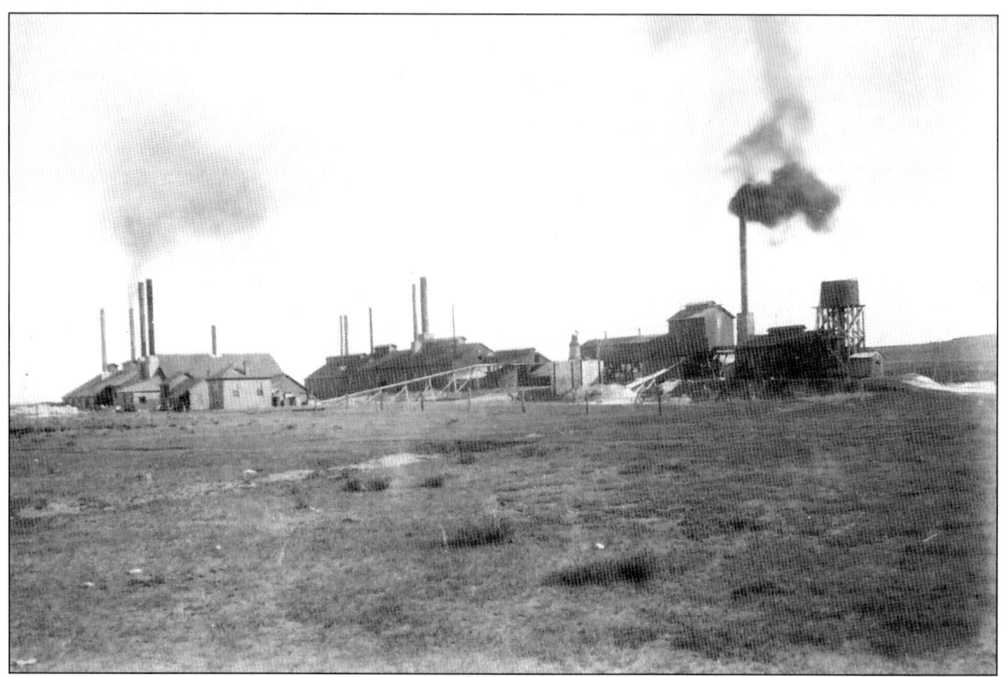

A chemical plant was located north of the present-day Curtiss Street Viaduct. Like many of the industrial facilities in early Laramie, it had a short and volatile life. Seen here around 1885, the plant was built in 1883, but it burned down two years later. It was rebuilt and then abandoned in 1886. (JHC.)

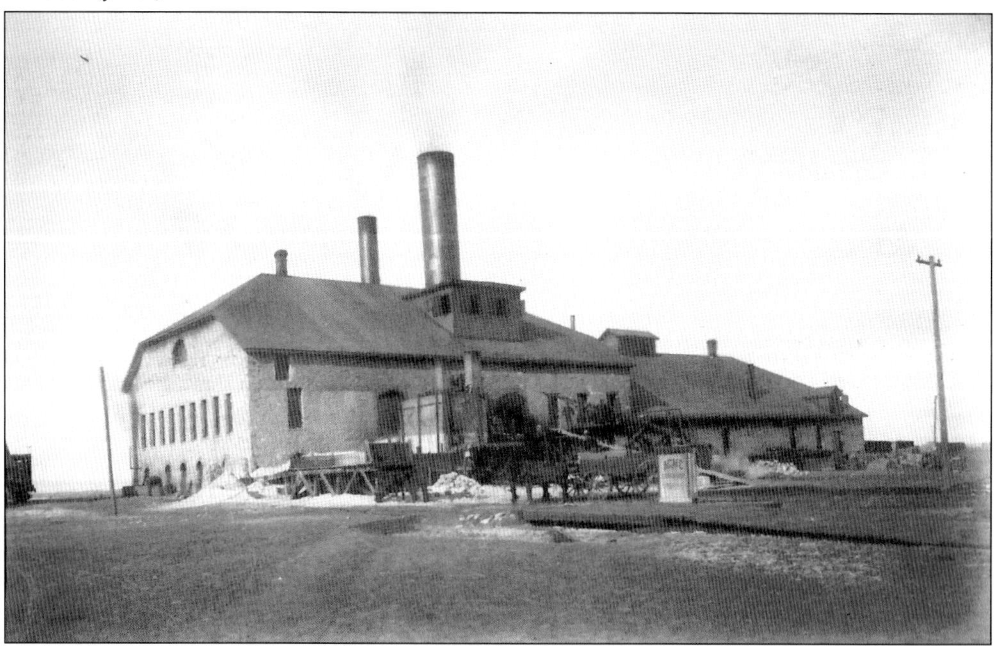

This building was the original glass factory. It was built in 1886 and began production in 1887. It continued life as a glass factory until 1890, when it was converted into the Acme Plaster Mill. The facility operated in that capacity until 1900. Both the glass factory and the plaster mill were served by the Union Pacific Railroad. It is seen here around 1905. (LPM.)

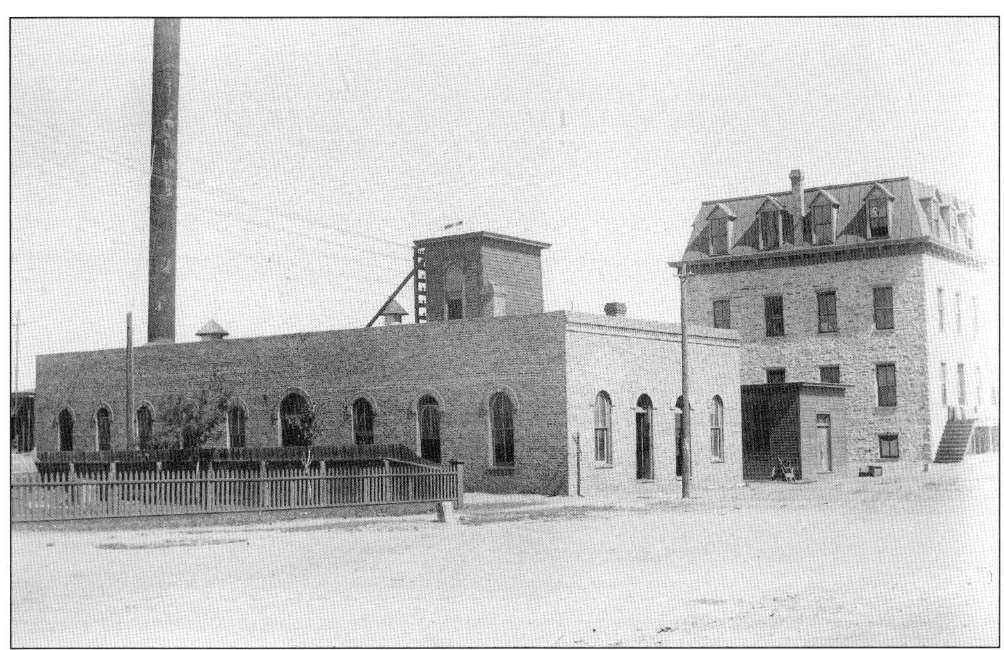

As the town continued to grow, industries that were not directly associated with the railroad began to sprout up. In the foreground of this c. 1892 photograph is Laramie's first electric plant, built in 1886. In the background is the Overland Cereals Company, a flour mill built in 1883. (LPM.)

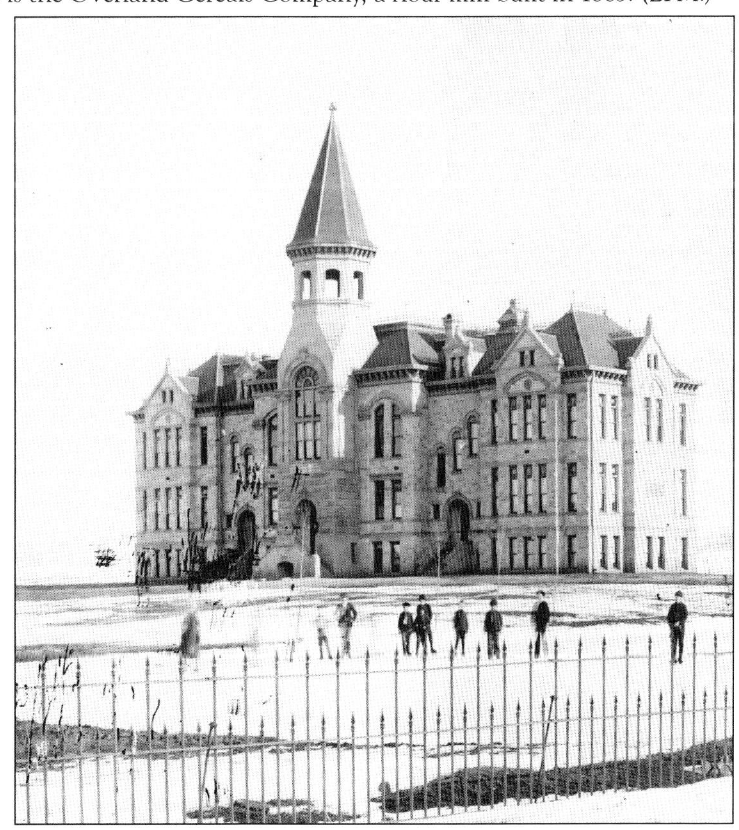

In 1886, a new source of revenue came to Laramie. The University of Wyoming was created, and the first structure, "Old Main," was built. It is seen here in its first years of existence. The university began small, but it now dominates the town's economy. Today, Old Main houses the administrative offices for a campus with 14,000 students. (Photograph by E.F. Burchard; US Geological Survey Collection.)

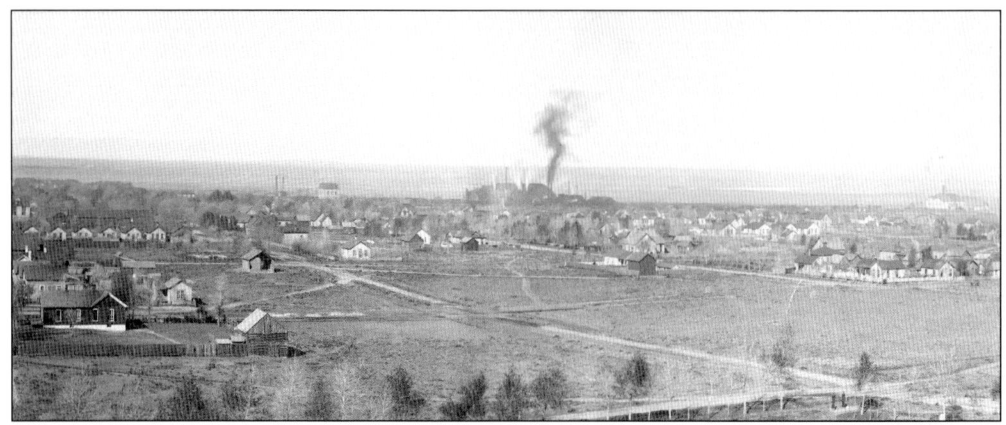

This 1900 photograph was taken from Old Main's tower, which was removed in 1916. The prominent structure billowing smoke in the distance is the Union Pacific Rolling Mills. In 1880, this mill employed an average of 174 males above 16 years old, 10 males under 16, and no females. The mill took old rail, melted it, and produced new rail. (Photograph by E.T.W. Weyle; LPM.)

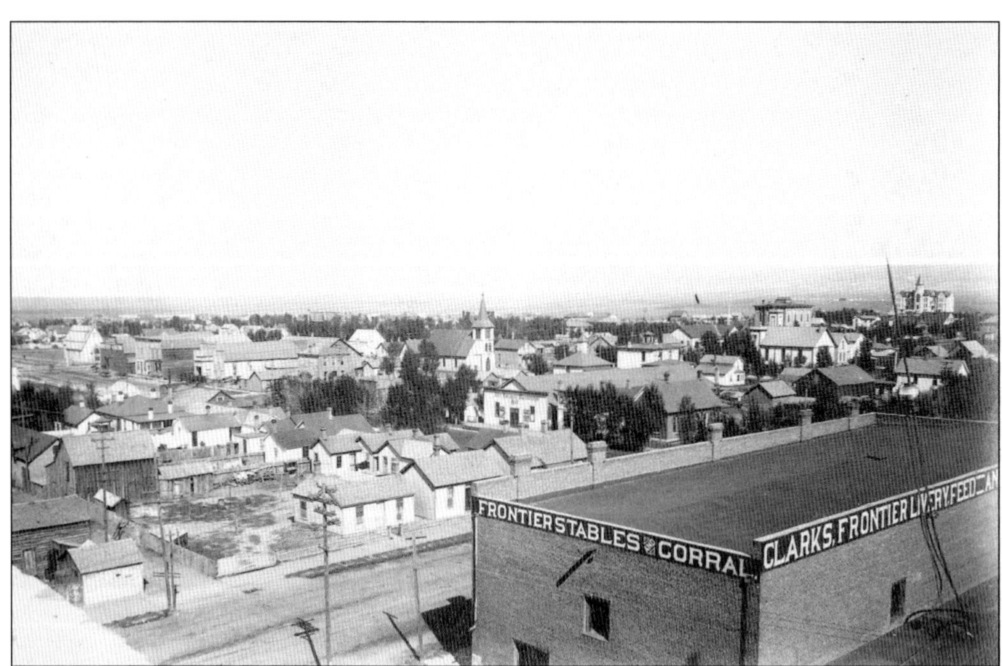

This photograph was taken from a roof on the edge of Laramie's historic downtown at the southeast corner of Third and Garfield Streets. The image dates to the first decade of the 20th century and looks to the northeast. Many shotgun-style houses can be seen in the foreground. On the edge of town, on the far right, is Old Main. (LPM.)

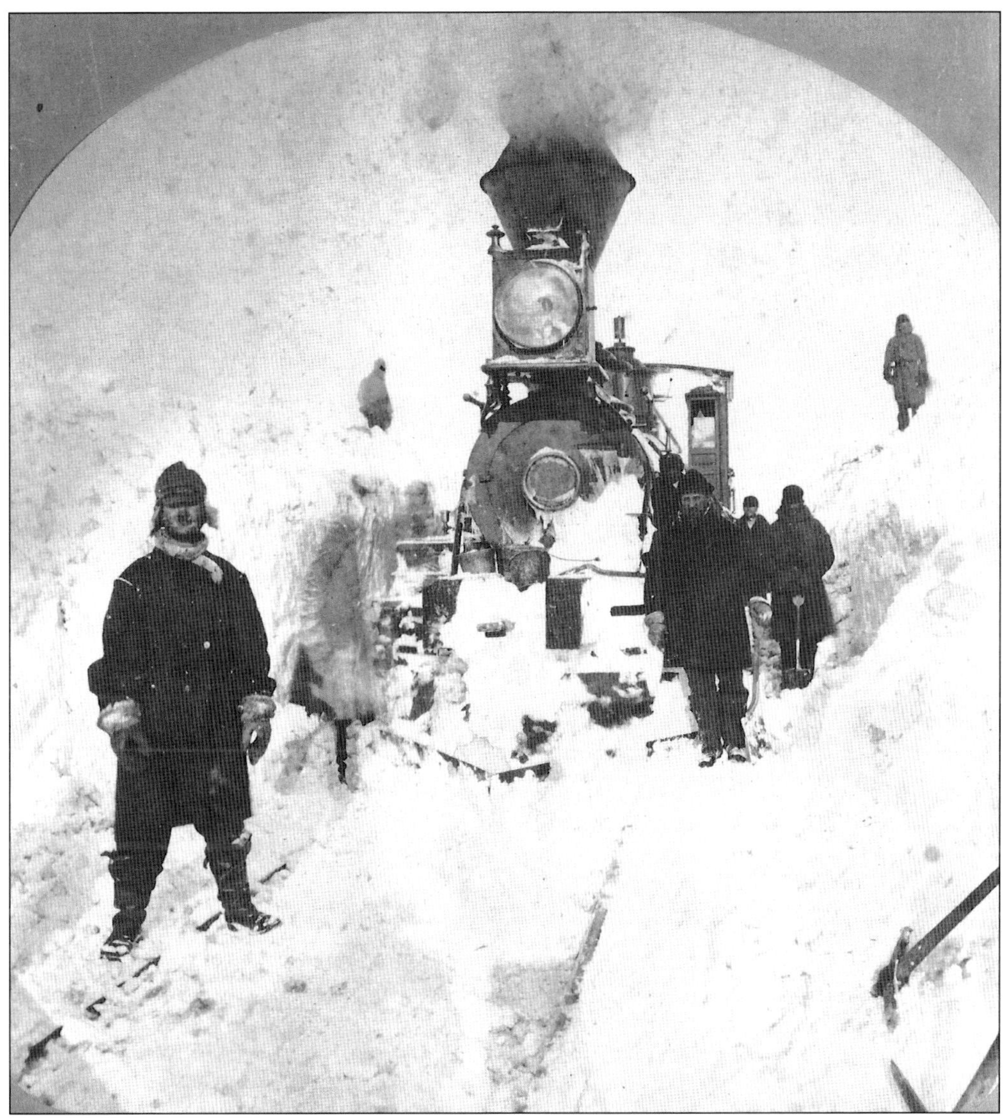

One of the worst snowstorms of Laramie's early years was the Schoolhouse Blizzard of 1888. The death toll throughout the Great Plains was 235; sixty people died in Wyoming. The blizzard hit unexpectedly, and many children in one-room schoolhouses were caught unaware. Transportation, including the Union Pacific, was brought to a standstill. This photograph was taken near the Cooper Lake Station. (JLEC.)

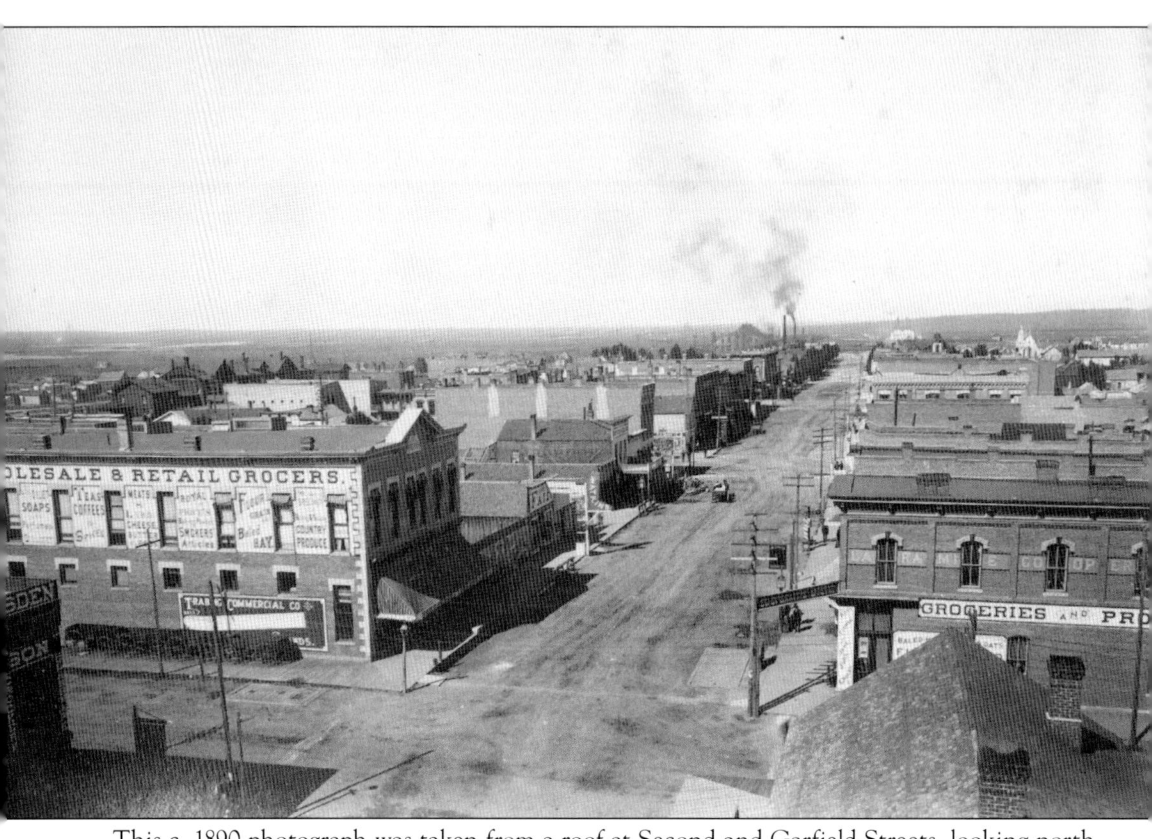

This c. 1890 photograph was taken from a roof at Second and Garfield Streets, looking north. The "Wholesale & Retail Grocers" was owned by a Mr. Trabing. A vacant lot beside it was owned by a Mr. Nadler, who wished to erect stables on the property. Not wanting stables so close to his store, Trabing bought the property. Additions to the structure wound up creating Laramie's first "superstore." (LPM.)

Three

1901–1930

Origins of the Smaller Railroads in Albany County

Though it was the first and is the only remaining railroad, the Union Pacific was not the only railroad in Laramie's history. Two smaller but significant routes saw their heyday in the early part of the 20th century. One of the railroads connected the gypsum mines to the local cement plant. The other wound its way through the mountains and passes of the nearby Snowy Range and connected the mine at Coalmont, Colorado, to the Union Pacific main line. Along the way, it also serviced many small timber communities in the Snowy Range area.

Of these two lines, the smaller was that which served the gypsum quarries. It was called the Laramie Valley Railway. It is significant in that it operated steam locomotives well into the late 1960s and early 1970s, longer than any other railroad in the United States other than tourist lines. The line to Coalmont saw several owners and name changes throughout the years. It began as the Laramie, Hans Peak & Pacific, went on to become the Laramie, North Park & Western, and for a time, it was bought by the Union Pacific and renamed the "Coalmont branch." It finally ended life as the Wyoming/Colorado Railroad (WyCo). Though primarily a line meant for freight, the Coalmont branch, in its various guises, was also used as an excursion train into the beautiful Snowy Range.

The early 1900s was also a time of great calamity in the town of Laramie. In an era prior to modern safety regulations and technology, fires and explosions were a common occurrence for the industrial and even nonindustrial buildings in town. Though many of these buildings had been damaged and rebuilt numerous times, the final end of several notable fixtures in town came about in the early 20th century. Affected by these fires and explosions were the original depot and hotel (Thournburgh Hotel), the rolling mills, and the glass factory. Calamity came to the area in the form of ice, as well. In 1917, a blizzard swept though the county that crippled the Union Pacific Railroad and humbled it for years to come.

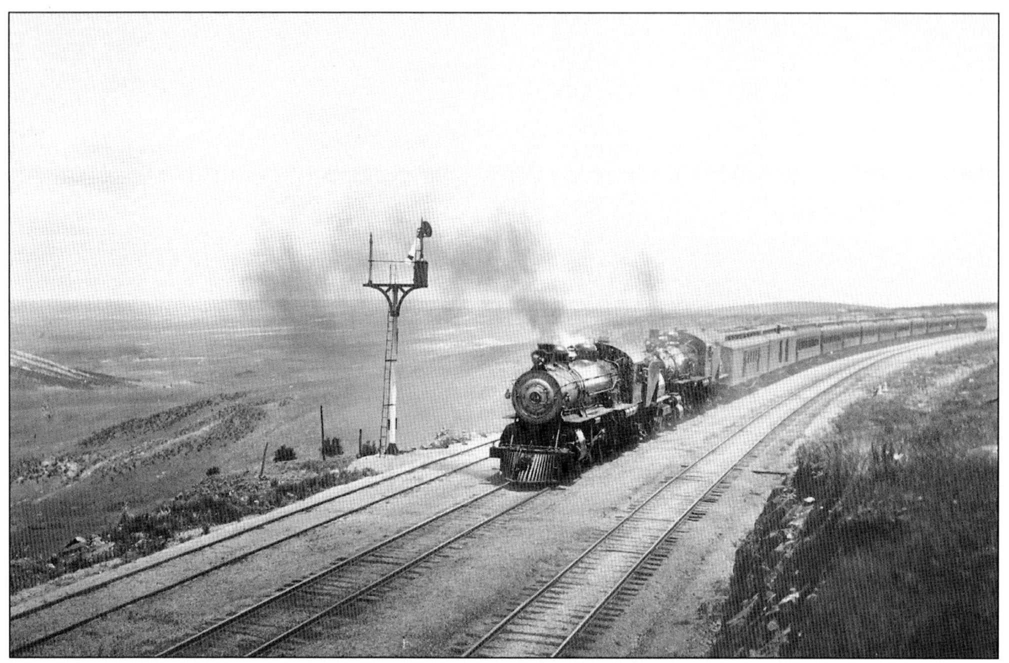

This 1911 photograph of the Western Pacific Express on the Gangplank, taken from the same location as the top photograph on page 13, faces east, to the plains. Here, the Rocky Mountains (behind the viewer) and the Great Plains are at the same elevation. To the north (left), the plains drop 300 feet to a 50-mile-long valley. (Photograph by J.E. Stimson; Wyoming State Archives.)

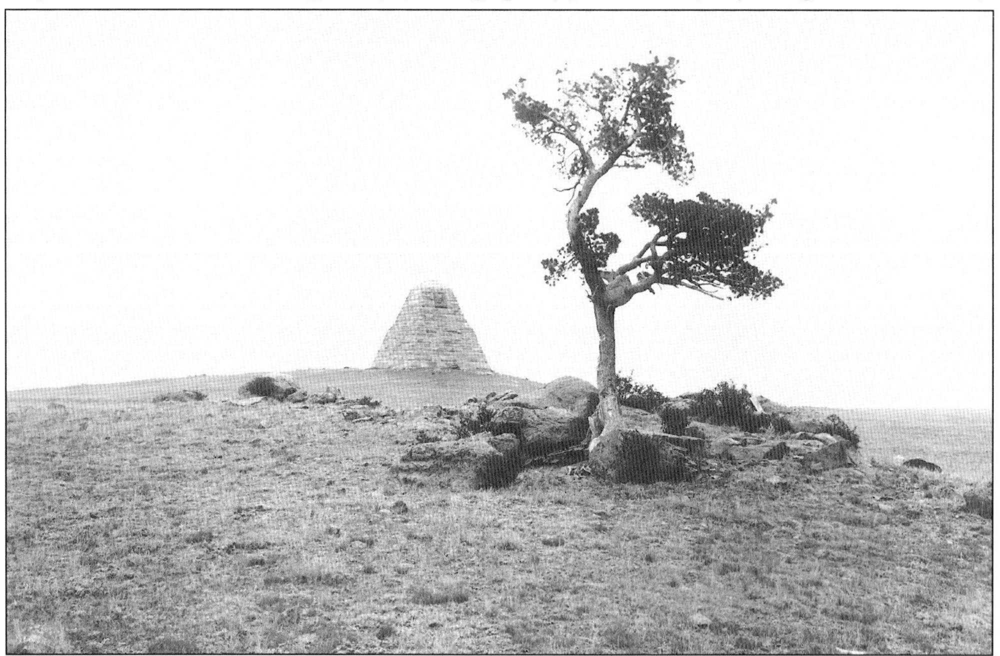

Photographs of the Ames Monument, much like this one taken in 1905, were commonly used as postcards sold to travelers along the Lincoln Highway. The highway, which opened in 1913, followed much of the same route as the original Transcontinental Railroad, and much of it was built directly atop the railroad right-of-way. (Photograph by J.E. Stimson; JLEC.)

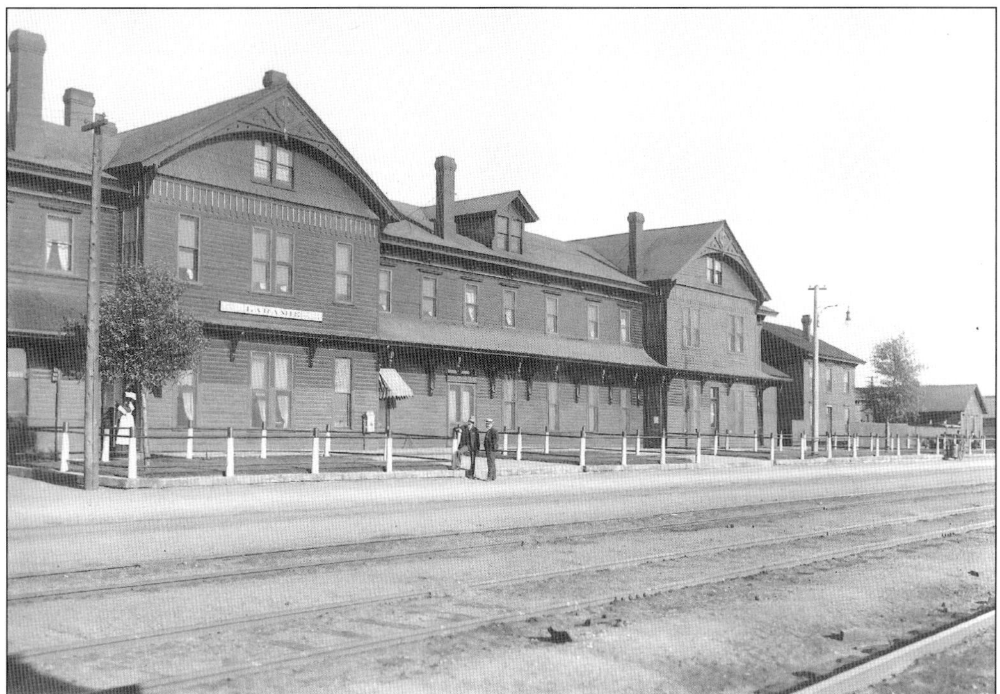

In 1885, dormers were added to the original hotel and depot, considerably changing its appearance. Nevertheless, this building, erected in 1868, continued to serve Laramie's passengers into the second decade of the 20th century. It is seen here around 1905. (Photograph by J.E. Stimson; Wyoming State Archives.)

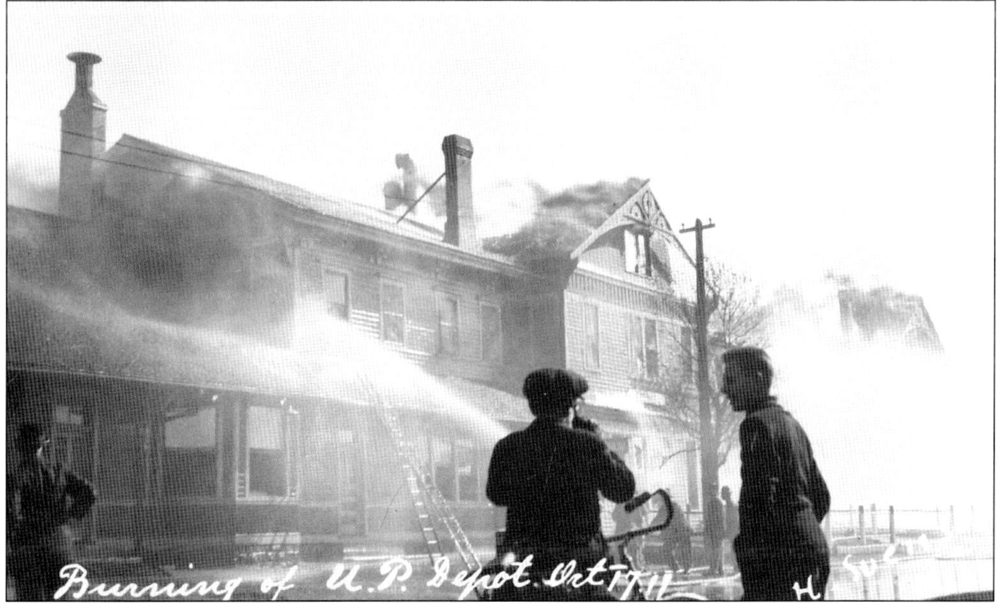

Due to its proximity to the tracks and a continual showering of embers from passing trains, the hotel/depot suffered many fires over the years. Finally, on October 17, 1917, a fire began in the kitchen that could not be quenched. After nearly 50 years of service, all but the northernmost part of the building burned down completely. (Photograph by H. Svenson; LPM.)

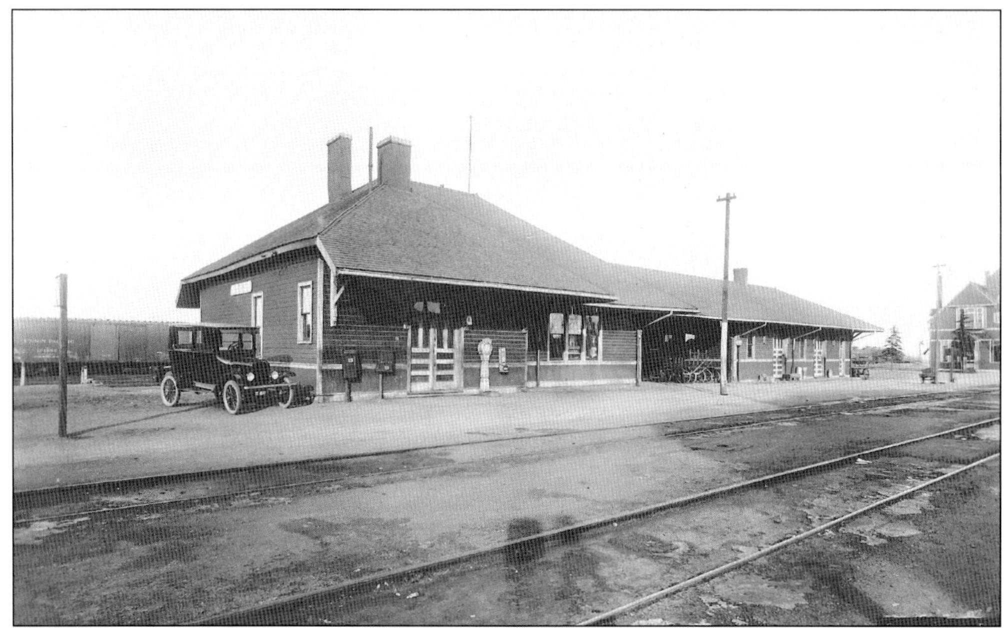

This building had been the women's waiting room on the north end of the depot/hotel. It was the only part of the structure that survived the fire of 1917 and was used as a temporary depot while the new one was being built. Note the Ford Model T parked next to it. This c. 1918 photograph faces northwest. (Photograph by Union Pacific; JLEC.)

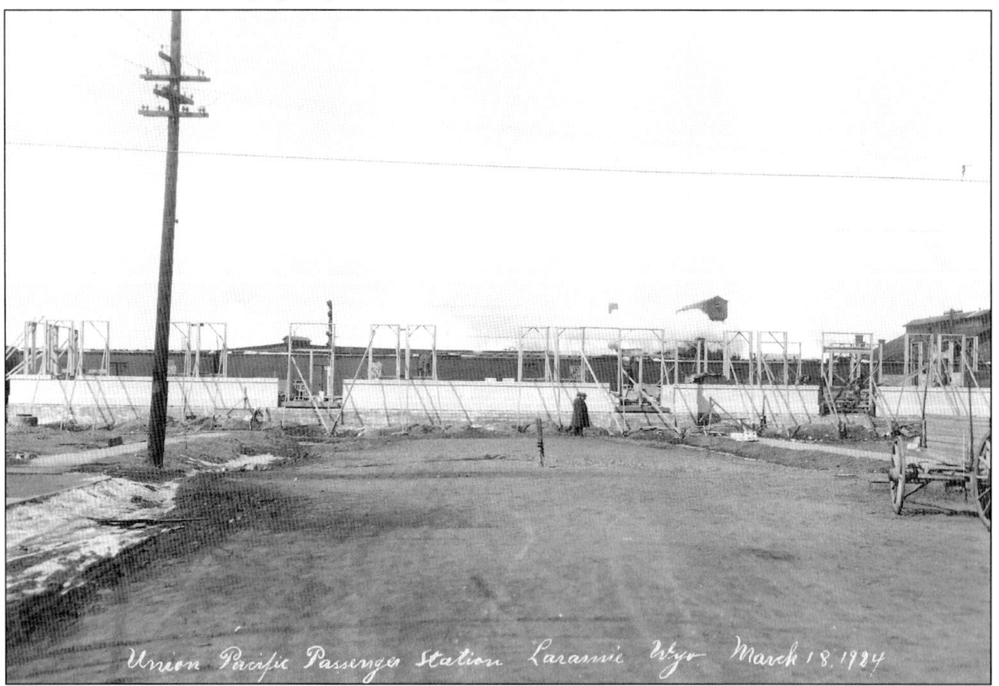

The American Construction Company was awarded the contract to build the new Laramie railroad depot. It was erected four blocks south and one-half block east of the original, at First and Kearney Streets. By mid-March 1924, the time of this photograph, the terra-cotta wainscot was complete, and the windows and doors were being framed. (Photograph by H. Svenson; JLEC.)

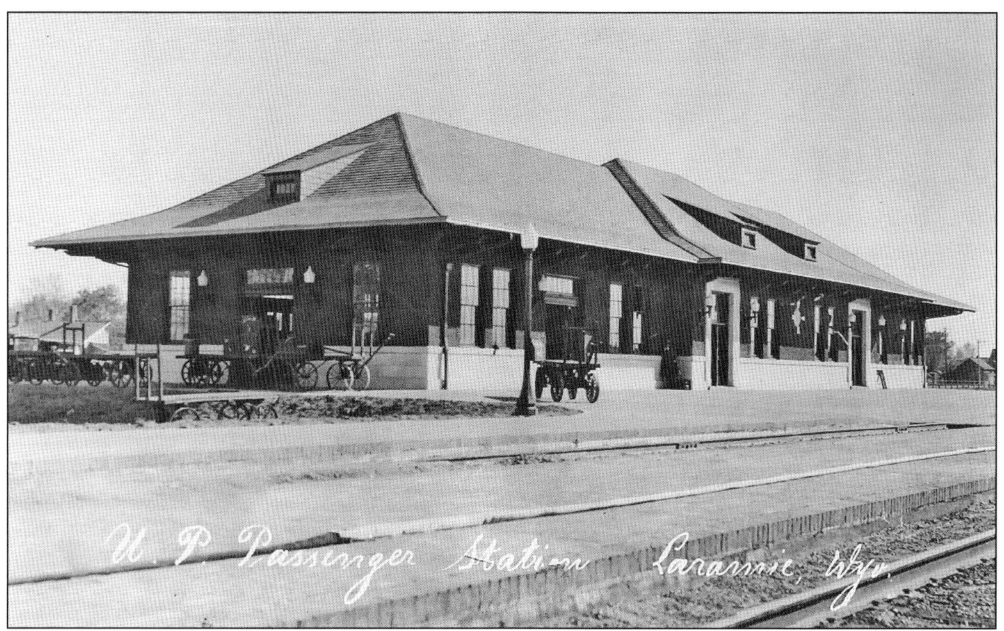

The new depot opened its doors to the public in October 1924. The two-tone exterior of red brick and white terra-cotta has helped the structure become one of Laramie's signature buildings. It stands today as a museum, community center, and graceful reminder of Laramie's railroad heritage. The handcarts in this 1953 photograph still exist and were recently restored. (Photograph by Union Pacific; JLEC.)

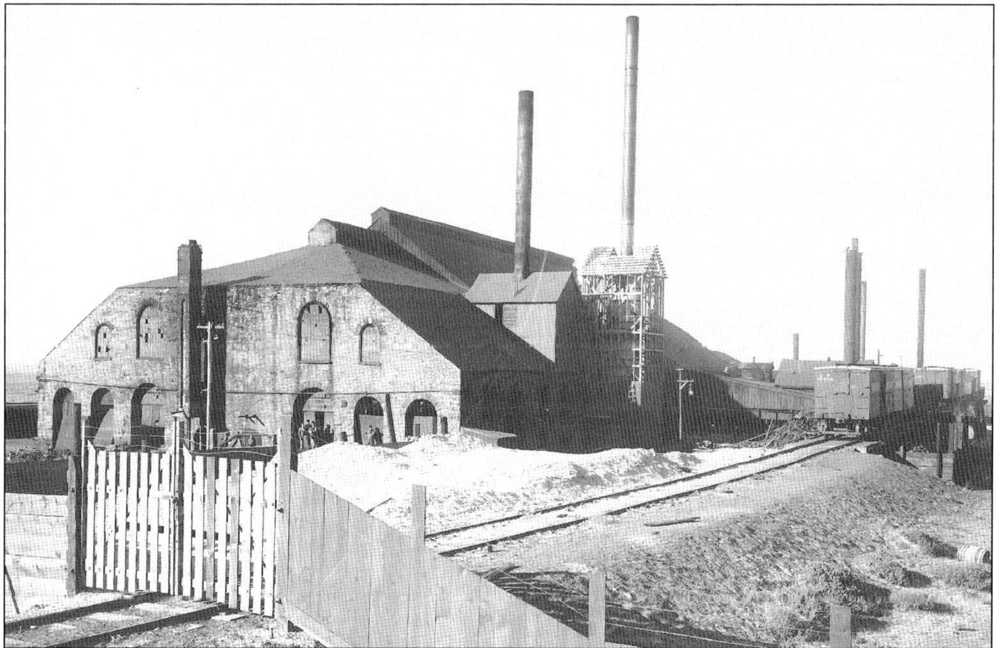

The Union Pacific Rolling Mills in Laramie, seen here in 1907, were the first such ironworks built west of the Mississippi River. The mill took old rail, melted it, and produced new rail. A pit filled with old rail, strewn like spaghetti, is visible to the left of the boxcar. (Photograph by J.E. Stimson; Wyoming State Archives.)

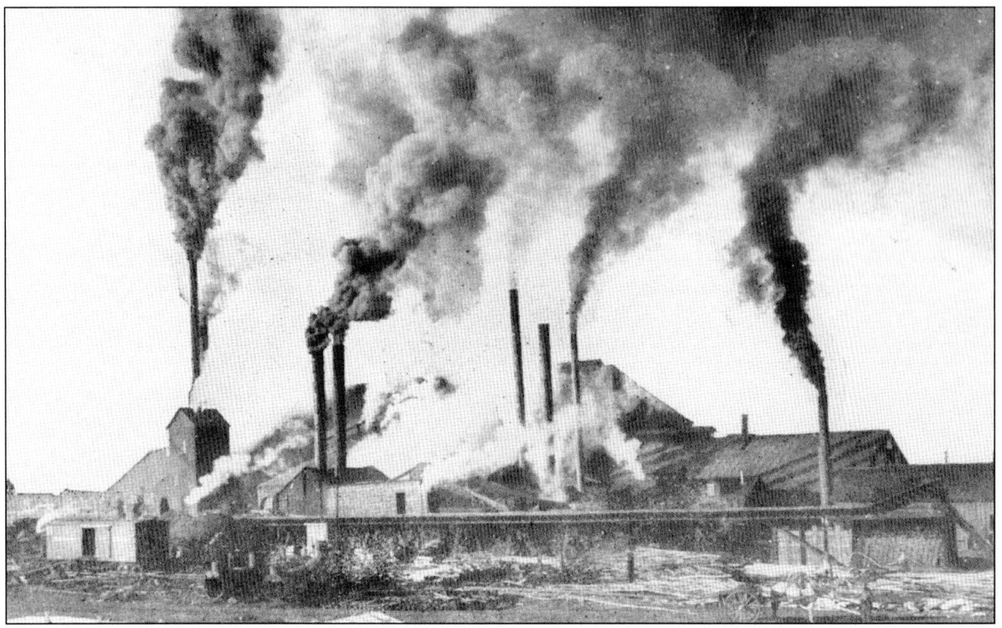

The rolling mill is seen here in full production around 1908. At the facility's peak of operation, smoke from the stacks could be seen from almost any point in the Laramie Valley. Like many of Laramie's early buildings and industry, the rolling mill was prone to fires and explosions. Note that many of these stacks were under construction in the previous photograph. (Photograph by Rogers; LPM.)

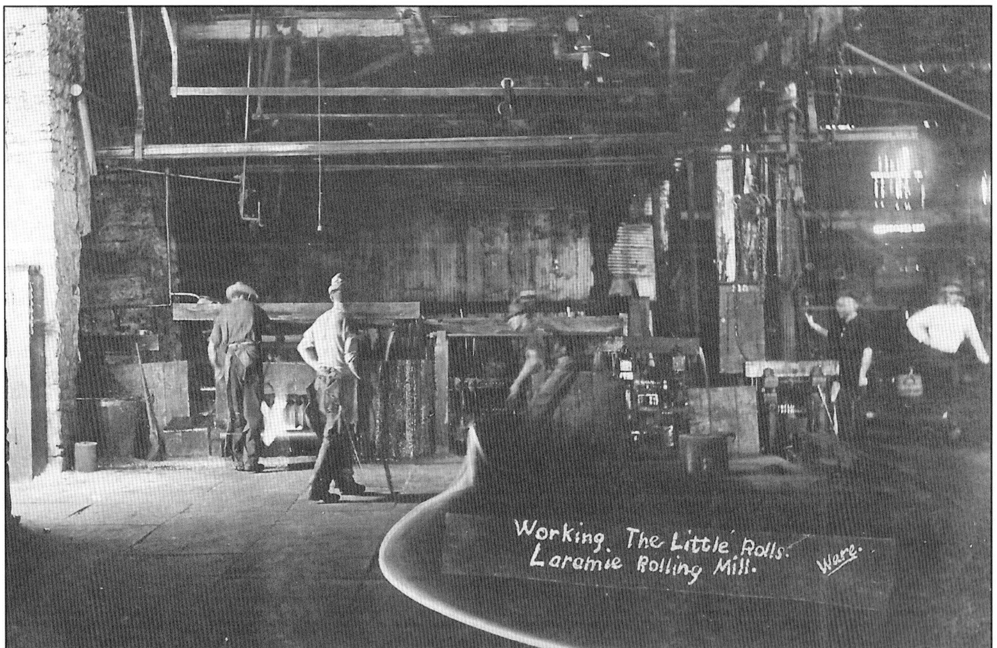

This c. 1912 postcard photograph shows men at work inside the rolling mill. The glowing line along the floor appears to be a piece of molten steel that was carried across the frame. The photograph was taken at a slow shutter speed, thus creating the ghostly appearance of the molten steel and some of the millworkers. (Photograph by Ware; JLEC.)

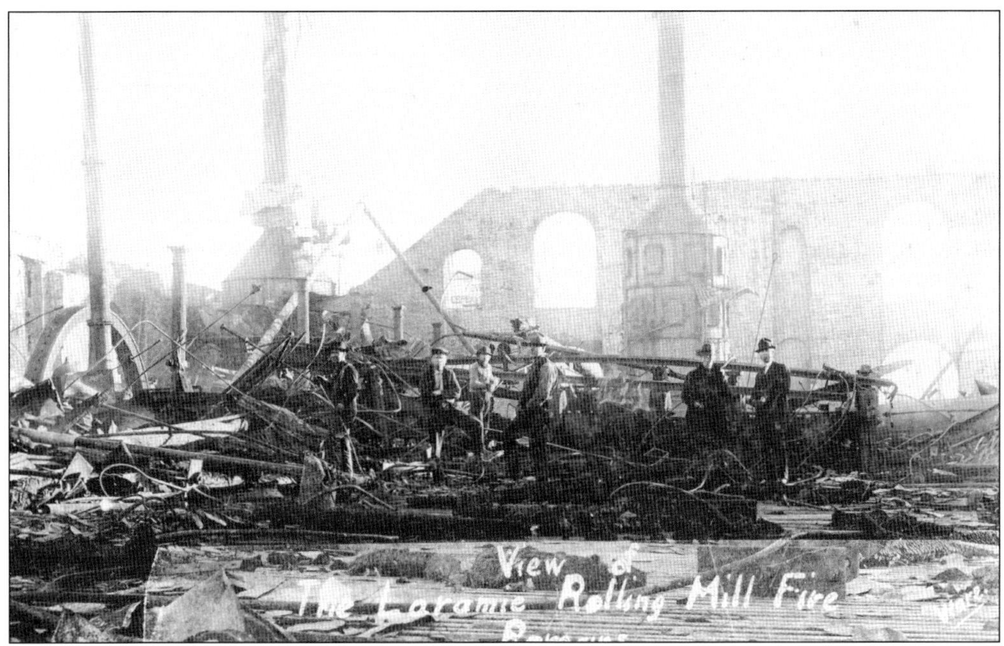

The rolling mills burned to the ground in 1910 and were never replaced. Boilers, smoke stacks, and a battered wall are the only things left standing in this photograph. The loss of this and other industrial concerns contributed to a major refocus of the town from railroading and manufacturing to the university community that it is today. (Photograph by Ware; LPM.)

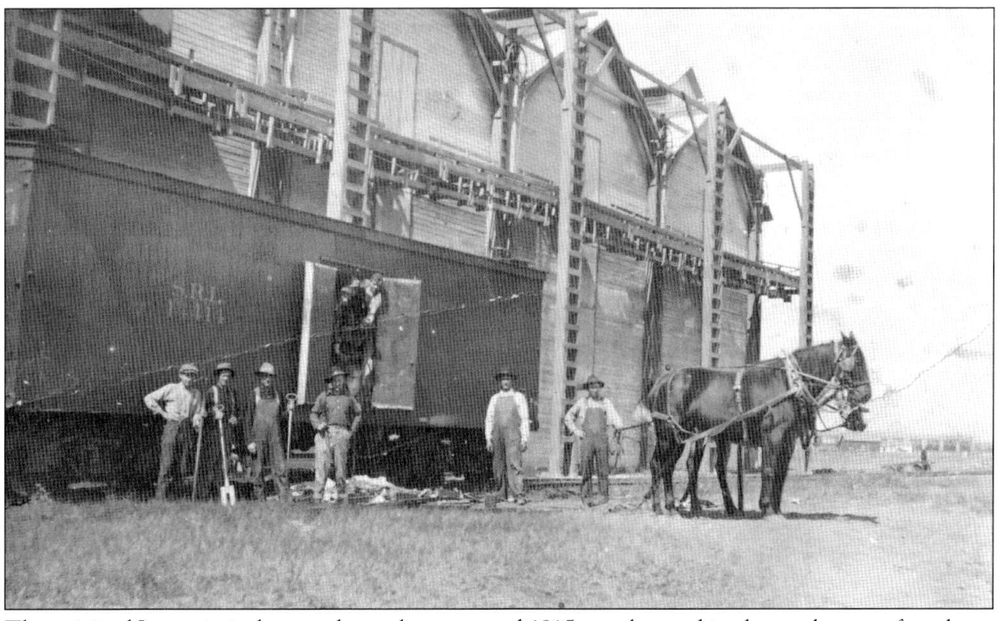

The original Laramie icehouse, shown here around 1915, was located in the yards west of modern-day Russell Street. Ice harvested from the Laramie River in the winter was stored to feed railroad refrigerator cars throughout the year. The facility, built in 1906, lasted until 1923. The horizontal runway behind the ladders could be raised and lowered as needed for access to the ice. (LPM.)

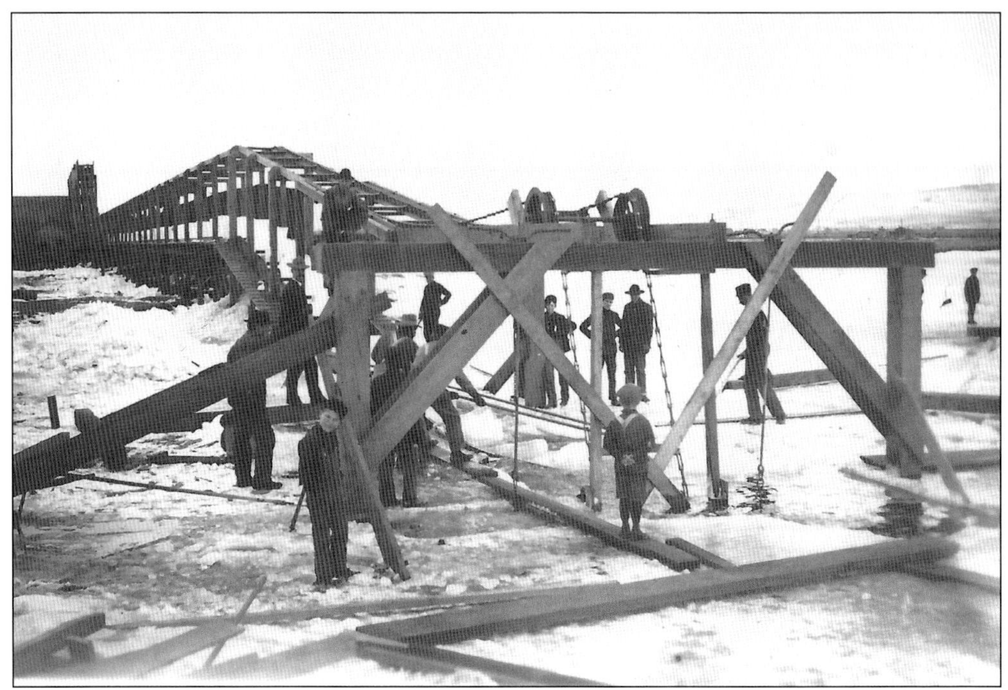

A pond west of the icehouse and along the Laramie River provided ice for this light industry. The conveyor system shown here carried ice from the pond to the facility. The conveyor burned down in 1918 and was not replaced. In an era before child labor laws, the children in this photograph, taken sometime between 1908 and 1912, were most likely working at the icehouse. (JLEC.)

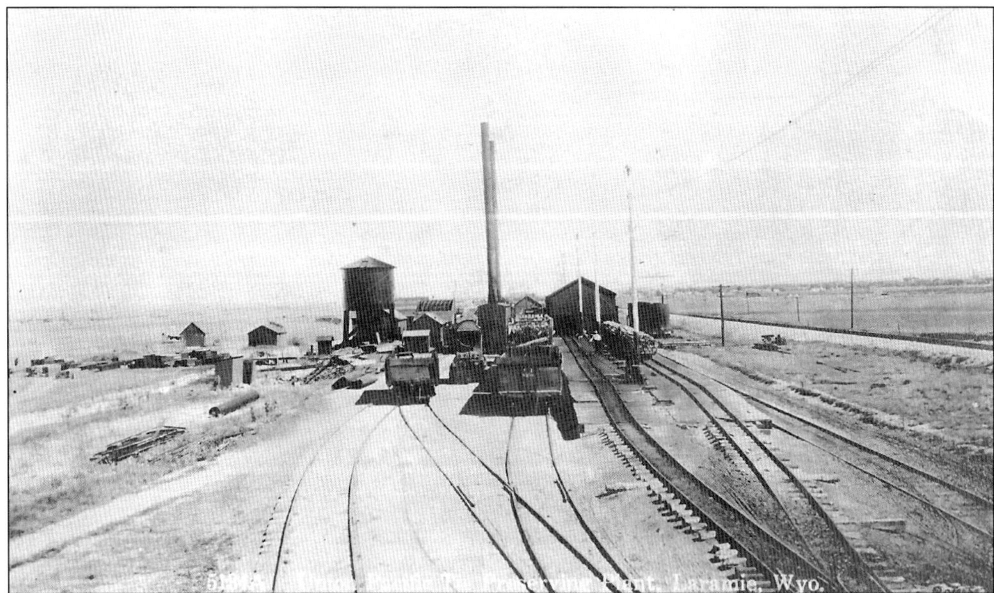

In addition to machine shops, turntables, roundhouses, and rolling mills, a critical support industry for the Union Pacific Railroad was the Union Pacific Timber Treatment Plant. In order to extend the life of wooden railroad ties, they were treated with creosote before being laid down to support rails. The plant, seen here on September 24, 1923, was located at the south edge of town. (JLEC.)

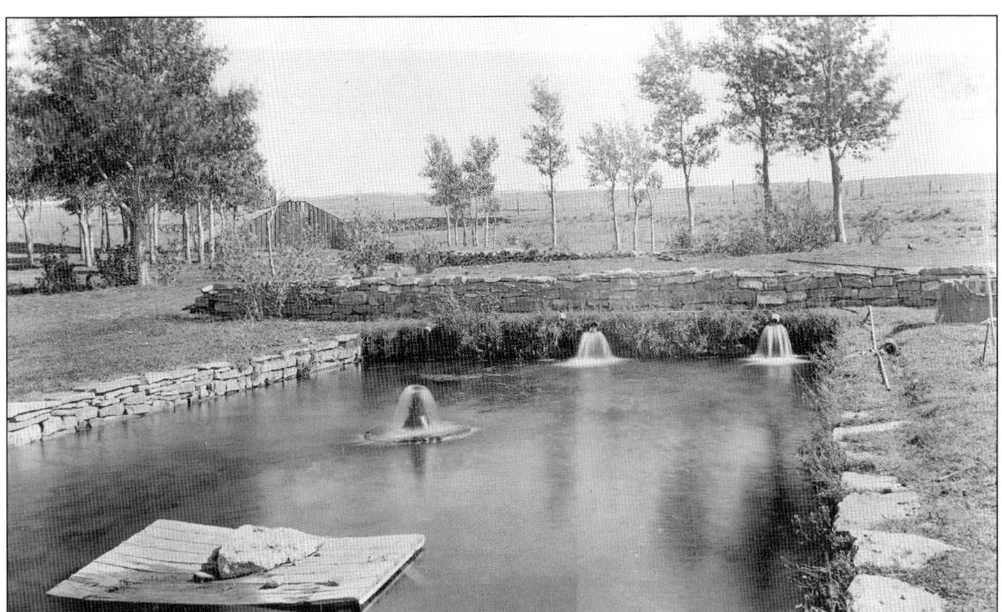

Wyoming's interest in supporting sports fisheries began before it was even a state. In an effort to enhance the fishing appeal of local lakes and rivers, the Territorial Fish Hatchery was established in 1884. It later became the State Fish Hatchery. Its Laramie branch, seen here around 1905, remained in operation south of town until 1922. (US Geological Survey Collection.)

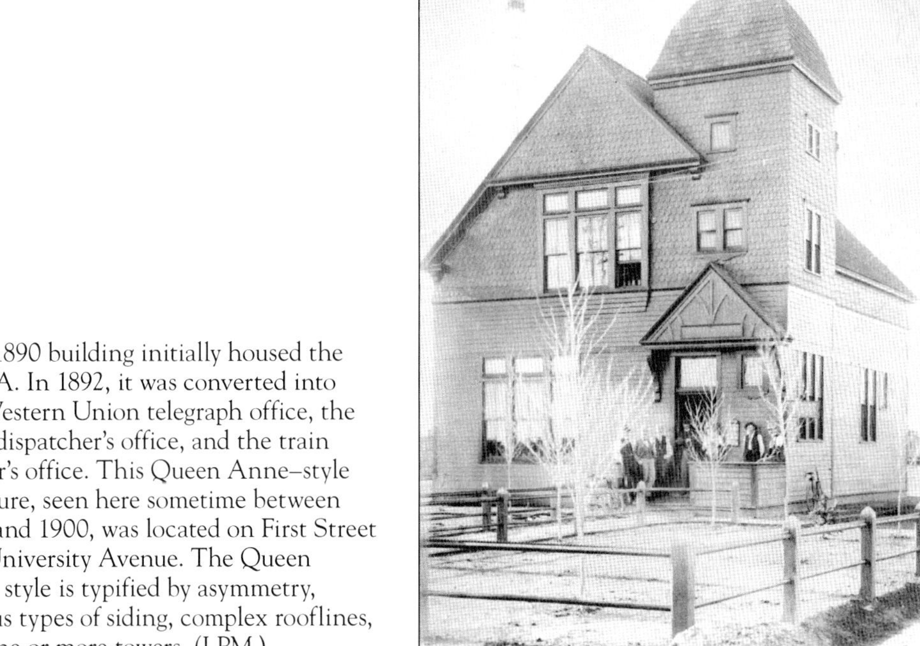

This 1890 building initially housed the YMCA. In 1892, it was converted into the Western Union telegraph office, the train dispatcher's office, and the train master's office. This Queen Anne–style structure, seen here sometime between 1894 and 1900, was located on First Street and University Avenue. The Queen Anne style is typified by asymmetry, various types of siding, complex rooflines, and one or more towers. (LPM.)

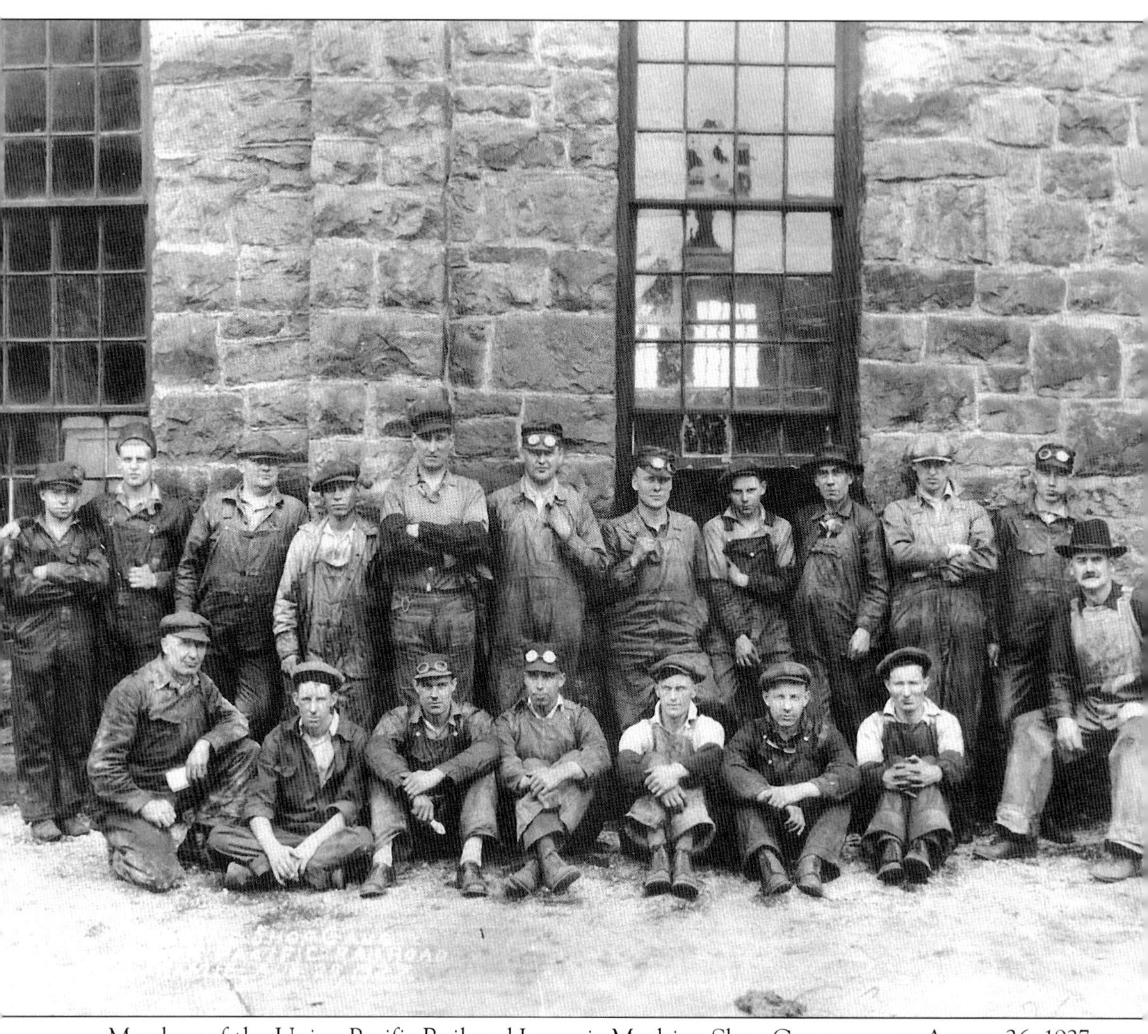

Members of the Union Pacific Railroad Laramie Machine Shop Gang pose on August 26, 1927. They are, from left to right, (first row) Clarence Hanson Sr., Harry Davis, unidentified, Walter Trautewig, Fred Barnes, Ray McAnnualty, and Lance "Snapper" Downing; (second row) Ralph "Red" Buesher, Hilary "Hi" Luthy, Gordon "Fat" Palmquist, Robert "Bob" Gonzalez, George Vass, Louis Miller, George Ruebling, Dwight "Kep" Kepler, Frank Hazlett, A.J. "Al" Heisey, Orville "Bugs" Peterson, and, sitting on the box, the machine shop foreman, Frank Davidson. The men are posing in front of the wall of the 1868 roundhouse. (Kay Kepler Schroeder Collection, Historic Laramie Railroad Depot.)

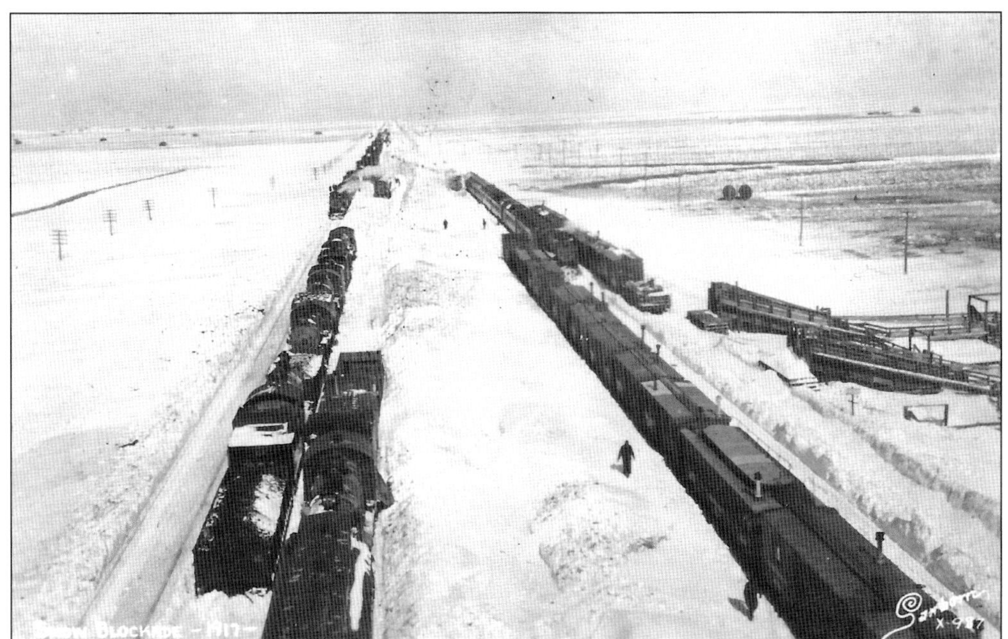

The second of the three most significant blizzards in Albany County's history was that of 1917. Unlike the blizzard of 1878, which affected several states, the 1917 storm was mostly confined to Albany County, Wyoming. And here, it was fierce. This photograph shows a bottleneck of trains stranded just outside of Rock River, Wyoming. (JLEC.)

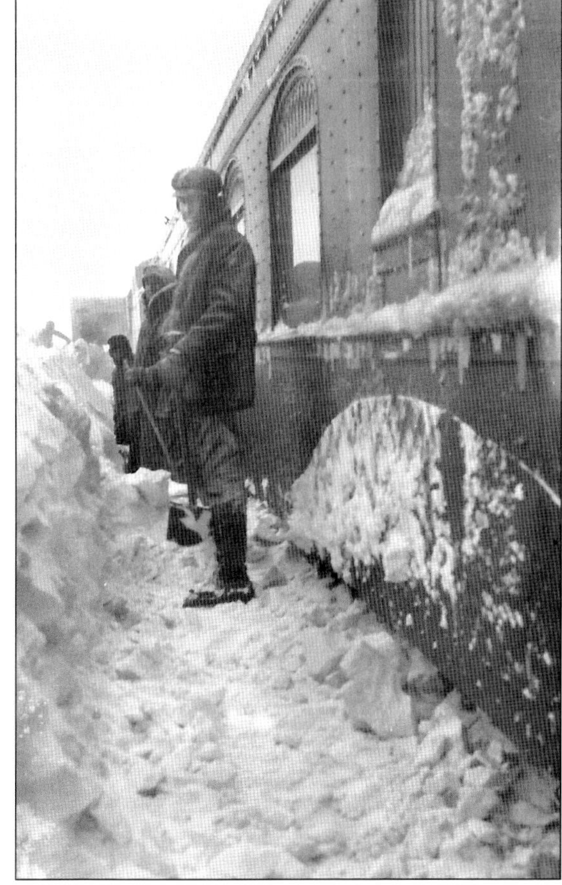

The storm hit early on January 22, 1917, and by midnight, nearly all railroad traffic was brought to a halt. Here, workers dig out a passenger train that was caught up in the blizzard. The work was backbreaking and tedious, and much of it had to be done by hand. Over 1,000 workers were brought in to help extricate the trains. (JLEC.)

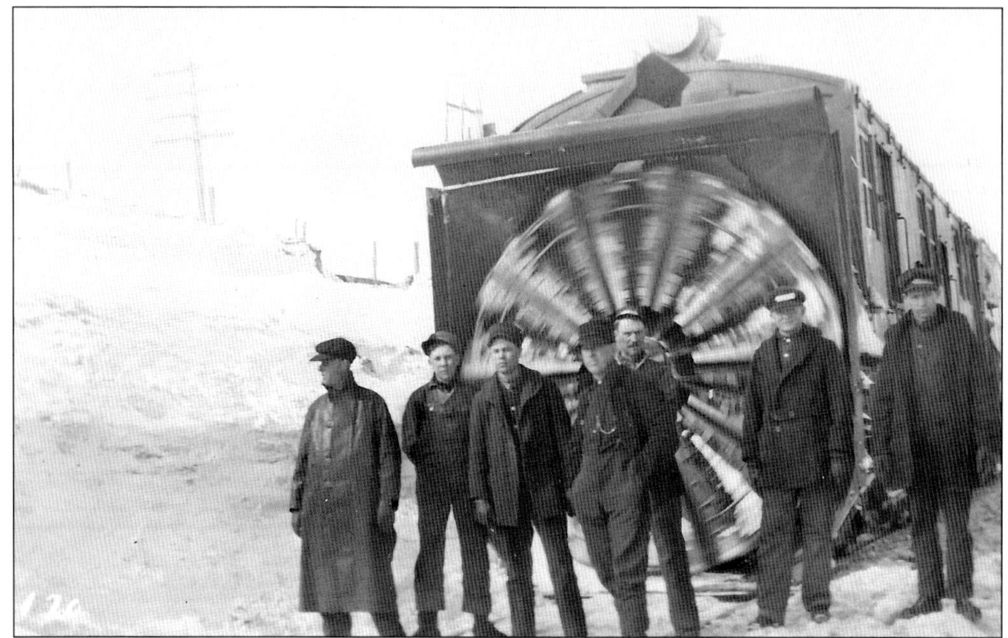

In addition to the manual labor required to dig the trains out of the snow, specialized equipment was used, such as this rotary snowplow. The plow was coupled to the front of a locomotive and pushed along the track. The powerful fan sucked in the snow and blew it out of the way through vents in the top. The plow is seen here in the aftermath of the 1917 blizzard. (JLEC.)

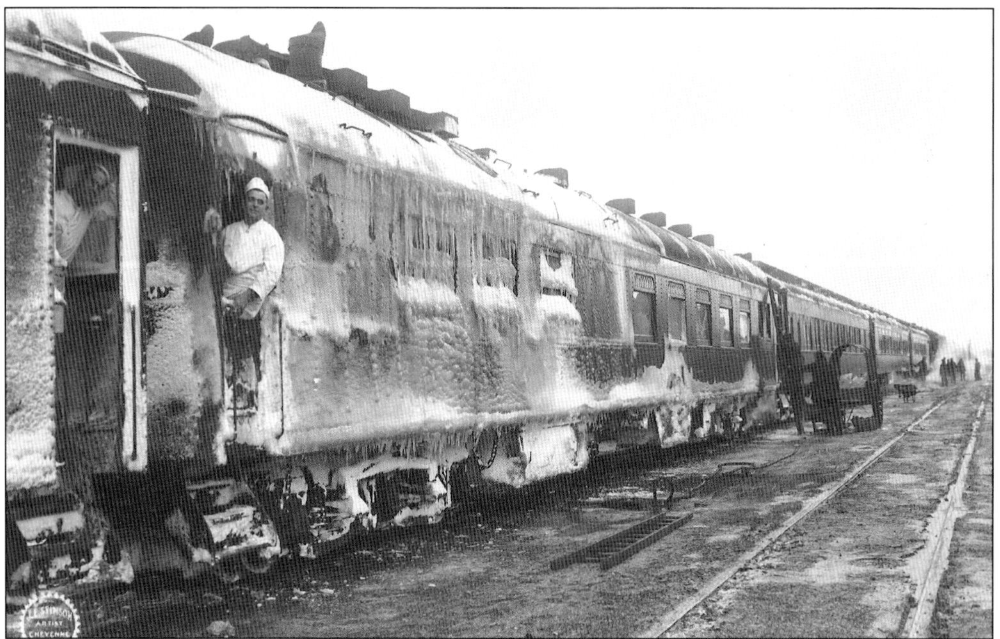

Rescuing passenger trains, such as the *Overland Limited* (shown here), was the highest priority during the blizzard. Here, the train pulls into the Laramie rail yards after surviving three snowbound days near Rock River. While freight service was suspended entirely during much of the blizzard, passenger service for the most part continued, albeit delays of up to 36 hours were common. (Photograph by J.E. Stimson; Wyoming State Archives.)

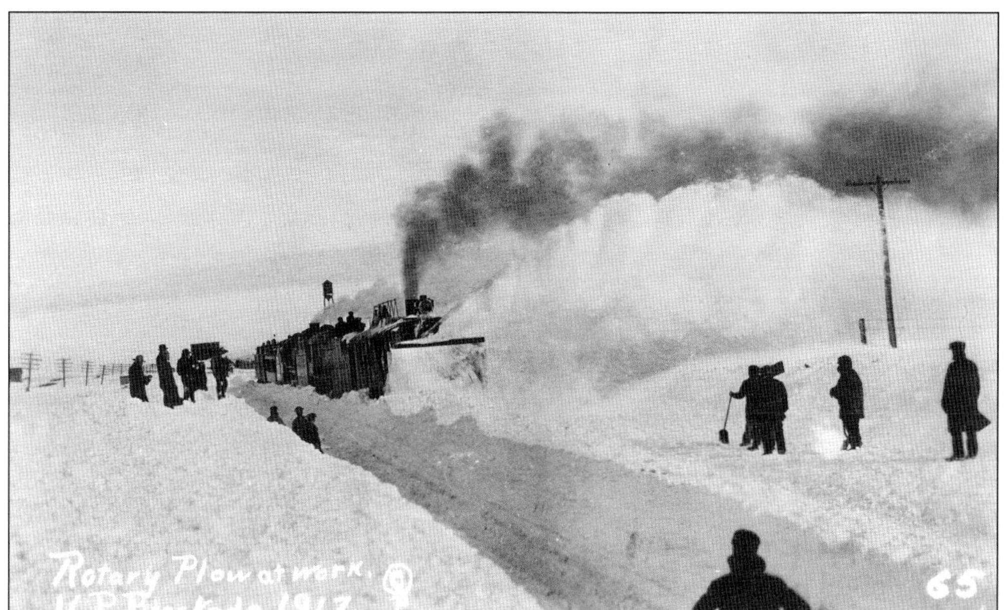

The line north of Laramie was double tracked, but during the blizzard, usually only one line could be kept open, and that only intermittently. Fighting the 1917 blizzard was a combined effort of man and machine. As seen here, manual laborers called in to shovel the snow by hand worked alongside the powerful rotary snowplow. (LPM.)

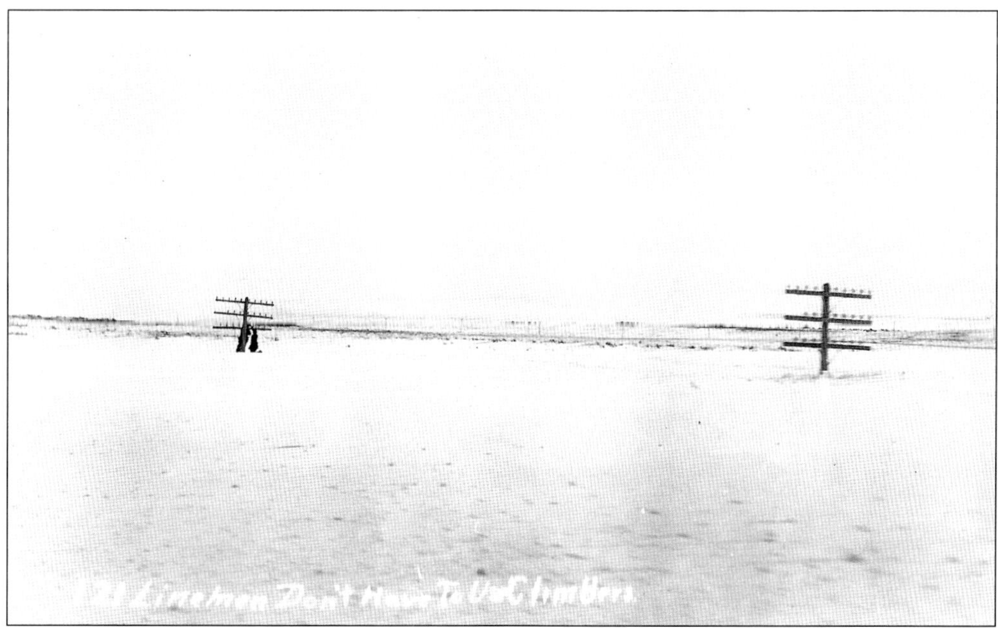

The magnitude of the 1917 blizzard is perhaps best illustrated by this photograph. The caption reads, "Linemen don't need to use climbers." Wind was a major problem, sweeping across the treeless Laramie Plains and dumping 20 or more feet of snow into cuts. Once dug out, the cuts might be refilled with snow in as little as half an hour. (JLEC.)

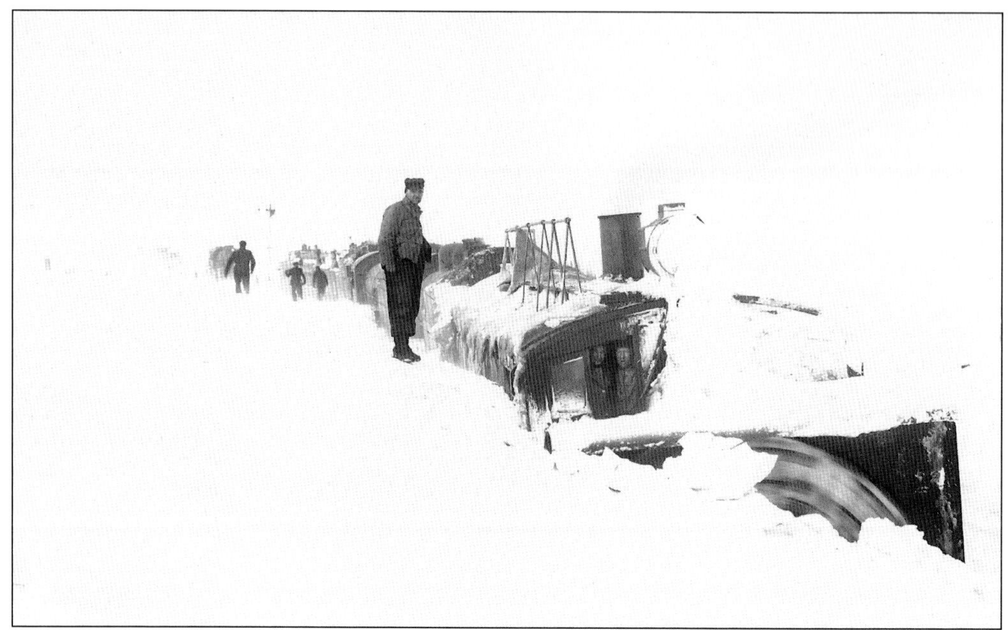

This photograph, taken along the Sulphur Lake Cut, shows that even the biggest machines can be humbled by nature. The burial of the rotary blade, approximately 11 feet tall, offers an indication of the immensity of the storm. Fighting the blizzard every hour for 15 days were five rotary plows, 11 wedge plows, and eight flangers. (Photograph by J.E. Stimson; Wyoming State Archives.)

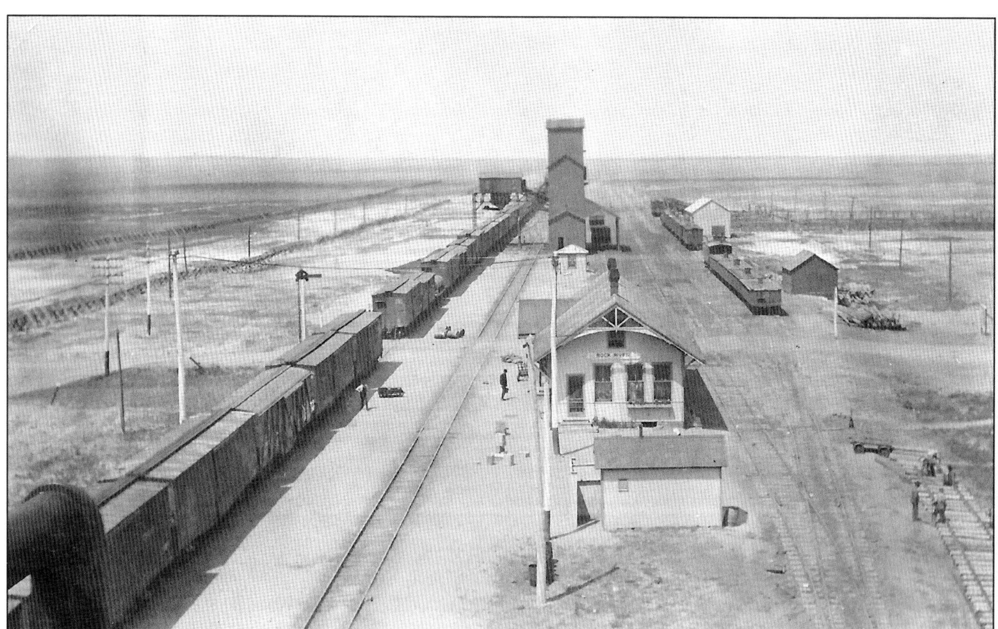

As a result of the 1917 blizzard, the Union Pacific built several snow sheds to keep snow off the tracks. The largest was at Rock River, the epicenter of the blizzard. The town's railroad facility is shown here in 1911, before construction of the shed began. As is evident, the surrounding topography offers little protection from the elements. The station in the center of the photograph appears on the next page, in a considerably changed environment. (JLEC.)

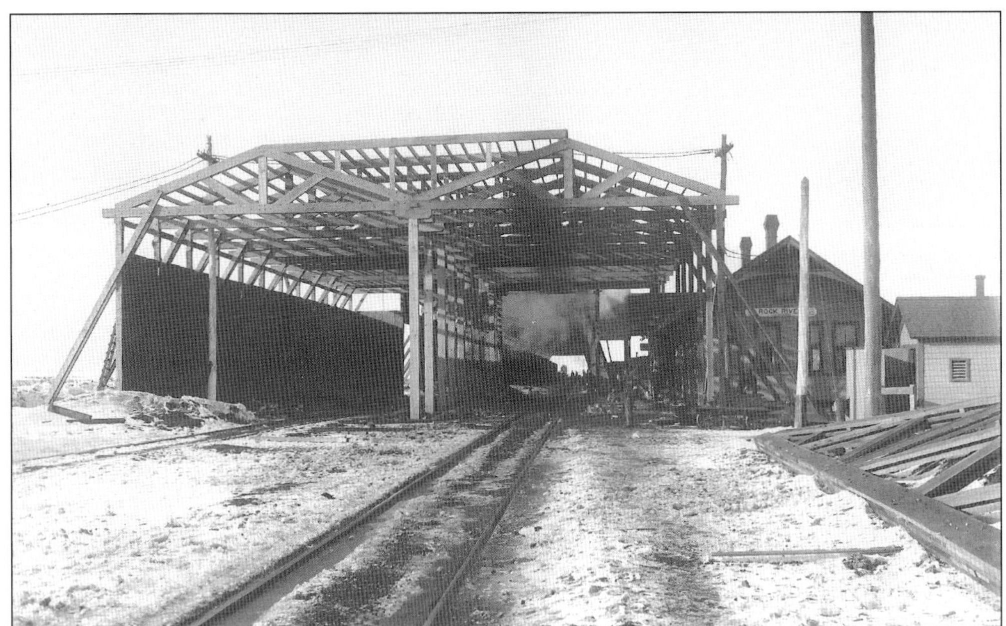

The blizzard of 1917 cost the Union Pacific hundreds of thousands of dollars. The railroad quickly decided that a snow shed would minimize some of the costs. As early as March of that year, a temporary wooden shed (shown here) was erected in Rock River. The building to the right of the shed is the station shown on the previous page. (Photograph by J.E. Stimson; Wyoming State Archives.)

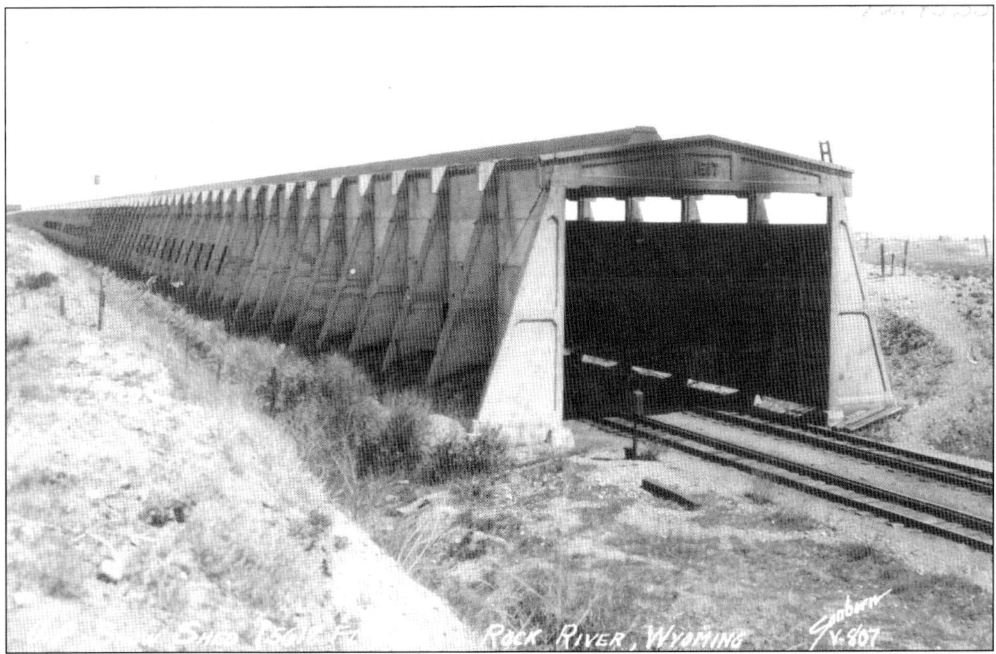

This permanent concrete snow shed was erected soon after the temporary wooden shed was built. Seen here around 1920, it was 5,618 feet long when it was finally completed. It lasted until 1948, when it was torn down. Ironically, its destruction came just one year before the third epic blizzard in Albany County. (Photograph by Sanborn; LPM.)

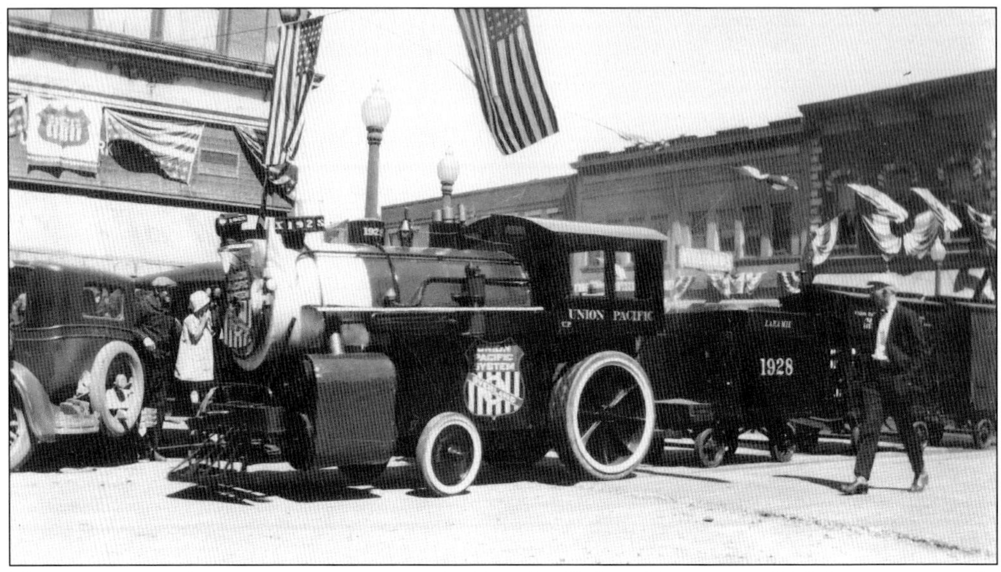

This unique parade car is participating in the Fourth of July celebration in 1928. It was essentially an ordinary automobile with the shell of a locomotive placed on it by the workers at the Union Pacific shop. This car was a staple of local parades well into the 1940s. (LPM.)

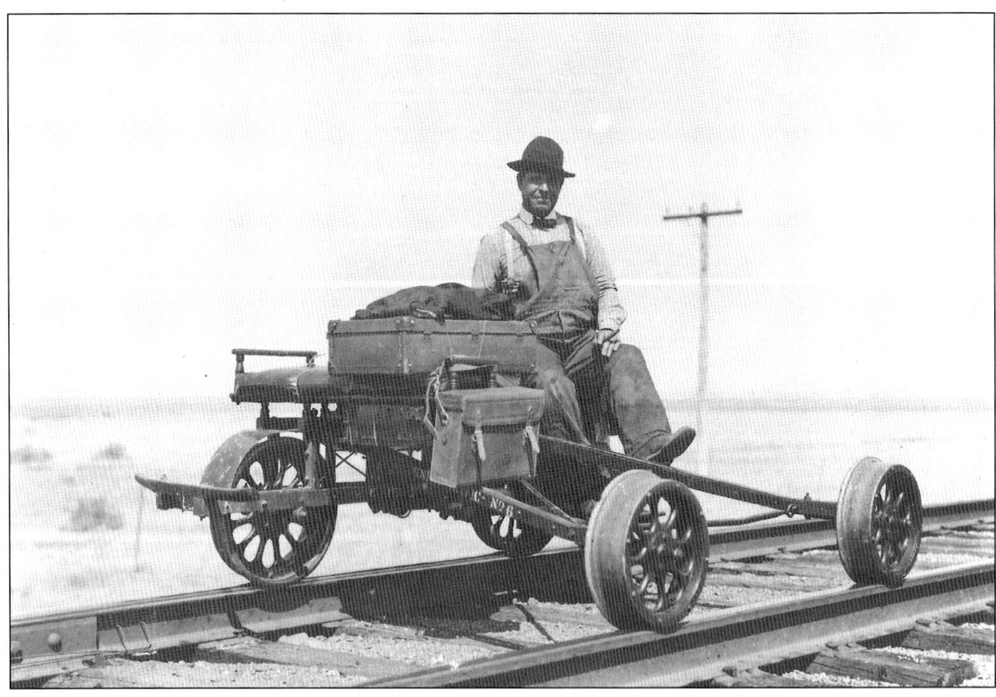

Developments in automotive technology were quickly adopted by the Union Pacific where appropriate. Shedding the lever-powered handcarts of previous decades, track inspectors and workmen could move about the line with much more freedom with motorized carts like the one seen here around 1901. (Photograph by M.F. Jukes; JLEC.)

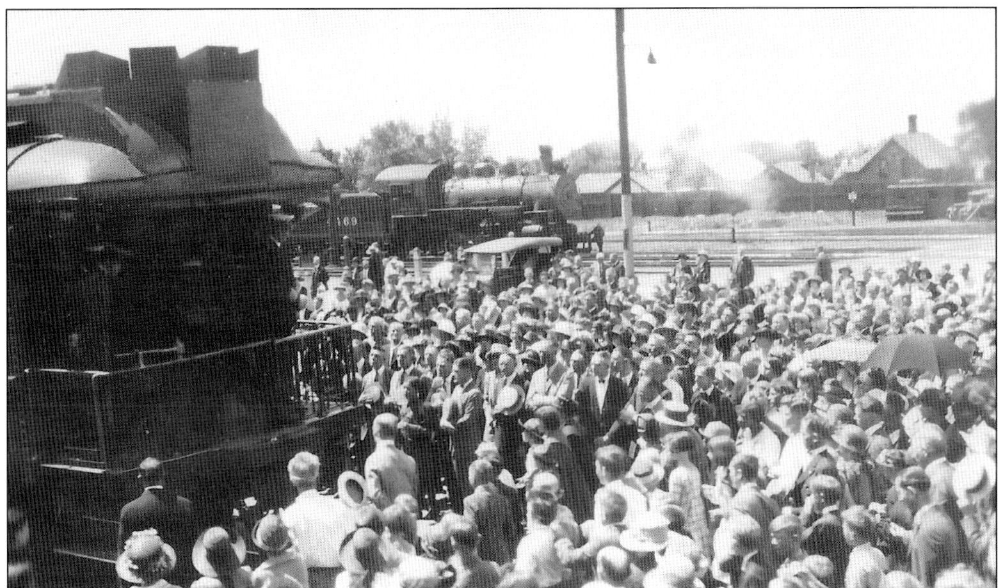

When Pres. Warren Harding suddenly passed away in 1923 on a visit to San Francisco, the train procession stopped in many towns along the route back to the East Coast. Here, the train stops in Laramie, and the citizens come out to pay their respects. (JLEC.)

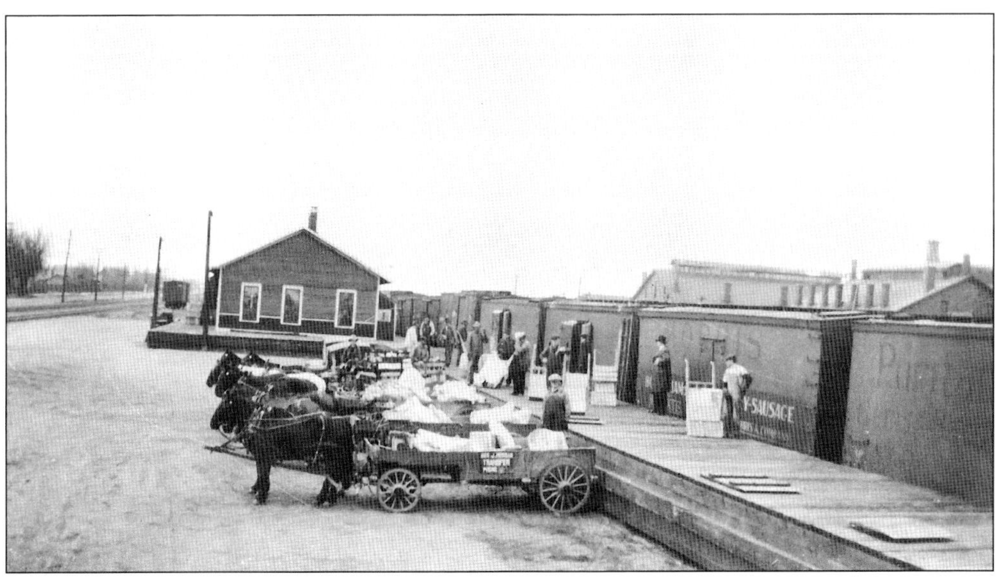

Draymen from the J. Noonan freight company and other local drayage firms load their wagons from the Union Pacific freight house around 1905. The freight house and the satellite firms were the predecessors of modern-day delivery services, such as FedEx and UPS. (Photograph by Union Pacific; Union Pacific Railroad Museum.)

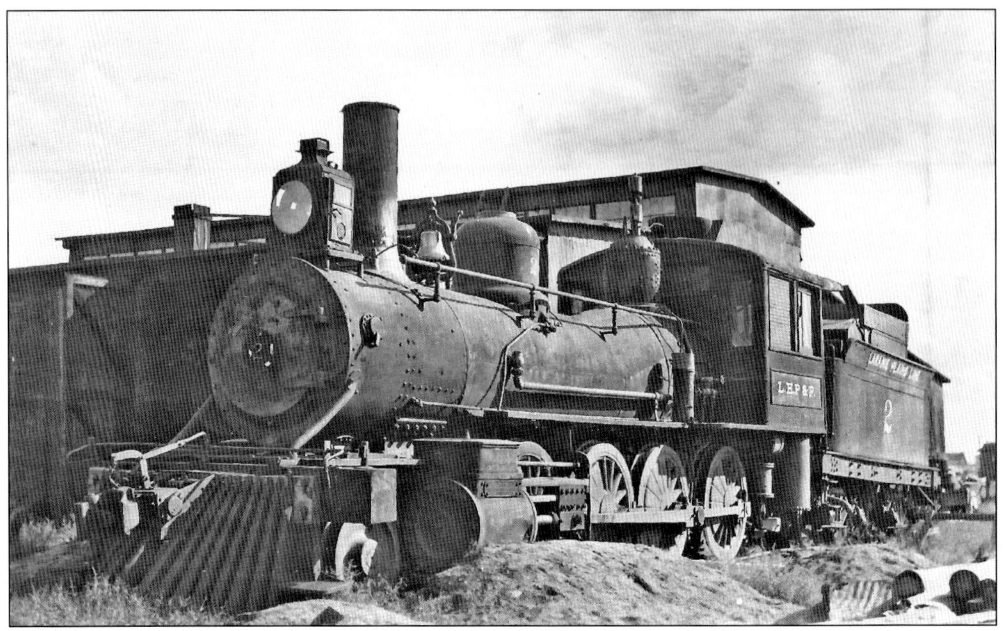

Several small railroads linked up to the Union Pacific main line in Laramie. The largest of these was the Laramie, Hahns Peak & Pacific (LHP&P), incorporated in 1901 by Isaac Van Horn of Boston and Fred A. Miller of Laramie. Shown here around 1916 is the LHP&P's No. 2 engine. Located behind it is the railroad's first small wooden engine house, which eventually burned down. (JLEC.)

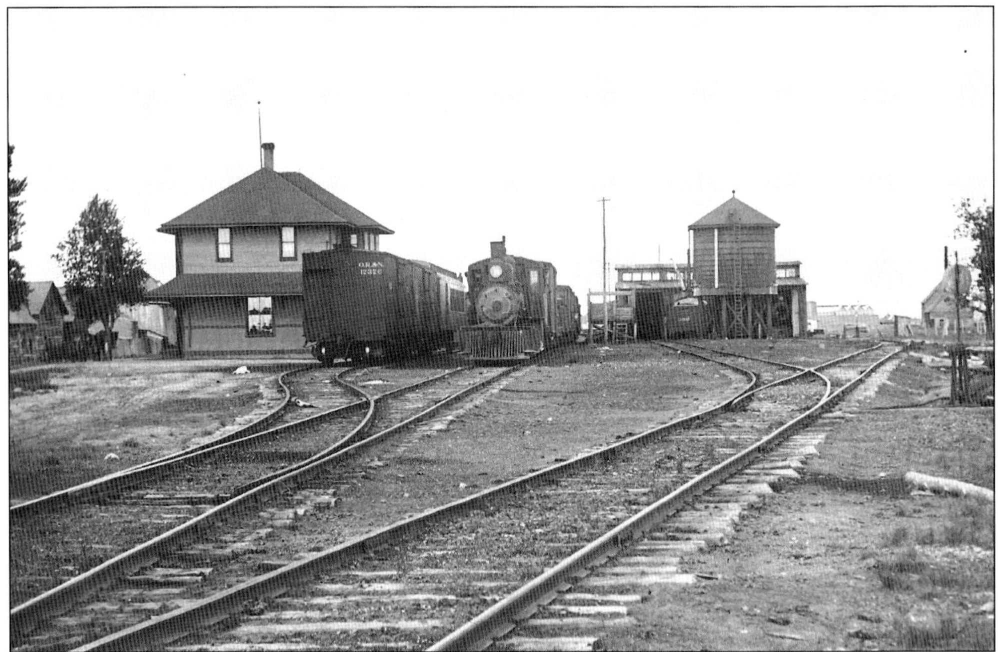

This 1912 photograph shows more of the Laramie, Hahns Peak & Pacific Railroad facilities. The original depot is to the left of the trains on the track. On the right are the water tower and original engine house. The station was located on Freemont Street, one block west of Cedar Street, on Laramie's west side. (JLEC.)

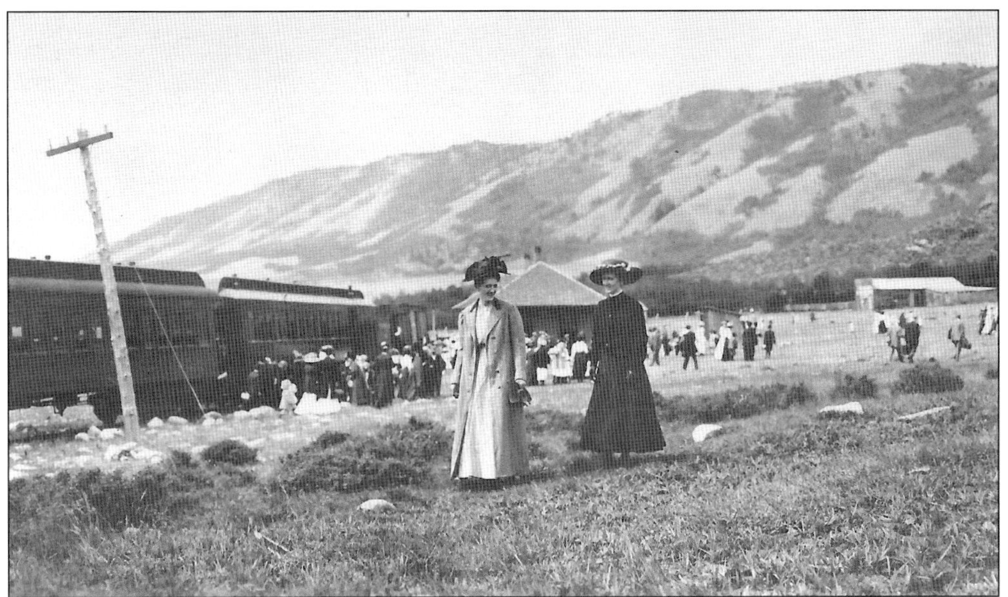

The Laramie, Hahns Peak & Pacific Railroad was lucky enough to operate in some of the most beautiful locations in Albany County. An excursion to Centennial, Wyoming, and often farther into the mountains, was an enjoyable outing for many of the town's residents. This scene was captured around 1907. (JLEC.)

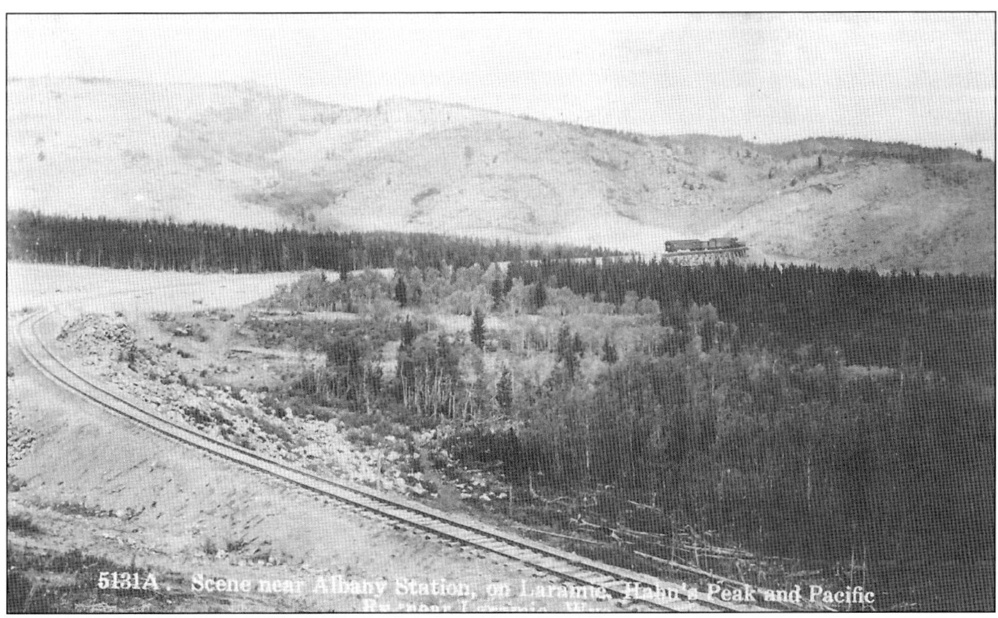

A train from the Laramie, Hahns Peak & Pacific Railroad approaches the town of Albany, Wyoming. The trestle the train is traversing was eventually replaced with a culvert and a fill. Though the track has since been removed, the fill remains. Shown here around 1910 is the No. 3 engine for the LHP&P, pulling two boxcars and a passenger car. (JLEC.)

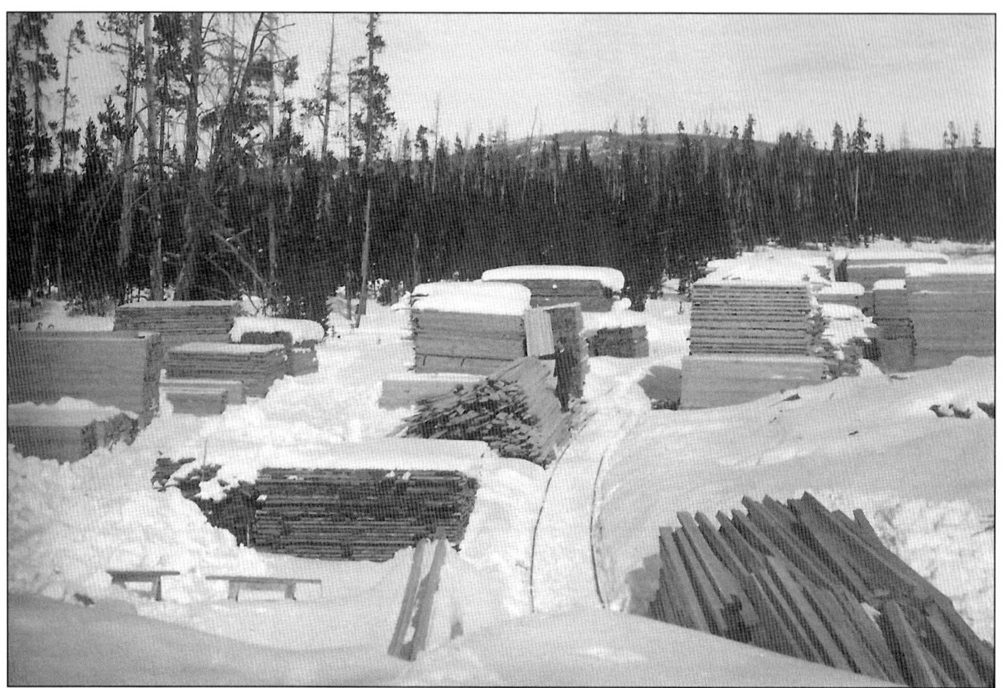

Written on the back of this postcard is the following: "Fox Park Wyo. Feb. 5, 1912. This is my lumber yard. It represents ten thousand dollars but not all mine. I have cleared about twenty five hundred $ from it this year & I have a better chance this coming summer. I am standing side of a timber pile in this picture. Your Friend E.A. Hamden." (JLEC.)

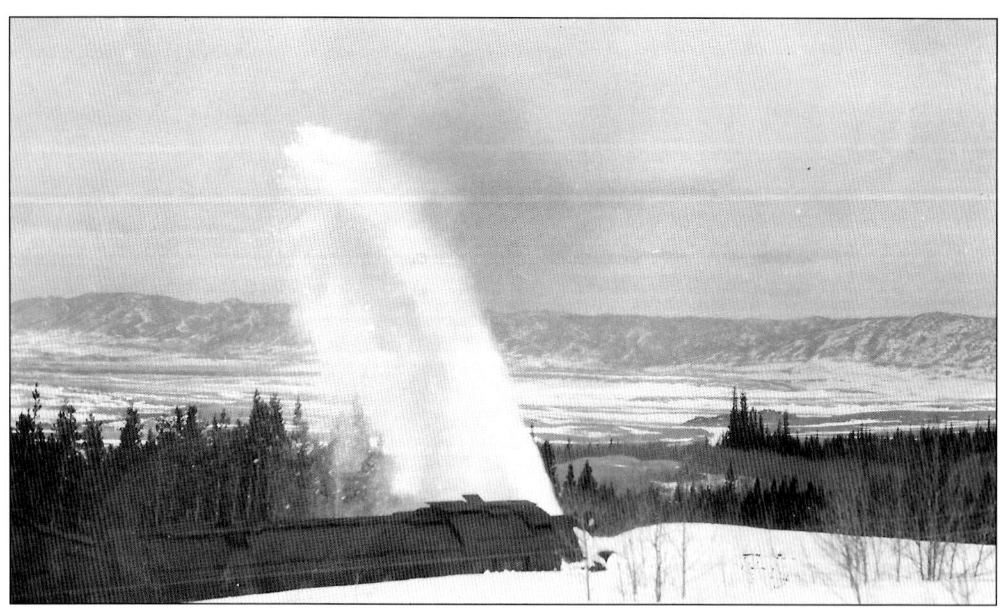

The amount of snow the Laramie Valley received in the blizzard of 1917 was an annual occurrence in the Medicine Bow Mountains, through which the Laramie, Hahns Peak & Pacific Railroad traveled annually, as here in 1922. Breaking through six- to 10-foot drifts, though never an easy task, was routine for the men and women who worked this line. (Photograph by Otto Kruger; JLEC.)

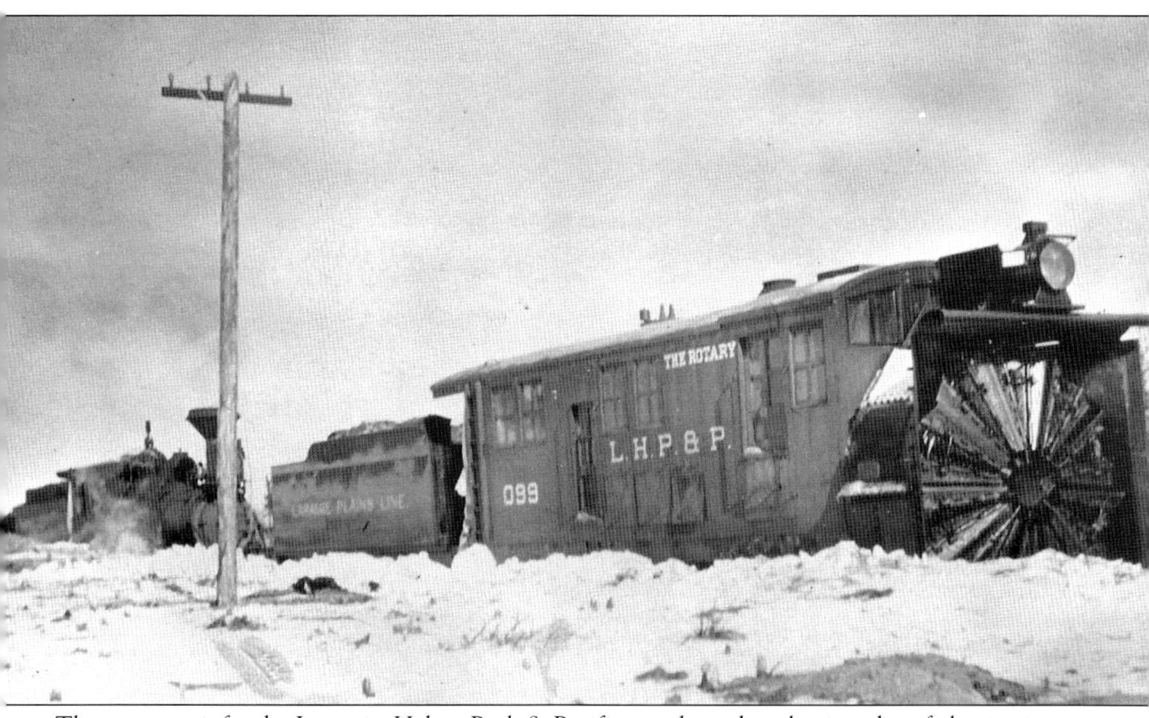

The rotary unit for the Laramie, Hahns Peak & Pacific stands ready to begin a day of plowing in 1911. The LHP&P engine is coupled behind rotary No. 099. Much of the company's equipment was purchased secondhand from the Union Pacific Railroad, but the rotary unit was purchased directly from Cooke Locomotive Works. (JLEC.)

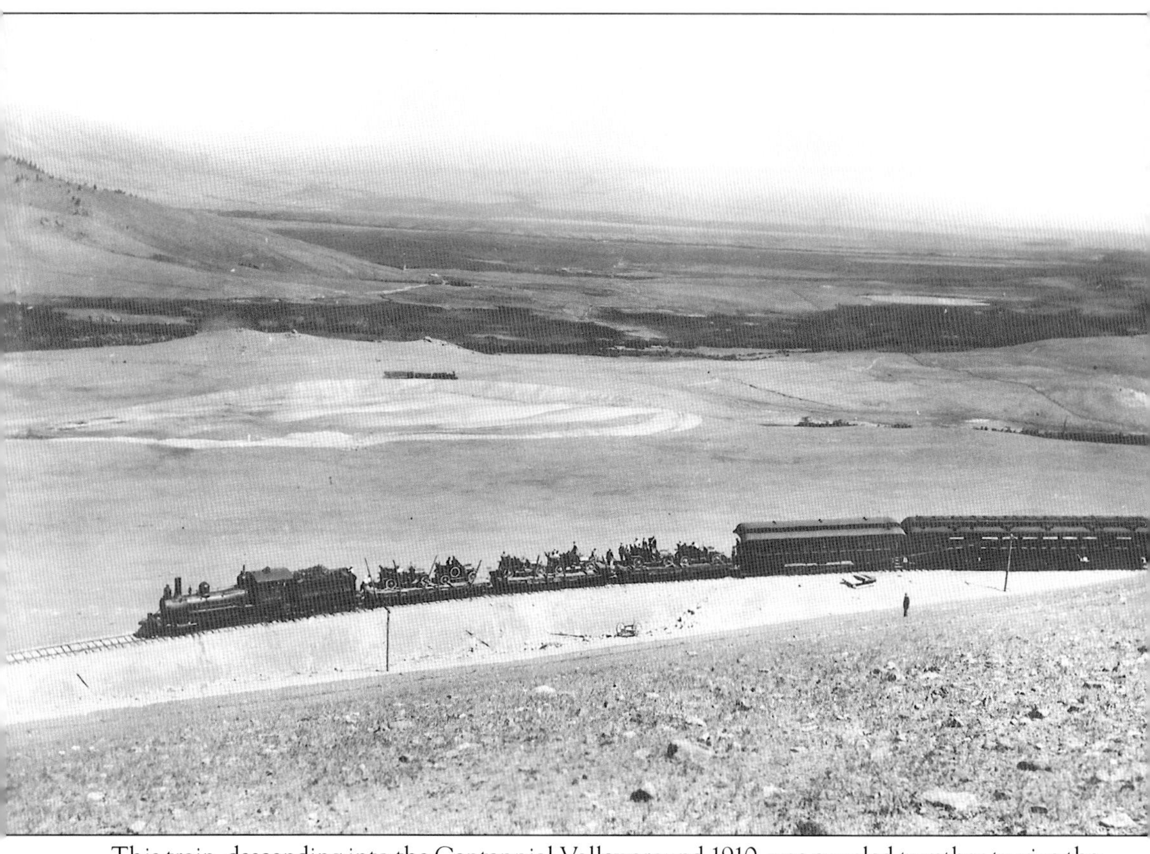

This train, descending into the Centennial Valley around 1910, was coupled together to give the owners and investors of the Laramie, Hahns Peak & Pacific a tour of the line. Sharp curves on a line were usually called horseshoes, but these were so sharp they were called mule shoes. The automobiles on the flatbed were being returned to Laramie from Coalmont, Colorado. (JLEC.)

Four

1903–1960

How the Loss of Steam Locomotives Changed Laramie

The inventions of the internal combustion engine and the diesel engine had a profound impact on the railroad and, subsequently, on Laramie. Experiments with diesel locomotives had been conducted on and off since the late 1800s, but by the mid-1920s, General Electric had a working prototype. The first true internal combustion locomotive to see active service with the Union Pacific Railroad was the M-10000. It was also the first "streamlined engine," which took aerodynamic concepts and applied them to a train. Its introduction in 1934 sparked a streamline craze in locomotive design that continued throughout the 1930s and 1940s. The streamlined look caught the public's attention, to the point that many steam locomotives were given streamlined shells. But it was the arrival of internal combustion that signaled the biggest change for the railroad. Diesel electric engines quickly caught up with steam engines in power and efficiency. The diesel engine's lower maintenance requirements effected Laramie most of all. Many of the town's railroad industries were built to service and maintain steam power, but as the Union Pacific gradually phased out steam power between the 1930s and 1960s, the primary economy of the town changed. Some of the town's founding industries, including the roundhouse, turntable, and machine shop, became obsolete. Railroad employment dwindled from hundreds to tens of workers. The new driver of the Laramie economy was the university.

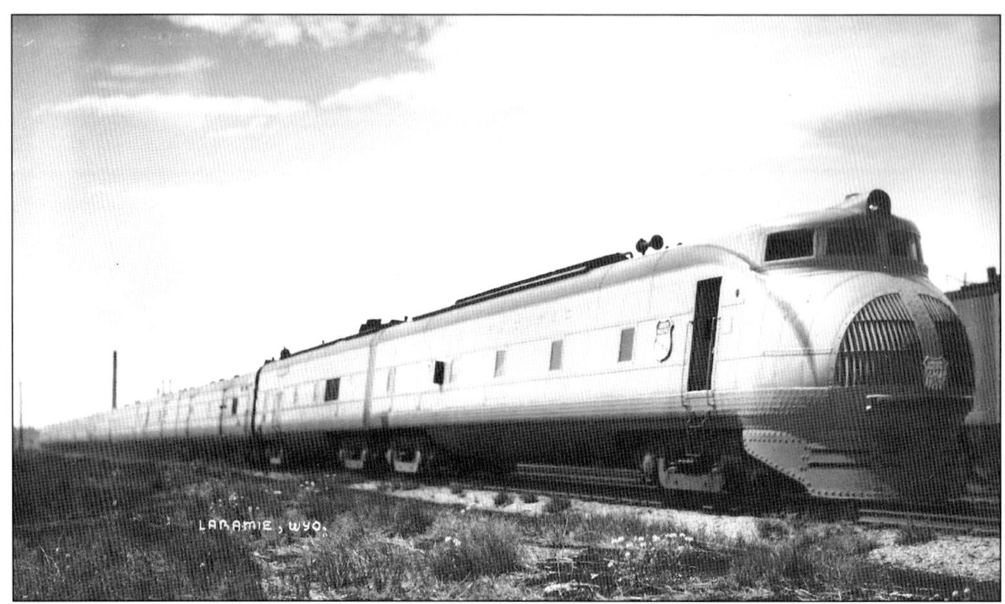

Struggling to reinvigorate its passenger train service as competition from airplanes and automobiles increased, the Union Pacific developed the world's first streamliner train. The M-10000, using an internal combustion engine and sporting an airplane-like shell, was delivered on February 12, 1934. It set the trend for passenger trains that would continue through the 1930s and 1940s. A streamliner is seen here around 1937. (Photograph by H. Svenson; Historic Laramie Railroad Depot.)

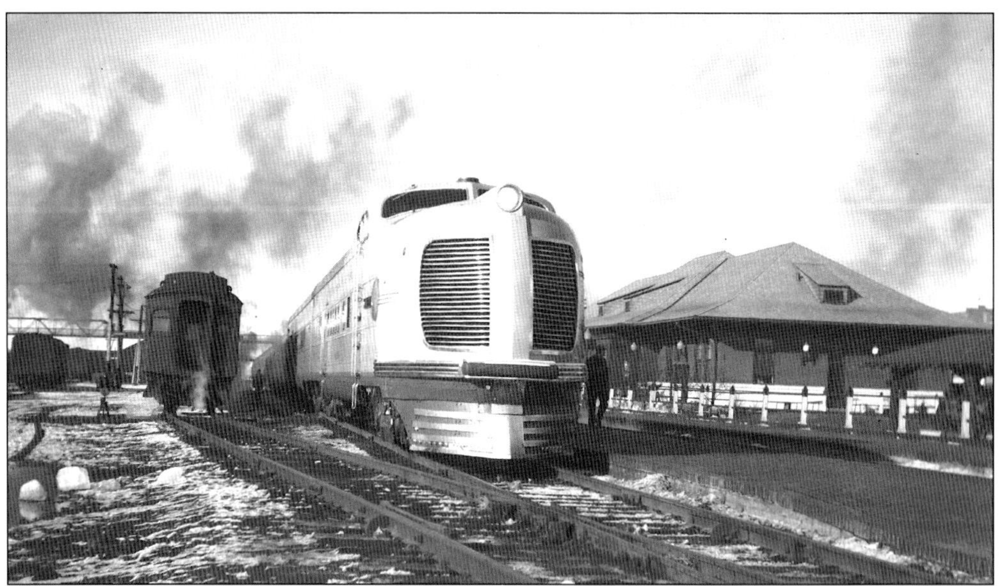
The M-10000, while not a practical success, had been a public relations victory. New streamlined engines and trains were soon to follow. The M-10004 was the first of four trains in a series. It was nicknamed "the Chevy" for its prominent grill. The photograph shows train No. 102, the eastbound train for the *City of San Francisco*. Train No. 101 followed the same route west. (Photograph by R.H. Kindig; AJWC.)

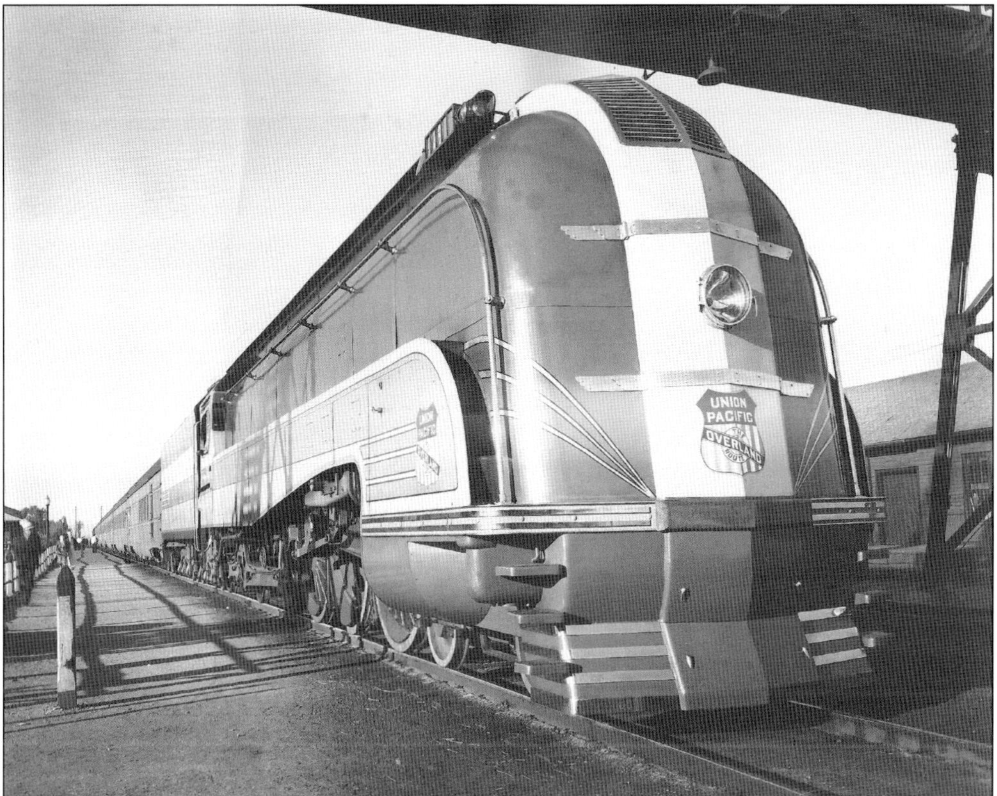

The adoption of the streamliner look outpaced new diesel-electric technology. In 1937, the Union Pacific streamlined a few steam engines. Engine No. 7002, seen here in July 1937, was used on the *49er* from Cheyenne, Wyoming, to Ogden, Utah. The *49er* train ran five times a month from Chicago to San Francisco and was used to complement the *City of San Francisco.* (Photograph by Union Pacific; JLEC.)

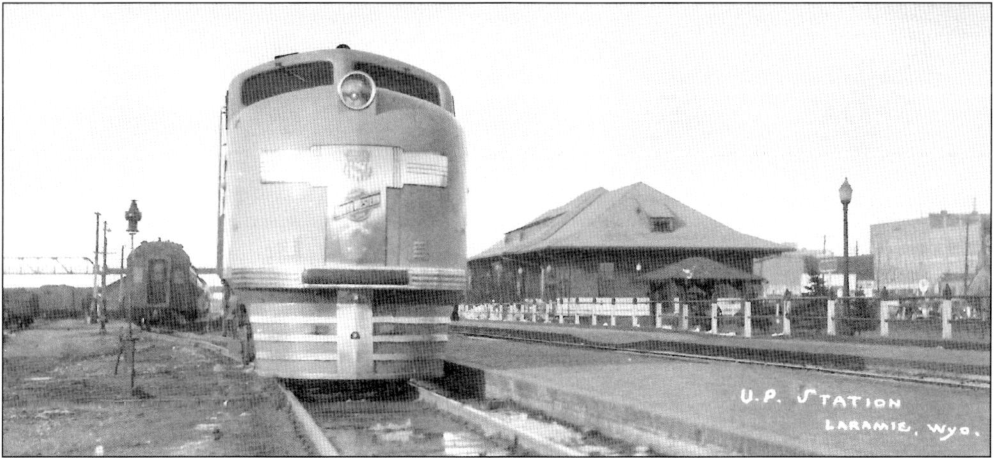

From 1937 to 1940, the passenger train *City of Los Angeles* (COLA) was pulled by a lash-up of diesel-electric E2s built by Electromotive Corporation. Here, the *COLA* is taking on passengers at the Laramie depot around 1940. The E series was in production until the early 1950s. Several of the E9s still run today as part of the Union Pacific's Heritage Fleet. No existing E2s remain. (JLEC.)

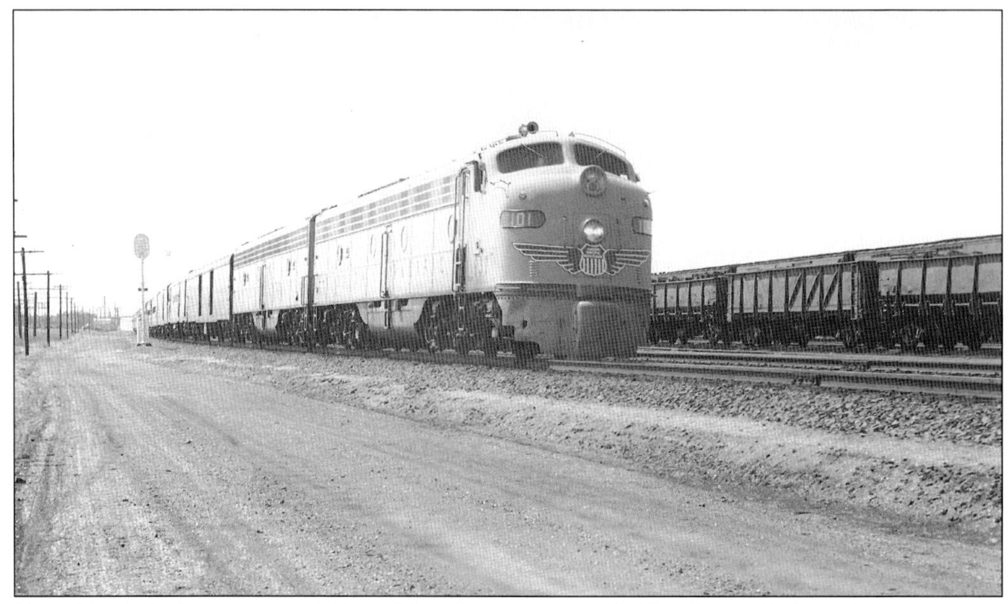

Train No. 101, the westbound *City of San Francisco,* is pulled by General Motors Electromotive Division E8 937. This photograph was taken just north of downtown Laramie in 1960. The distinctive "bulldog nose" of the later E units was a common sight across America until the 1970s. (Photograph by A.J. Wolff; AJWC.)

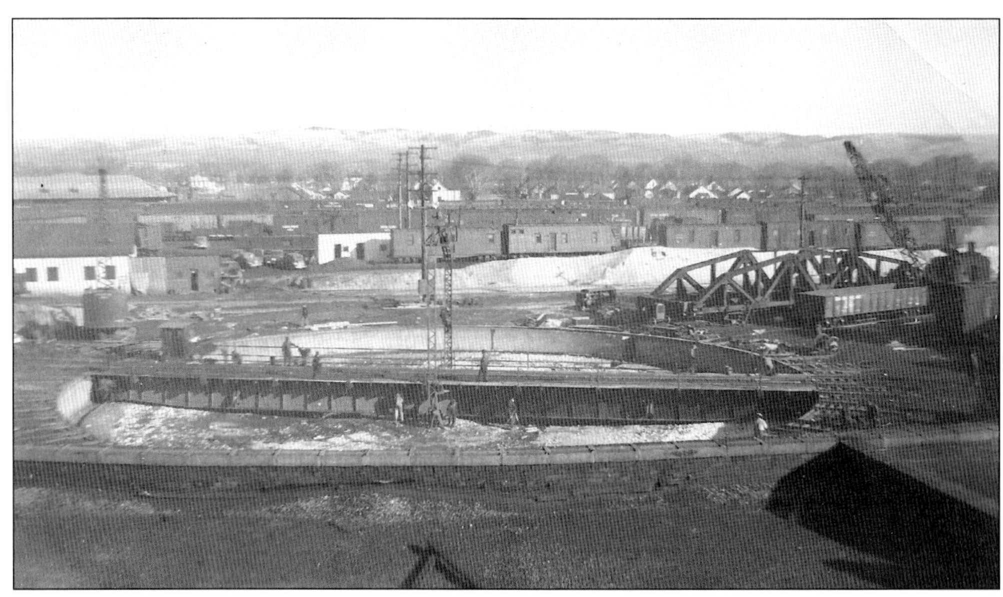

The 1940s and 1950s were a time of giant steam locomotives, notably the Challengers and Big Boys. To accommodate the length of these massive engines, the turntable for the Laramie roundhouse was increased from 100 to 135 feet. Here, the conversion is in progress in 1941. The old, truss-style turntable bridge is at right, and the new, deck-style bridge is in the pit. (JLEC.)

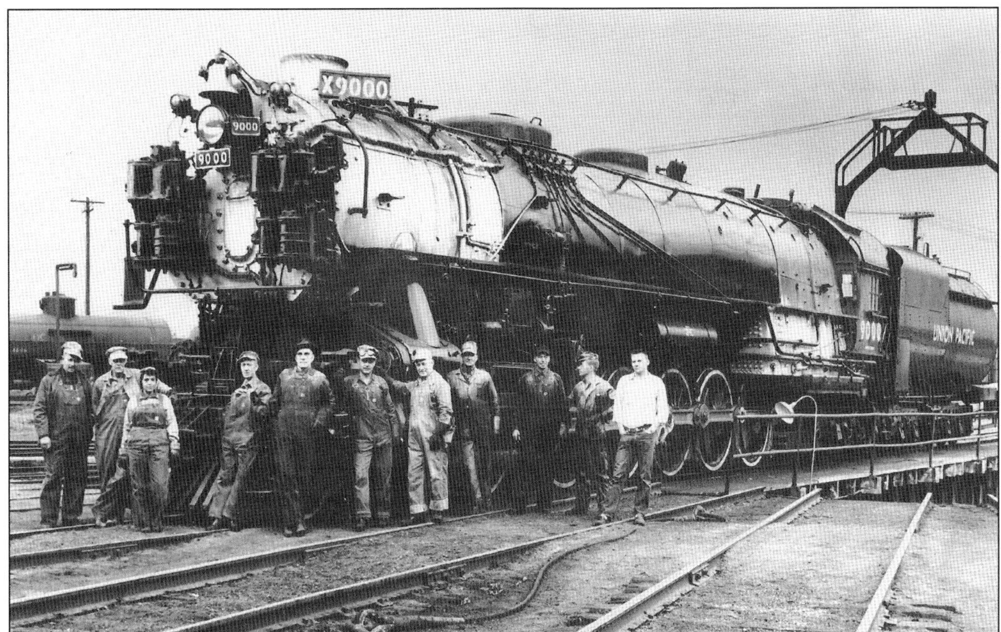

Union Pacific Engine No. 9000 sits on the Laramie turntable with its crew and some of the roundhouse workers in 1950. The 9000 was built in 1926, the first of a series of 88 engines. These were the largest rigid-frame engines ever built, and the class was called "Union Pacific." This engine is on display at the Los Angeles County Fairplex in Pomona, California. (JHC.)

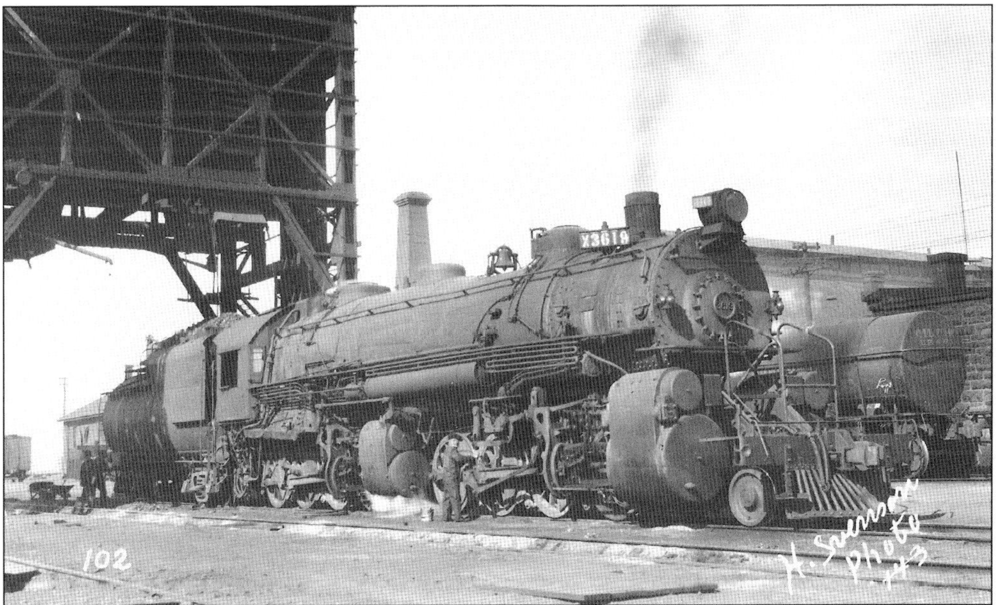

Union Pacific engine No. 3619 takes on coal from the Laramie chute sometime between 1935 and 1940. For this compound Mallet engine, steam was first pumped to the smaller, high-pressure cylinders in the rear and then sent to the larger, low-pressure cylinders in the front. Mallet engines were built for power more than speed and were generally used to haul freight. (Photograph by Henning Svenson; Historic Laramie Railroad Depot.)

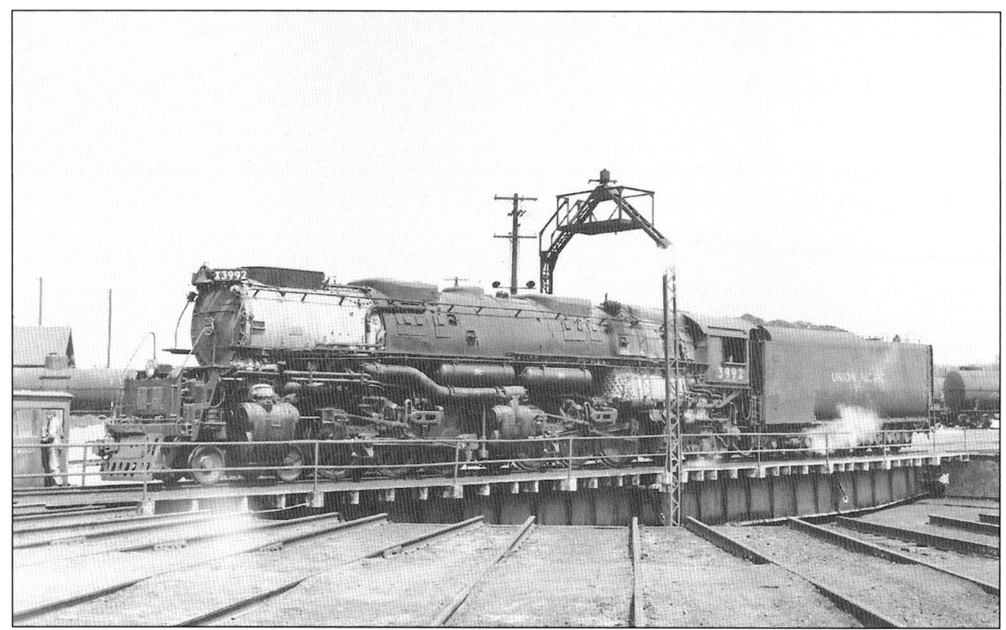

Union Pacific No. 3992, a 4-6-6-4 locomotive, spins on the Laramie turntable on May 17, 1953. A sister to the 3985, which still operates, it was built by the American Locomotive Works of Schenectady, New York, in 1943 and served until 1960. Though not a technically accurate term, most laypeople referred to them as Challengers. (Photograph by Neil R. Miller; Klinger Collection.)

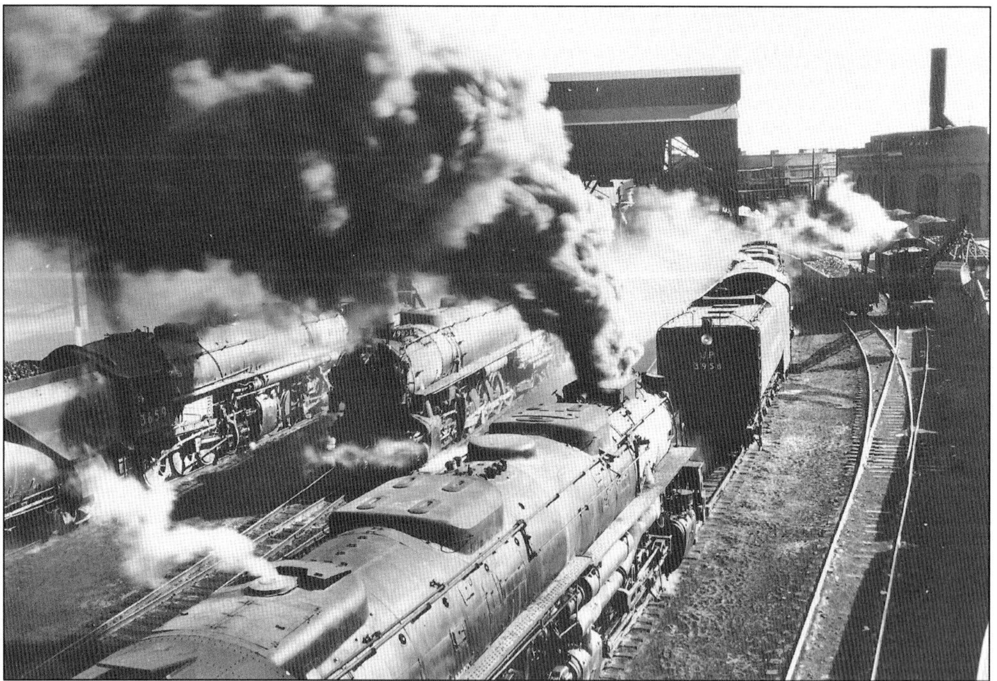

At the peak of World War II, steam-powered freight engines were critical to the war effort. It was one of the busiest times for the Laramie yards. In this c. 1943 photograph, the coal chute is under repair, and a backlog of locomotives waits for the steam-powered clamshell (far right) to load the tenders with coal. (Photograph by Union Pacific; L. Ostresh Collection.)

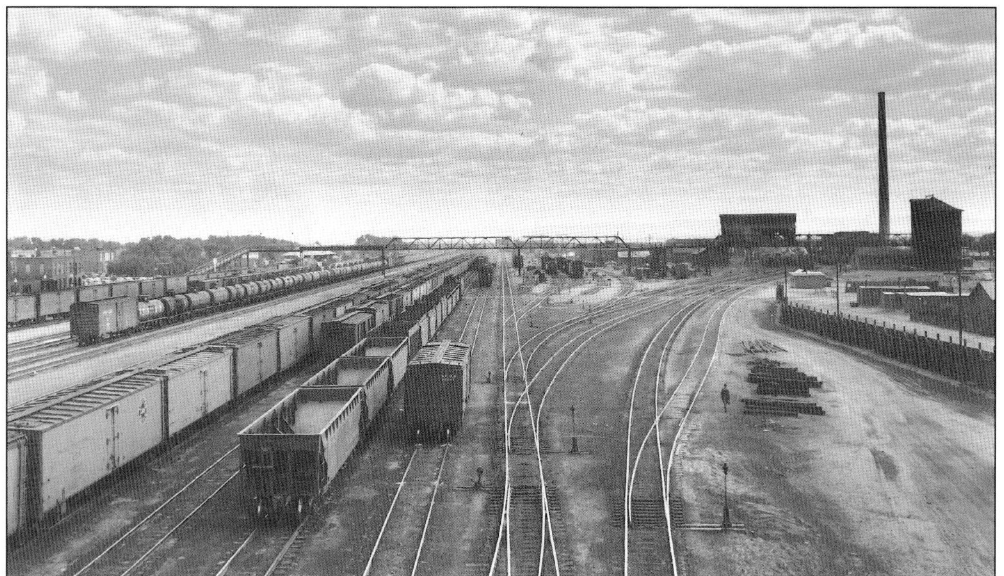

This photograph from the 1940s shows an expanded view of the Laramie rail yards. The three mainline tracks are on the left. The tracks at right lead to the storage yards or terminal facilities. The area on the far right is dedicated to locomotive maintenance. (Photograph by Henning Svenson; Historic Laramie Railroad Depot.)

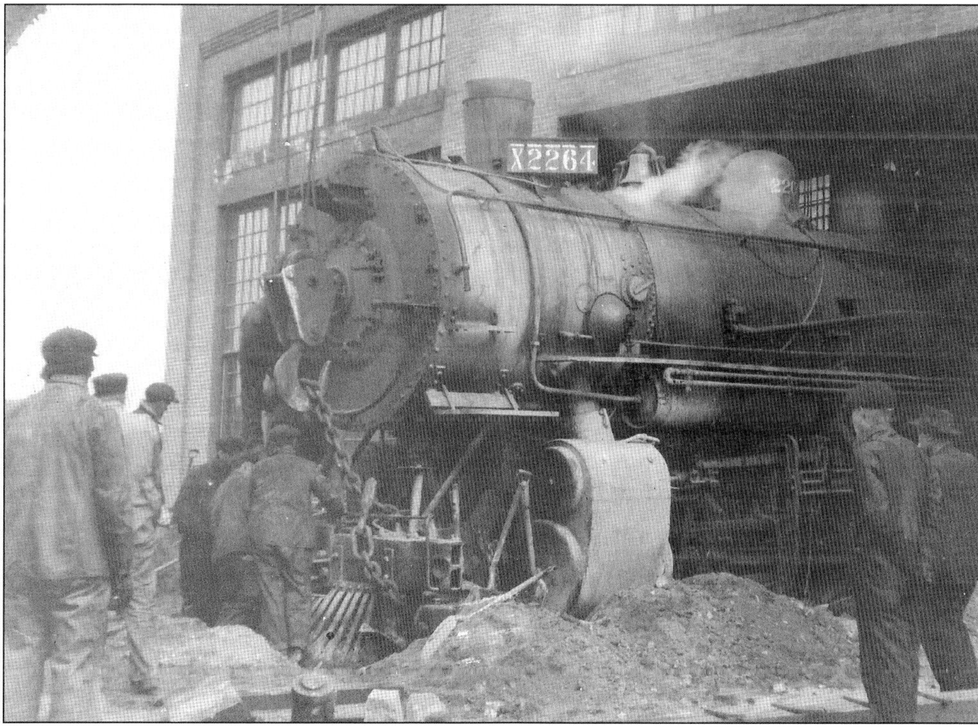

Locomotives do not stop on a dime. After a brief loss of control, engine No. 2264 crashed through the back of the Laramie roundhouse in 1940. Here, workmen attach heavy chains to the derrick hook in an attempt to hoist the engine back onto the tracks. Though train locomotives are the most powerful moving machines on land, they are quite helpless when off their track. (JHC.)

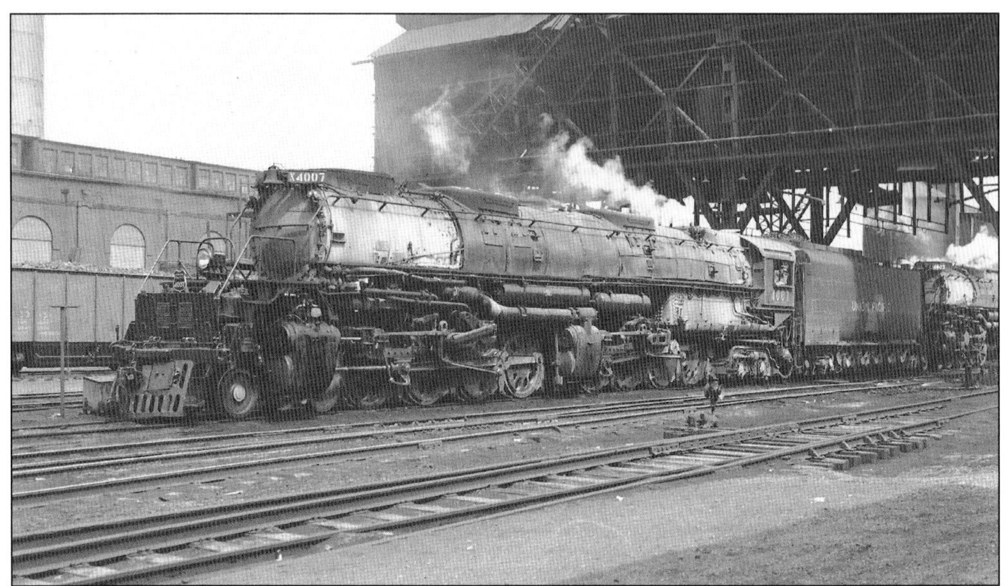

The apex of the American steam locomotive was the 4-8-8-4 Big Boy. At a total length of over 132 feet, it was one of the largest steam engines ever made. Here, No. 4007, built in 1941 by American Locomotive Works (ALCO), takes on coal from the Laramie coaling tower on May 8, 1954. Just behind it is No. 4003. (Photograph by F.G. Gschwind; AJWC.)

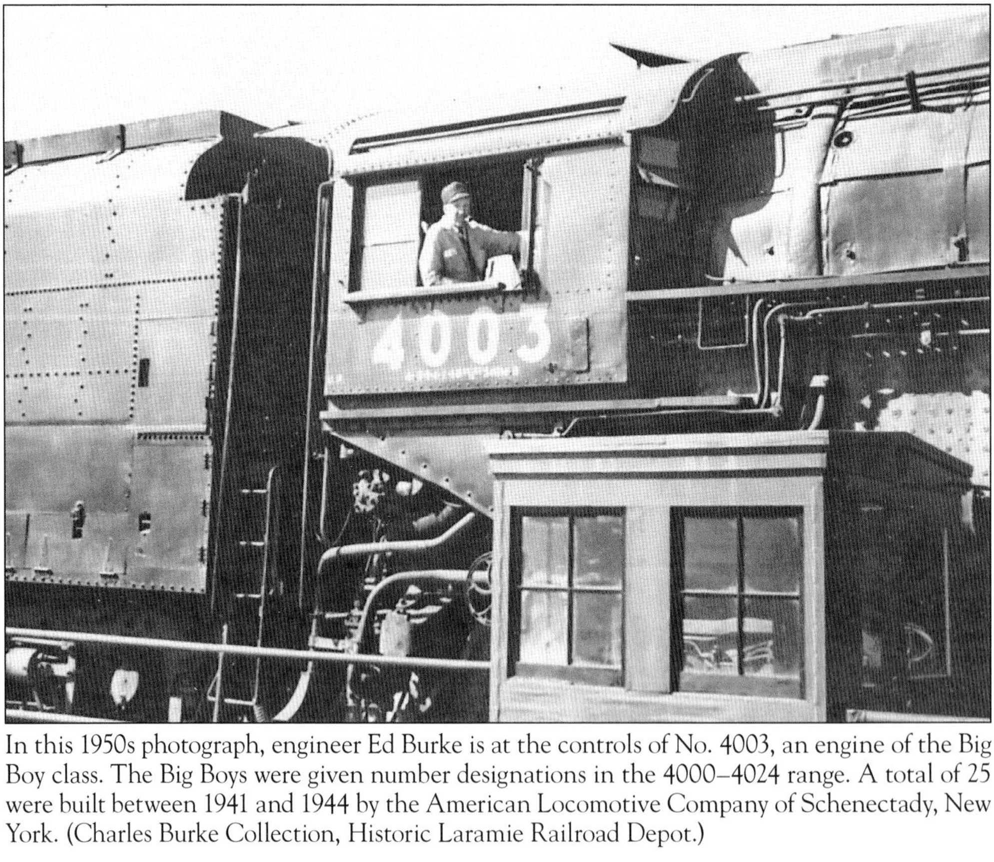

In this 1950s photograph, engineer Ed Burke is at the controls of No. 4003, an engine of the Big Boy class. The Big Boys were given number designations in the 4000–4024 range. A total of 25 were built between 1941 and 1944 by the American Locomotive Company of Schenectady, New York. (Charles Burke Collection, Historic Laramie Railroad Depot.)

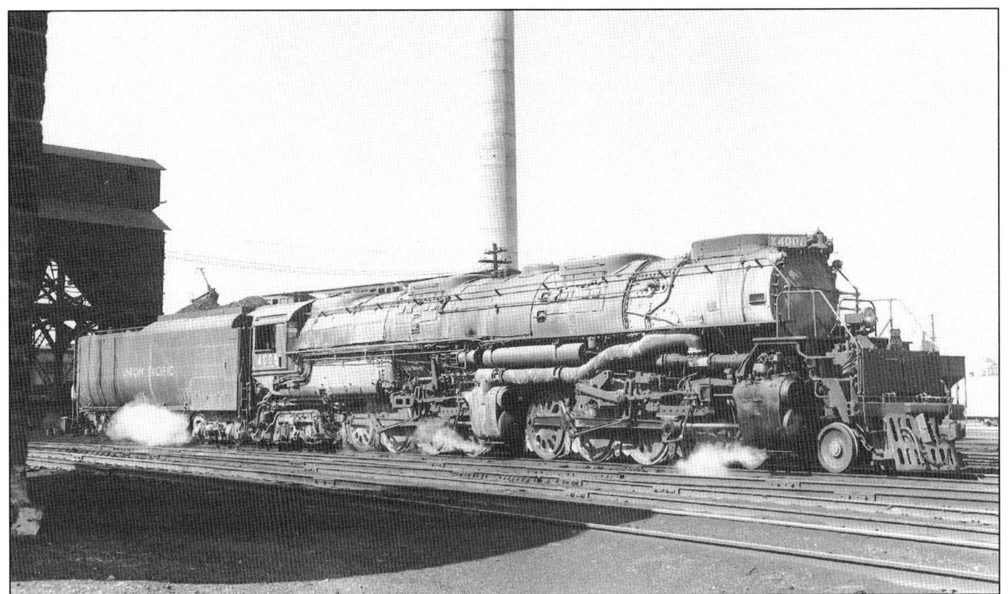

On August 18, 1956, engine No. 4006 emerges from the Laramie coal chute after being refueled. The Big Boys were designed specifically to haul freight at sustained speeds of 60 miles per hour. Originally designed for the Wasatch Mountains, the locomotive was eventually extended across the plains to Cheyenne. This was no small feet, considering the altitudes and grades they were expected to surmount. (Photograph by F.G. Gschwind; AJWC.)

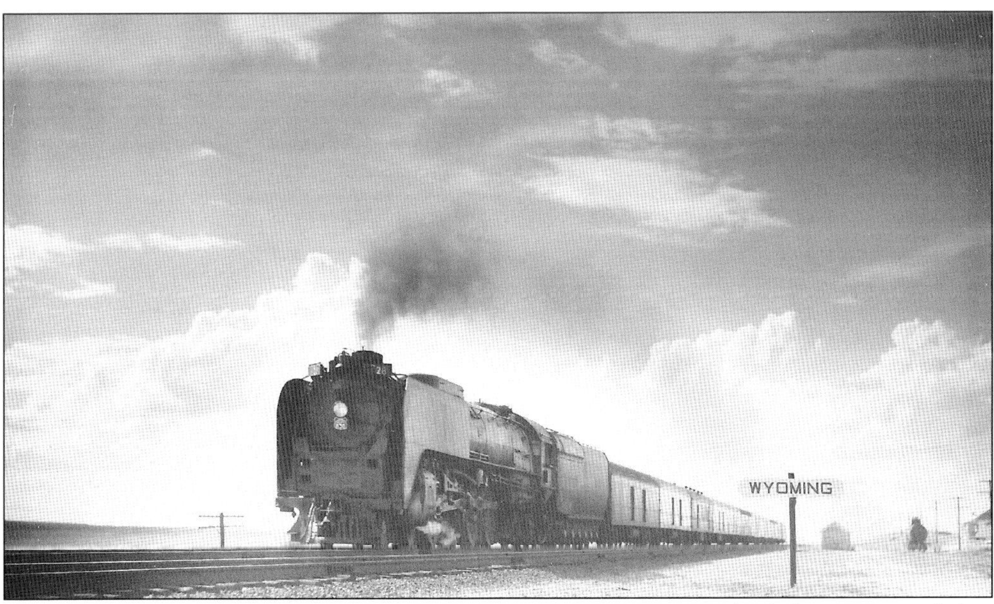

The cowlings on each side of the smoke box of engine No. 830 are smoke deflectors, intended to lift the smoke away from passenger cars. They are often called "elephant ears." Here the No. 830, a 4-8-4 Northern built by ALCO, pulls a 10-car passenger train through Wyoming at 75 miles per hour on July 13, 1957. (Photograph by R.H. Kindig; James L. Ehernberger Collection.)

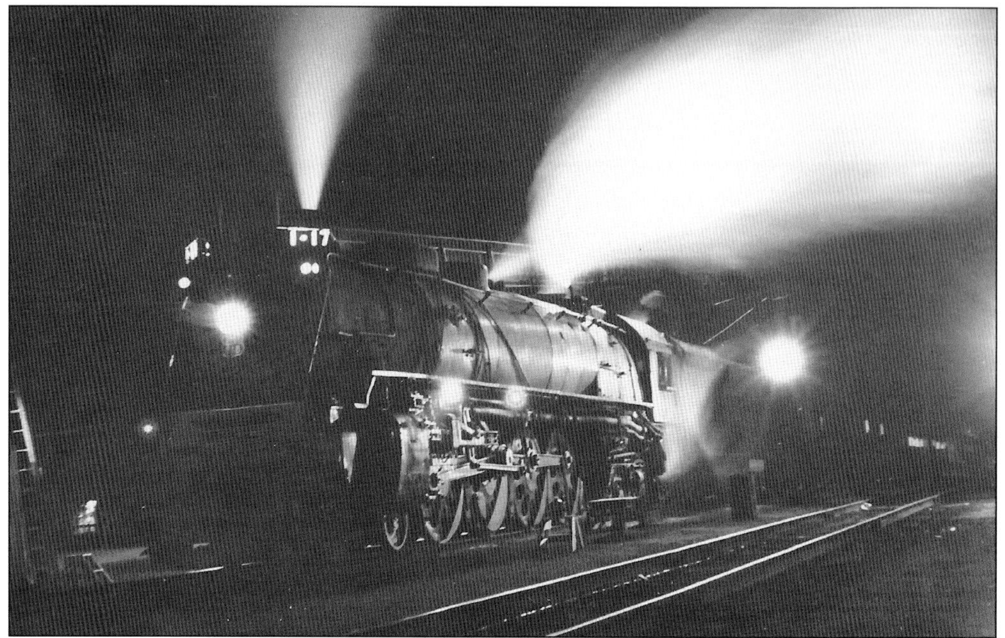

Engine No. 818 pulls into Laramie on the night of May 21, 1951. It was pulling the first section of the *Portland Rose* train service. Just visible above the boilers is the footbridge over the Laramie rail yards. The Union Pacific Railroad kept a tight schedule, and the speeds of passenger trains like this one were carefully regulated. (Photograph by F. Zahn; JLEC.)

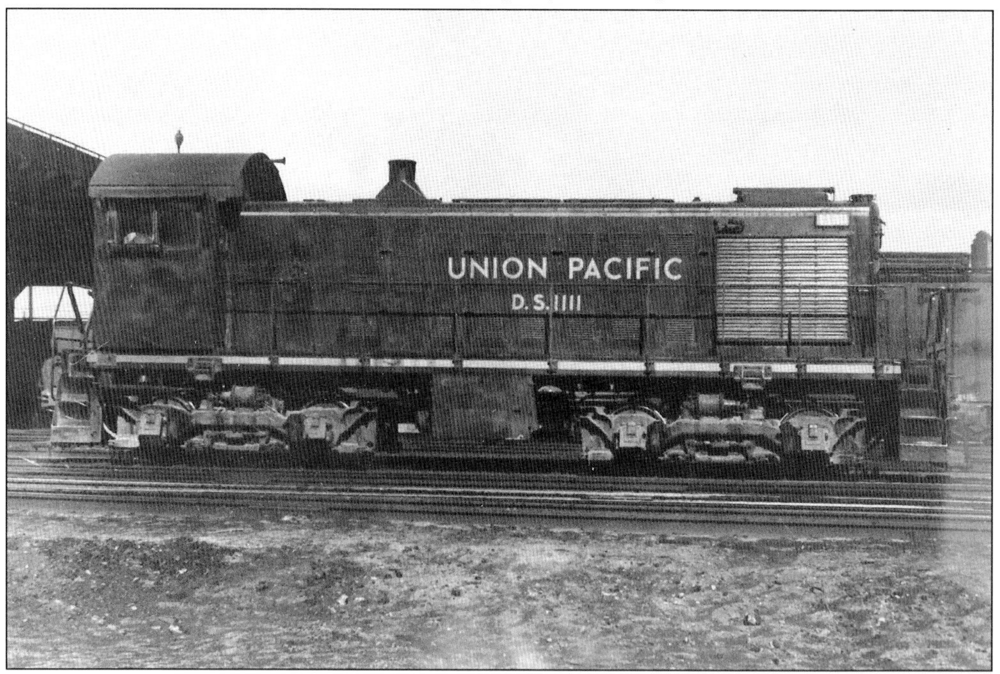

Seen here around 1947, this was the first diesel switcher in the Laramie yards. For many years, the job had been relegated to old steam engines, but this small engine, an S-2 built by ALCO in 1943, was designed specifically for the task. Initially painted black, in 1948, the engines acquired the armour yellow and harbor mist gray livery still used throughout the UPRR fleet. (JLEC.)

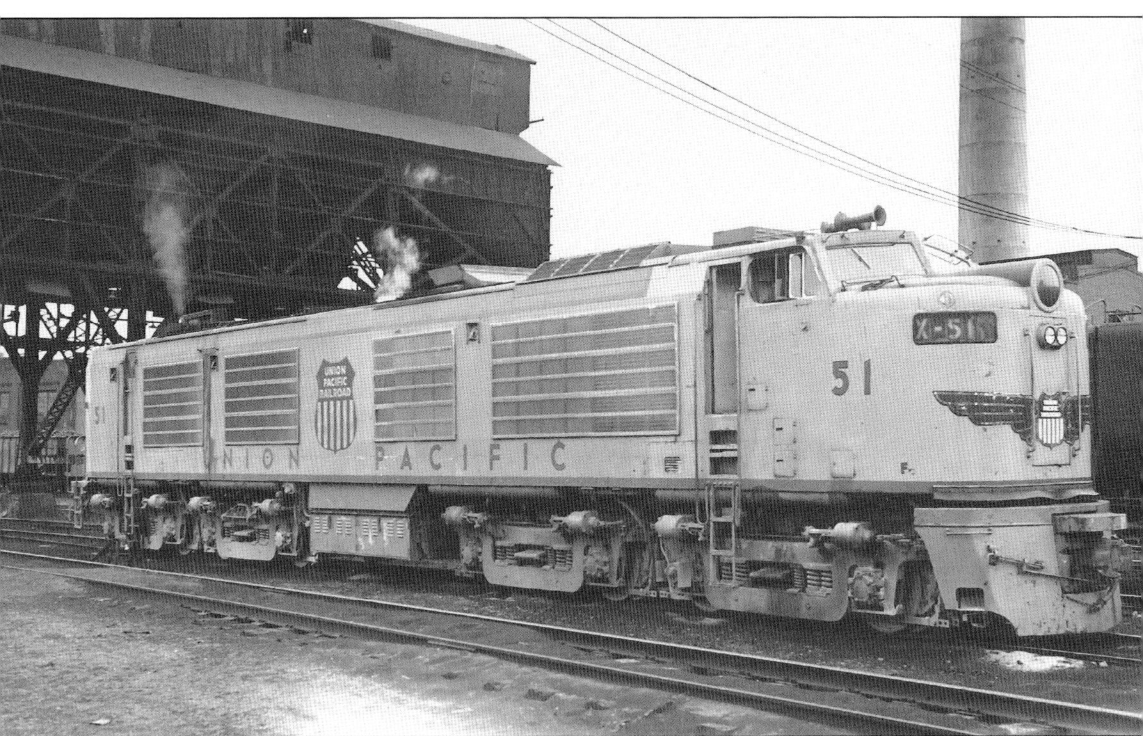

Engine No. 51, seen here on May 8, 1954, was known colloquially as a "Big Blow." This was the very first of the Union Pacific's gas turbine electric locomotives (GTEL) to be produced after the original No. 50 prototype. The first-generation GTELs, Nos. 51 through 60, were produced between 1952 and 1953. (Photograph by F.G. Gschwind; AJWC.)

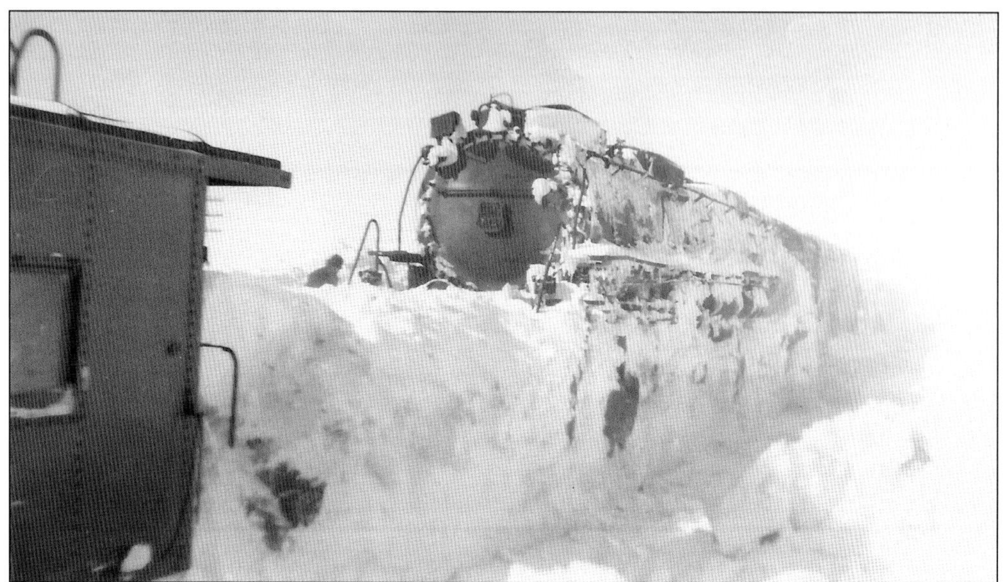

The Laramie Valley is no stranger to severe blizzards, but there were a few that stand above the rest. For Laramie, the blizzards of 1878, 1917, and 1949 were historic. This photograph shows Challenger No. 3932 trapped in the snow during the 1949 blizzard. (Charles Burke Collection, Historic Laramie Railroad Depot.)

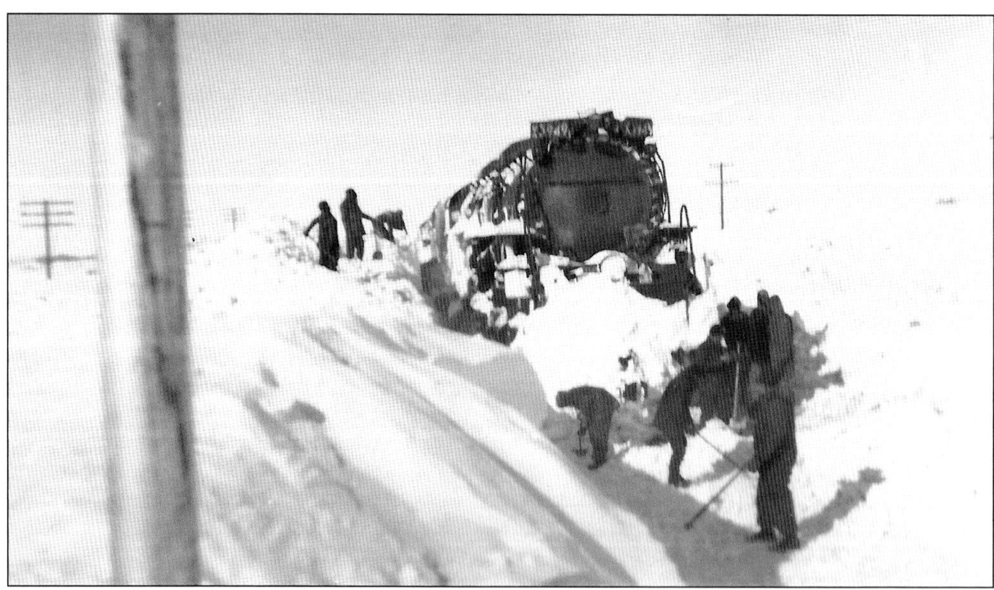

Here, engine No. 3949 is being manually shoveled out of an extreme snowdrift. The blizzard struck southeastern Wyoming during January and February 1949. Within 24 hours of the initial onslaught, thousands of motorists and rail passengers were stranded. Snowfall measured 30 inches, and drifts were over 20 feet high. (Charles Burke Collection, Historic Laramie Railroad Depot.)

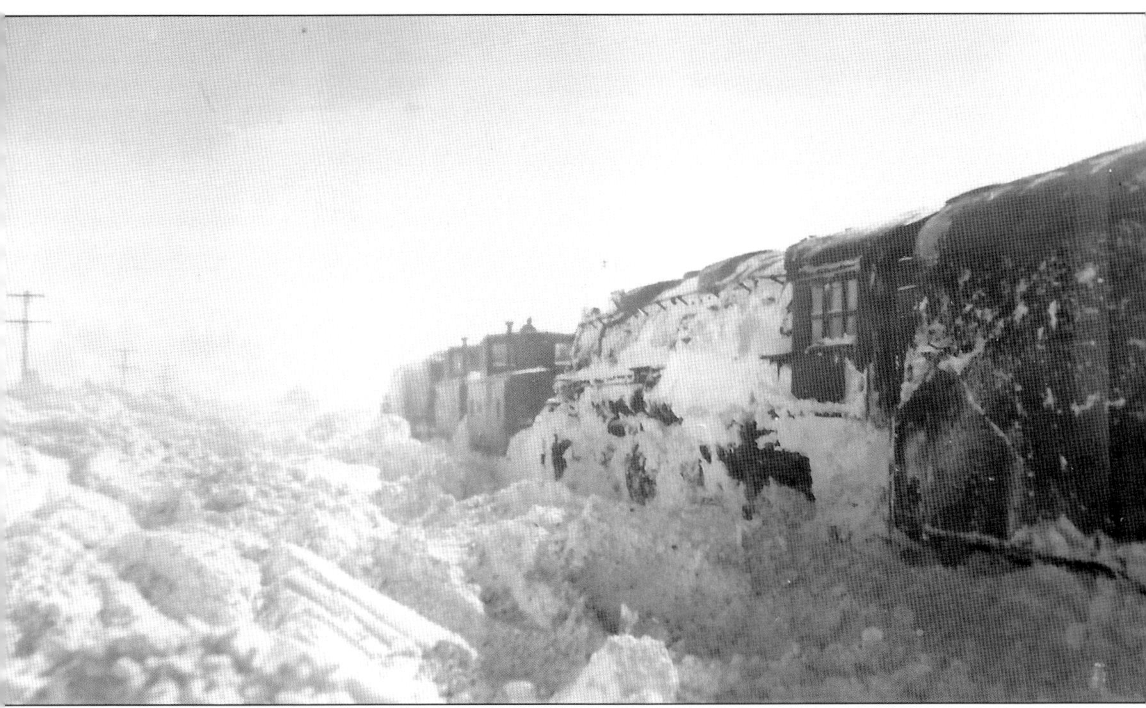

The 1949 blizzard brought transportation to a stop throughout much of Wyoming, Nebraska, South Dakota, and Colorado. It killed 17 people in Wyoming, 55,000 head of cattle, and over 105,000 sheep. Here, two engines have been partially dug out, but it will be a while before they can start moving. (Charles Burke Collection, Historic Laramie Railroad Depot.)

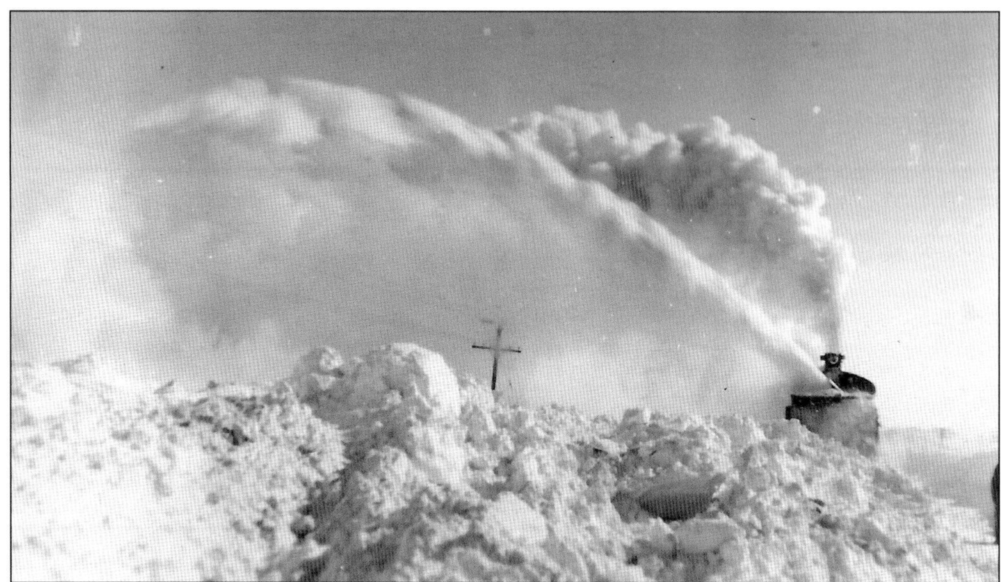

A rotary snowplow hurls snow up to 200 feet away in order to clear the tracks. As the 1949 storm continued, stores began to run out of food. The Union Pacific and other railroads played a vital role in bringing provisions to the storm-battered cities and towns throughout the region. (Charles Burke Collection, Historic Laramie Railroad Depot.)

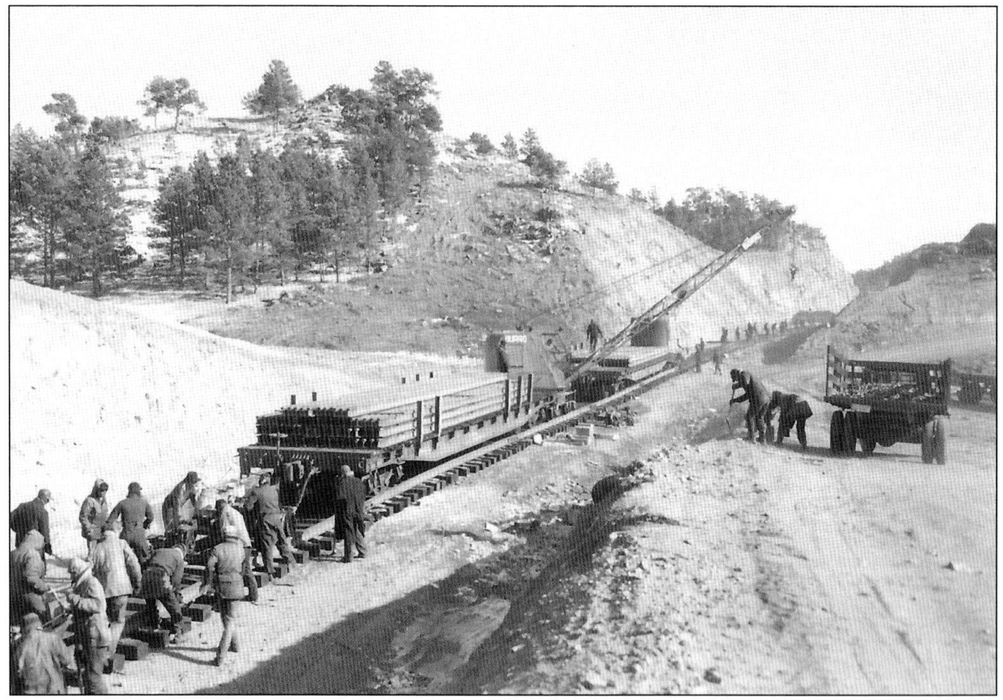

In 1951, the Union Pacific Railroad expanded the Harriman route by adding a third line from about Cheyenne to Dale Junction. In this c. 1951 photograph, railroad workers known as "gandy dancers" offload rail from a flatcar in preparation for spiking it into the ties. Track No. 3 is 10 miles longer than the other tracks, but its gentler grade (.82 percent versus 1.51 percent) makes it a more efficient line for westbound traffic. (Photograph by Union Pacific; JLEC.)

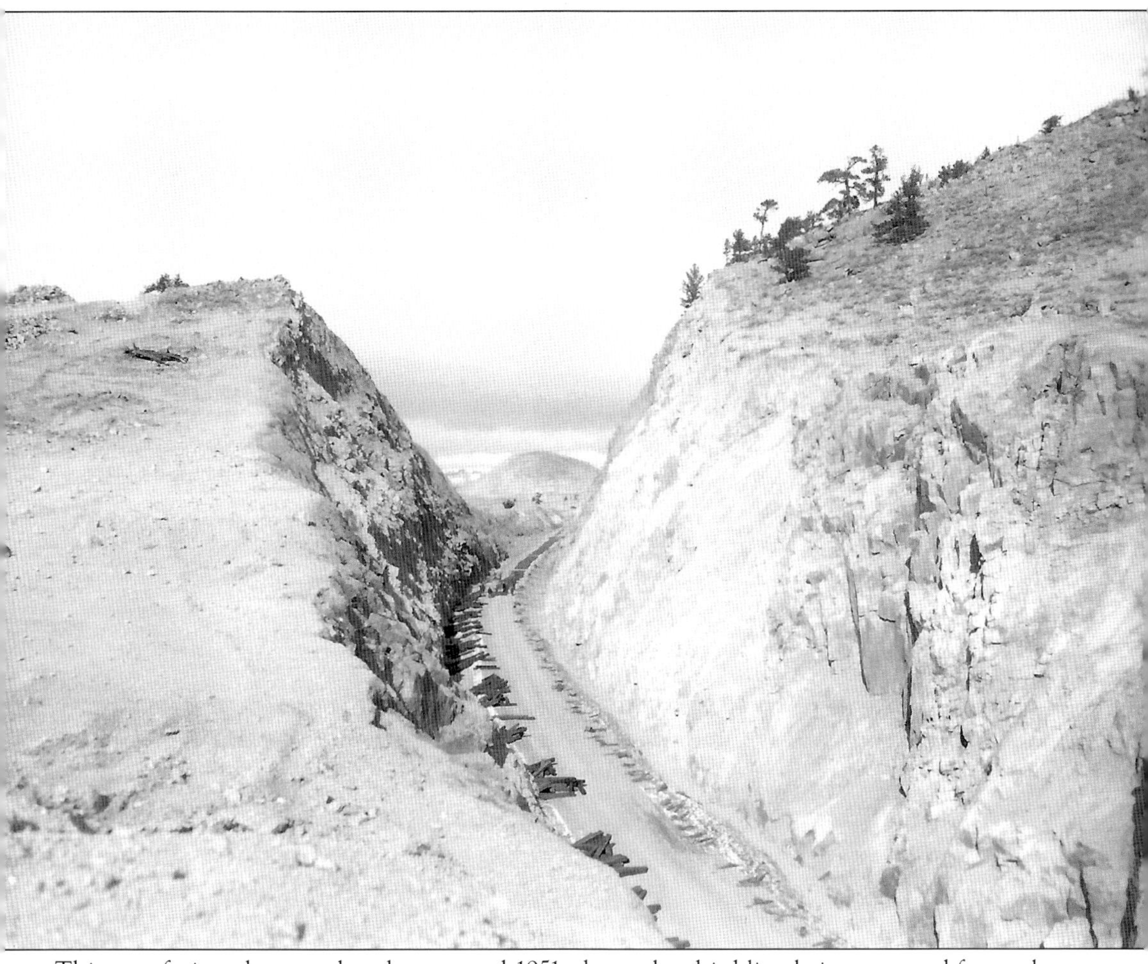

This west-facing photograph, taken around 1951, shows the third line being prepared for track laying in Dale Creek Cut. Ties are lined up, and a team of workers is laying rail. The cut is 120 feet deep and pierces solid granite, a feat that would have been impossible with the technology and equipment available to the builders of the Transcontinental Railroad in the 1860s. (Photograph by Union Pacific; JLEC.)

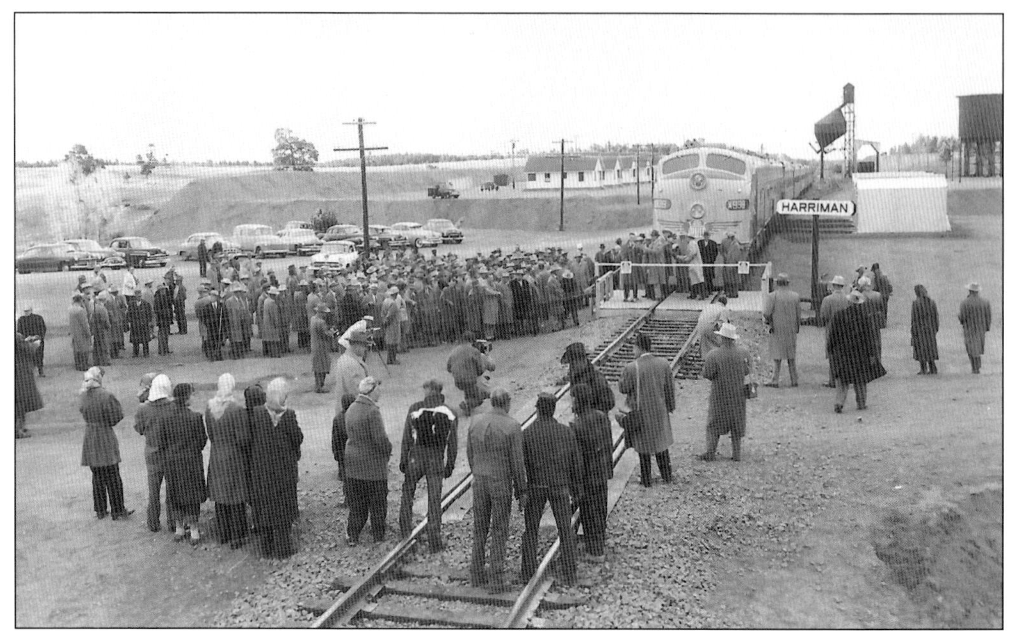

This is the opening ceremony for track No. 3 at Harriman, Wyoming, on May 12, 1953. A train brought officials from Union Pacific and Morrison-Knudsen (builders of the line) together with dignitaries for the celebration. Harriman was named for Union Pacific board chairman E. Roland Harriman, not Edward Harriman, whose leadership saved the company in the early 1900s. The water tower and section houses still stand as of 2013. (Photograph by Union Pacific; JLEC.)

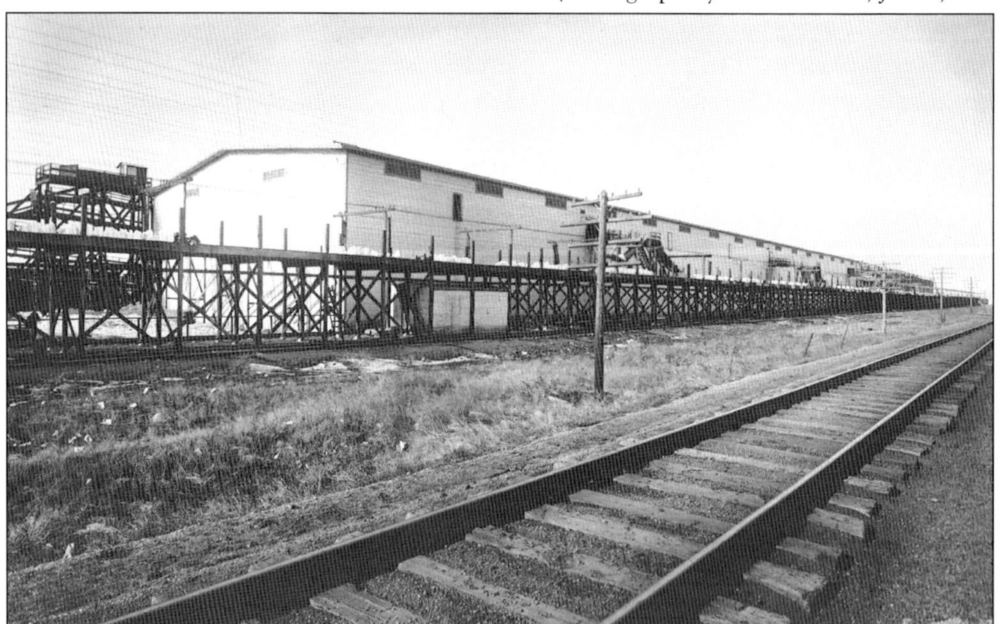

The new Pacific Fruit Express (PFE) icehouse north of Laramie, built after the original one was destroyed by a flood in 1923, is believed to have been the largest ice-storage facility in the world. It was 900 feet long, 108 feet wide, and 34 feet high. Ice harvested from nearby ponds during the winter was used in refrigerator cars throughout the year. The icehouse is seen here in 1923. (Photograph by Union Pacific; JLEC.)

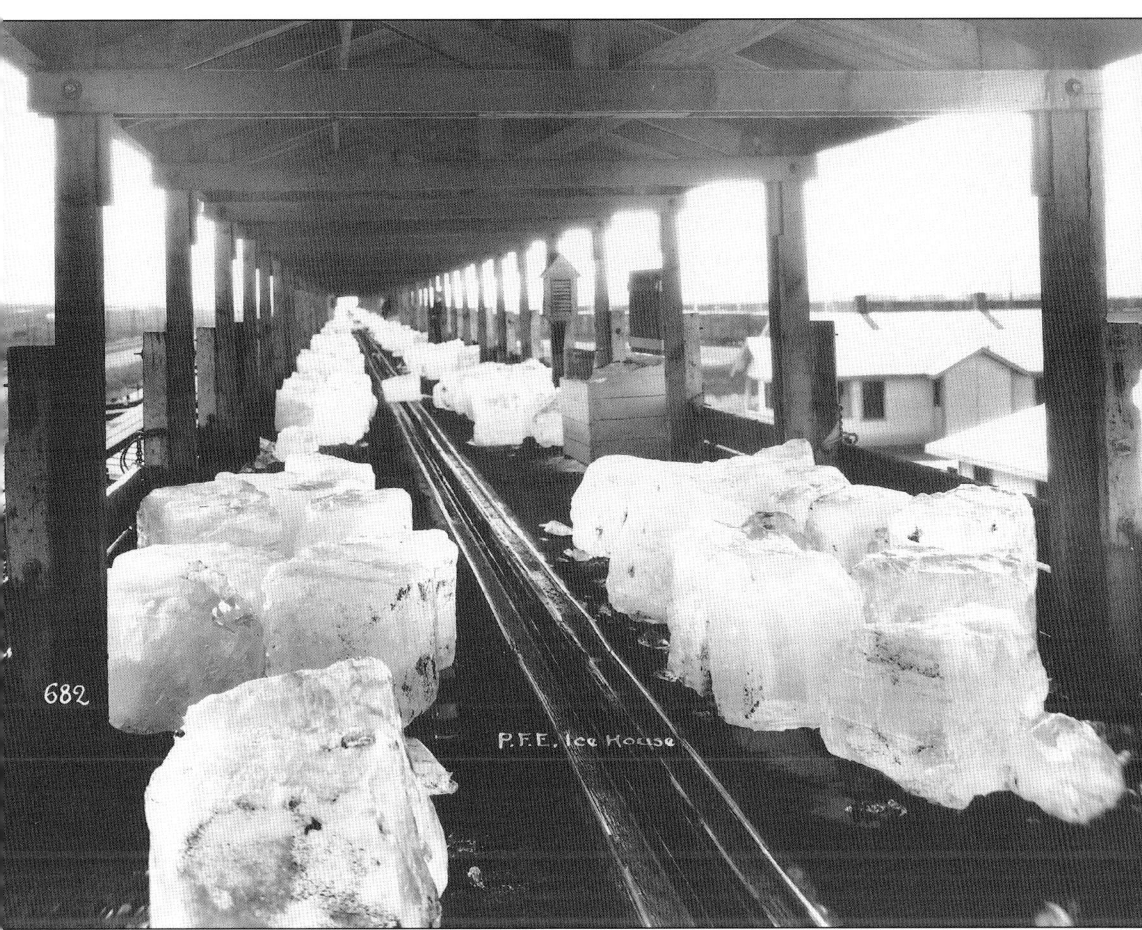

Seen here around 1940, the platform on the east side of the icehouse next to the tracks was originally roofed and could handle a train 80 cars long. Ice from the ponds was cut into 22-inch by 22-inch blocks, stored in the house, and then sent down the platforms to be loaded into cars as needed. (Photograph by H. Svenson; Historic Laramie Railroad Depot.)

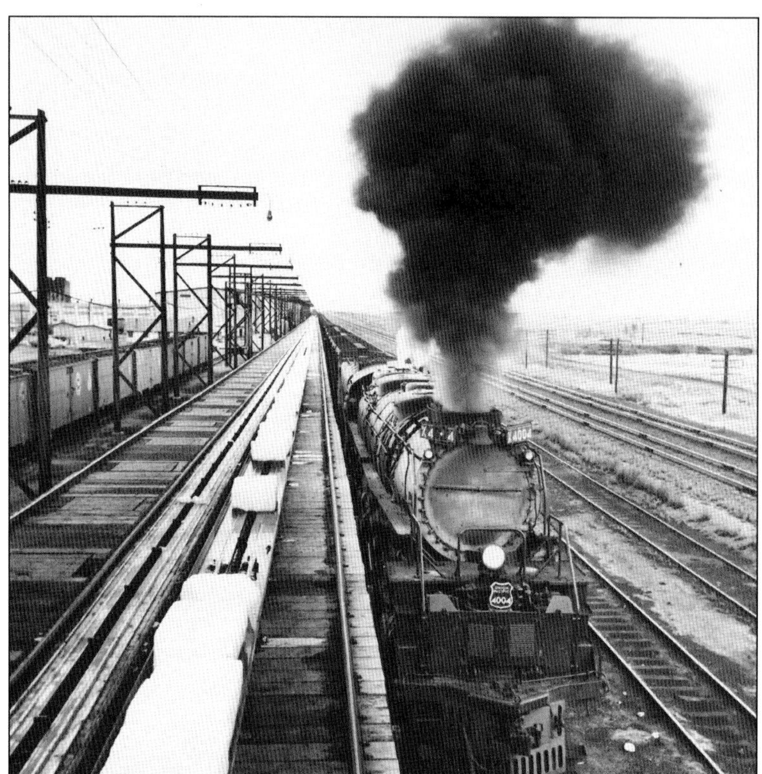

Big Boy No. 4004 waits at the icehouse platform as its train of refrigerator cars takes on ice in this c. 1954 photograph. Often, entire trains consisted of such "reefers," most of them PFE. Produce from the West Coast headed for Eastern markets on the eastbound trains, and empty reefers ran westbound. A Big Boy at the head of such trains was a common sight throughout the 1940s and 1950s. (JLEC.)

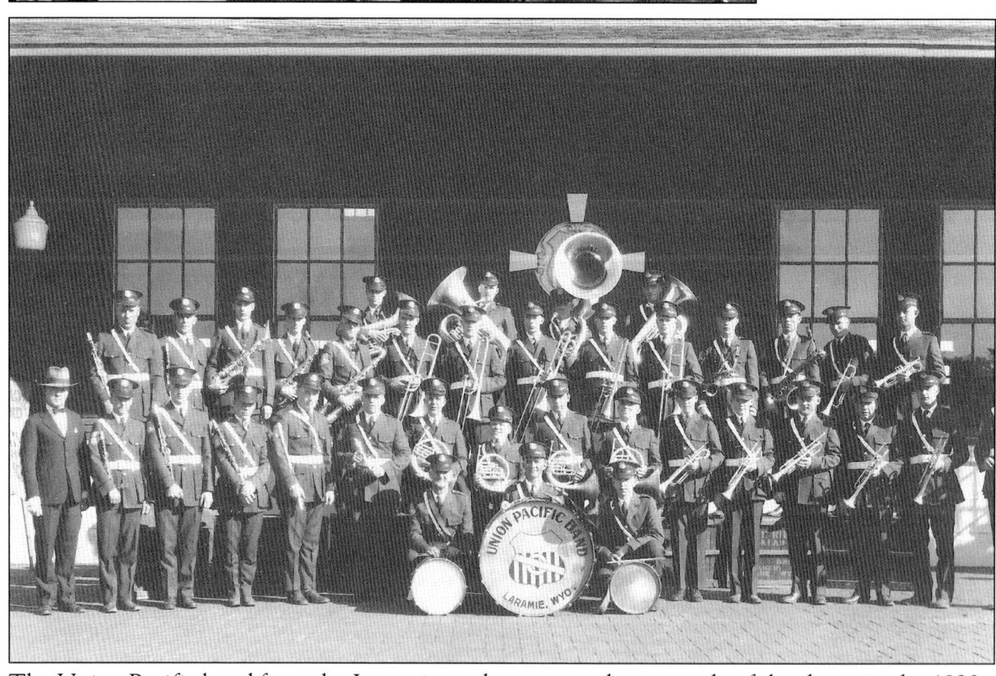

The Union Pacific band from the Laramie yards poses on the west side of the depot in the 1920s. UP bands were located in most major terminal facilities along the line. Common in the 1920s and 1930s, they often participated in local parades and celebrations. (Photograph by Henning Svenson; Historic Laramie Railroad Depot.)

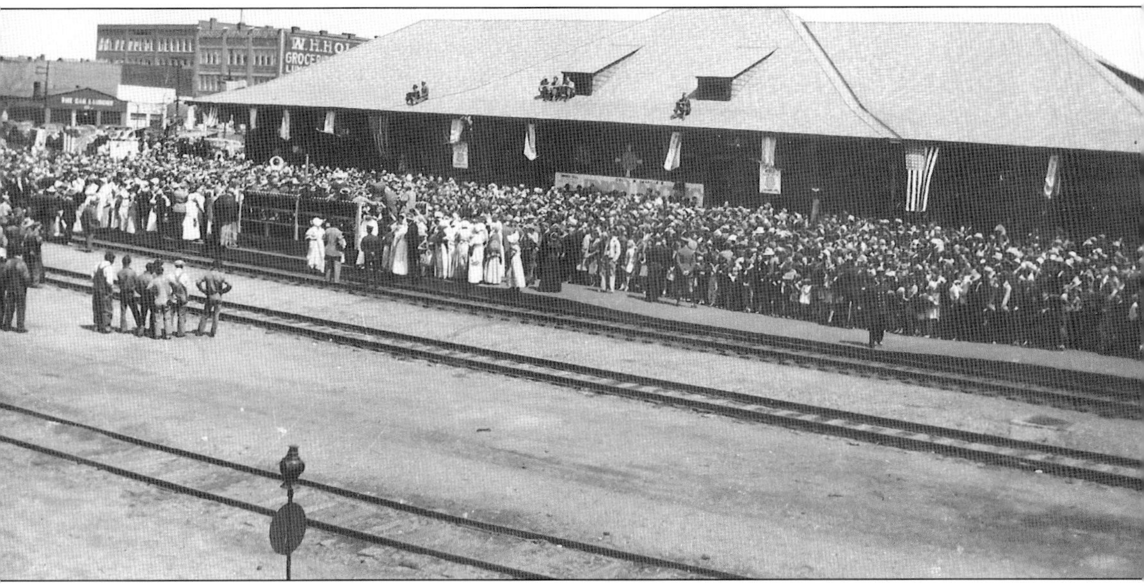

Crowds gather to see a train promoting the Cecil B. DeMille movie *Union Pacific* in 1939. The movie was loosely based on the building of the Transcontinental Railroad in the 1860s. The film created history in its own right, as it and John Ford's *Stagecoach* were credited with transforming Western films from low-grade "B" movies into top-grossing films with all-star casts. (JLEC.)

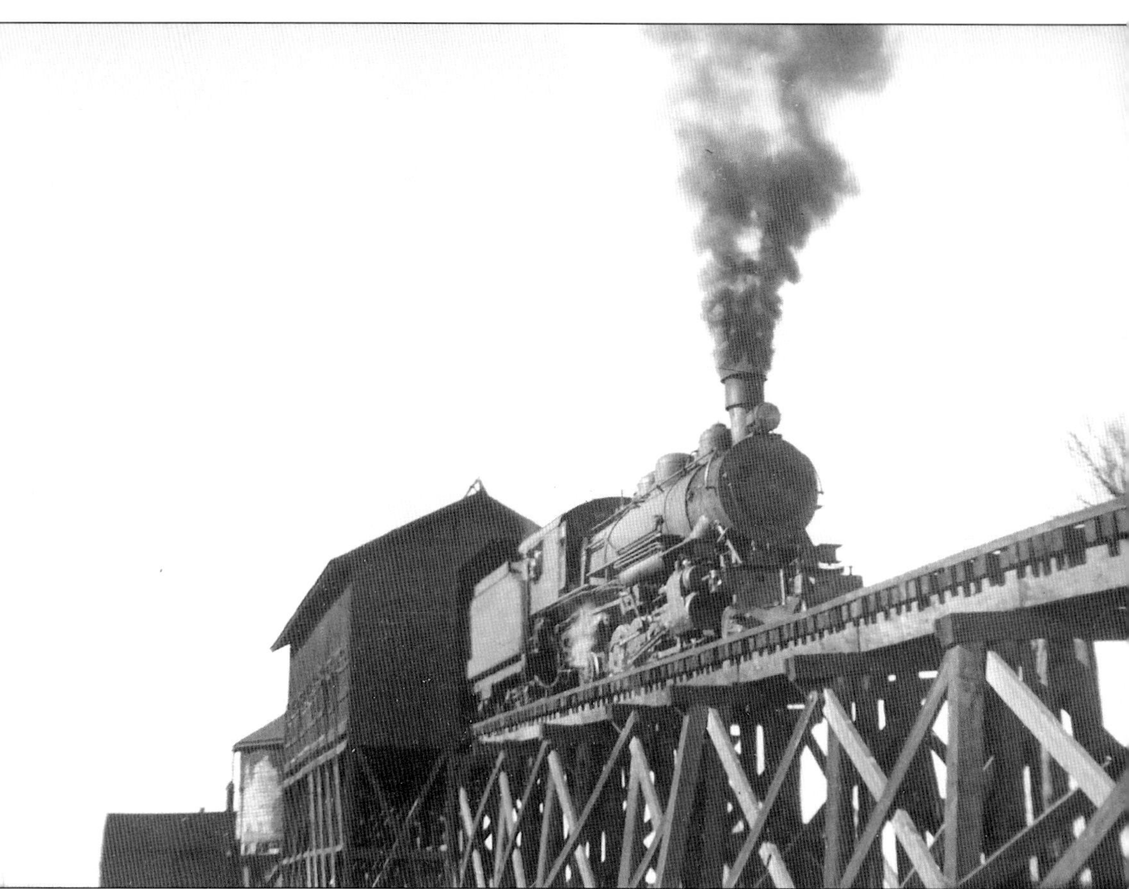

The Laramie, Hahns Peak & Pacific Railroad went through several reorganizations and name changes. At the time of this photograph in the 1930s, it had become the Laramie, North Park & Western (LNP&W). The company's engine No. 8 is filling the small four-pocket coal chute the railroad used. Loaded coal cars were brought to the chute, where they unloaded their cargo. They were then brought down empty. (JHC.)

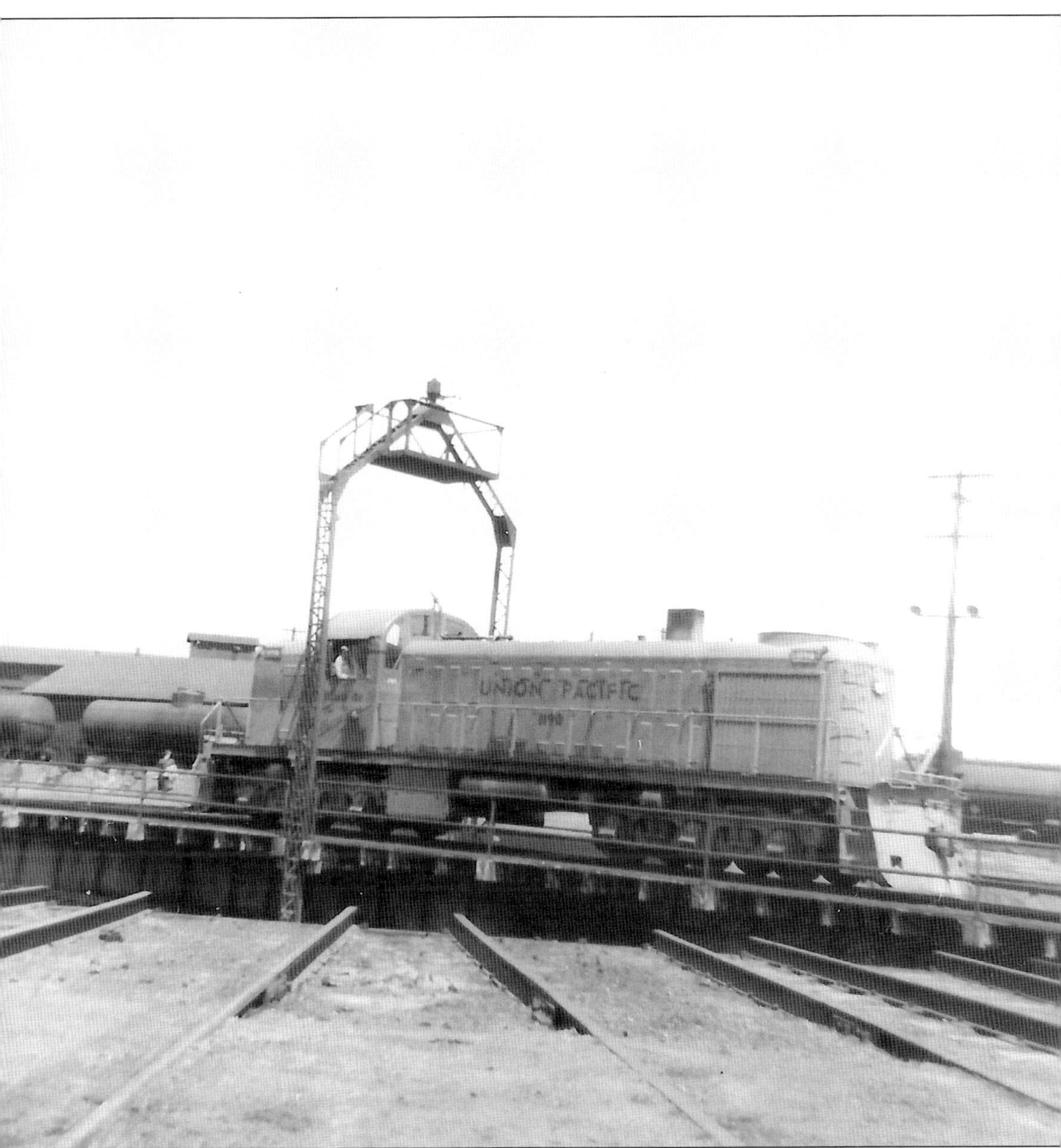

Union Pacific engine No. 1190 sits on the Laramie turntable on May 17, 1953. This was the first diesel road engine used on the Union Pacific Railroad, and it was run on the LNP&W line. The railroad used it for testing, because Foxpark was the highest elevation in the entire UP system. It had to lighten its ballast in order to make the Foxpark run. (JLEC.)

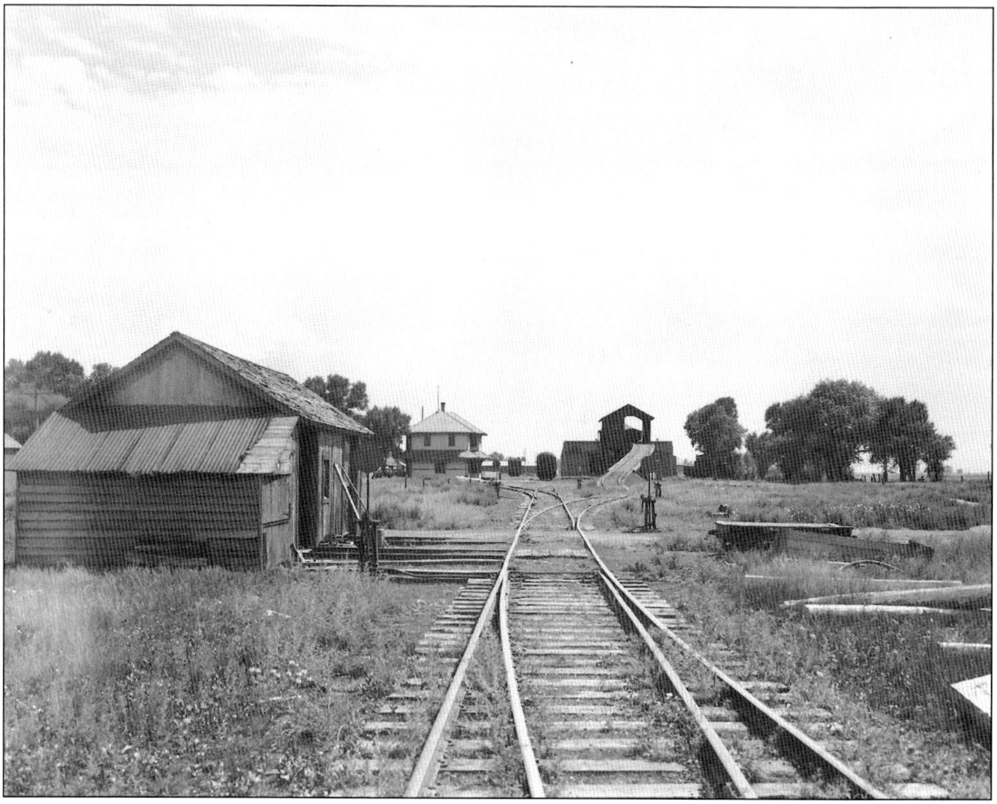

The yards for the Laramie, North Park & Western are seen here around 1941. In the foreground is a small shed used to store a motorized cart, also called a speeder. In the background, left of the tracks, is the depot. To the right are the coal chutes. (Photograph by Union Pacific; JLEC.)

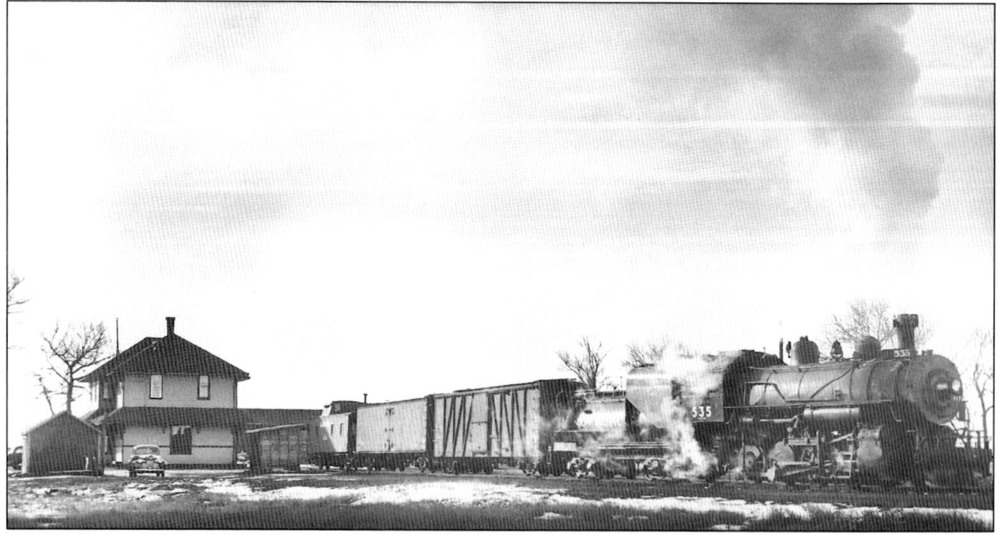

Engine No. 535 is a locomotive with a long history in Laramie. Starting out on the Oregon Short Line in 1903, it was moved to the Laramie area in 1947 and began working on the LNP&W line. In this November 1948 photograph, it is leaving the LNP&W depot for its long climb up to Foxpark. (Photograph by Donald Duke; JLEC.)

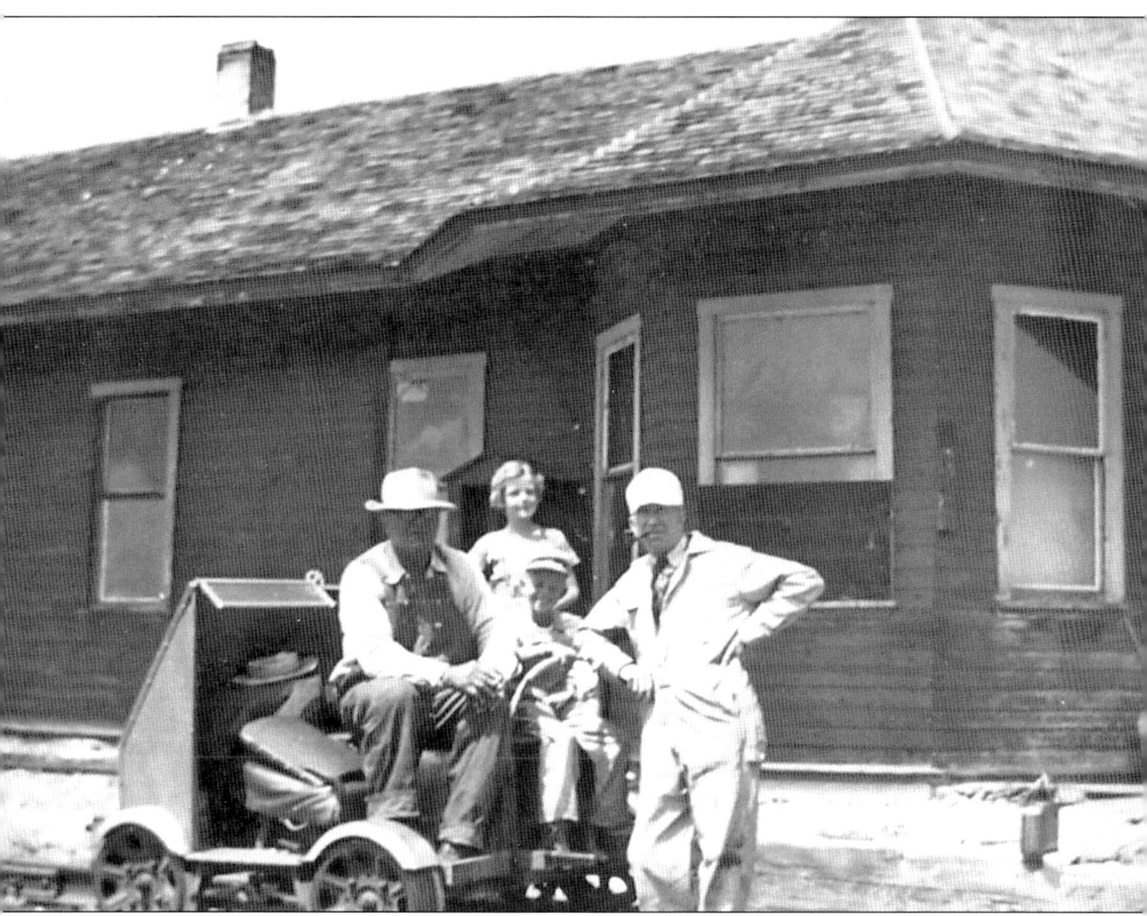

This 1950s photograph shows the depot in Centennial, Wyoming. Ed Burke, a Union Pacific engineer (right) is shown with his family, seated in the small self-motorized "speeder" car. (Charles Burke Collection, Historic Laramie Railroad Depot.)

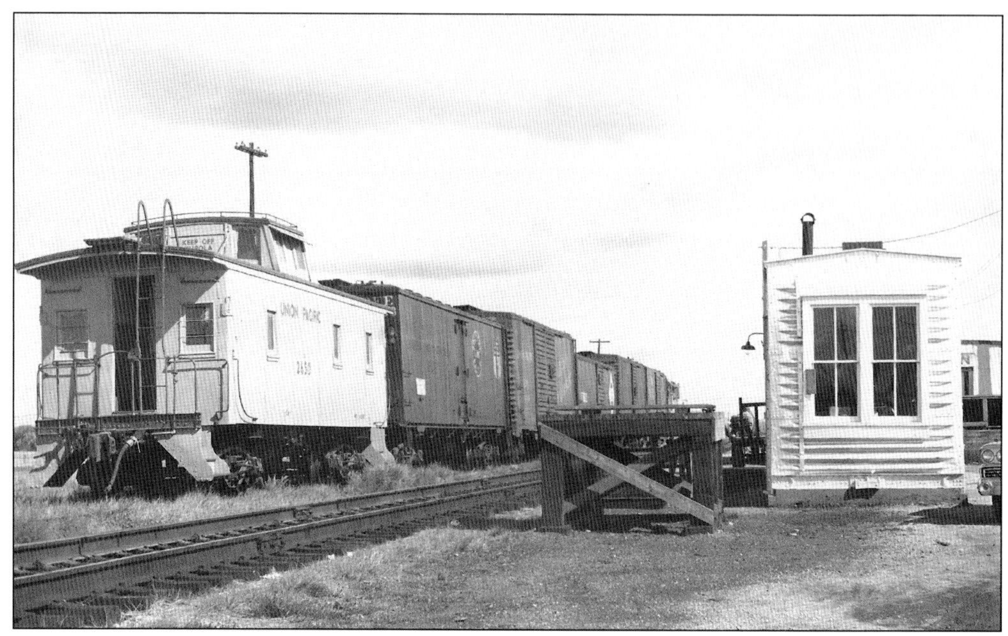

A freight train on the Laramie, North Park & Western line sits at Foxpark about 1960. The refrigerator car ahead of the caboose remained with the train, going back and forth between Laramie and Coalmont, Colorado. It was used to carry small amounts of freight to and from the various stations along the line. Because it was refrigerated, it could handle frozen goods and ordinary freight. (JHC.)

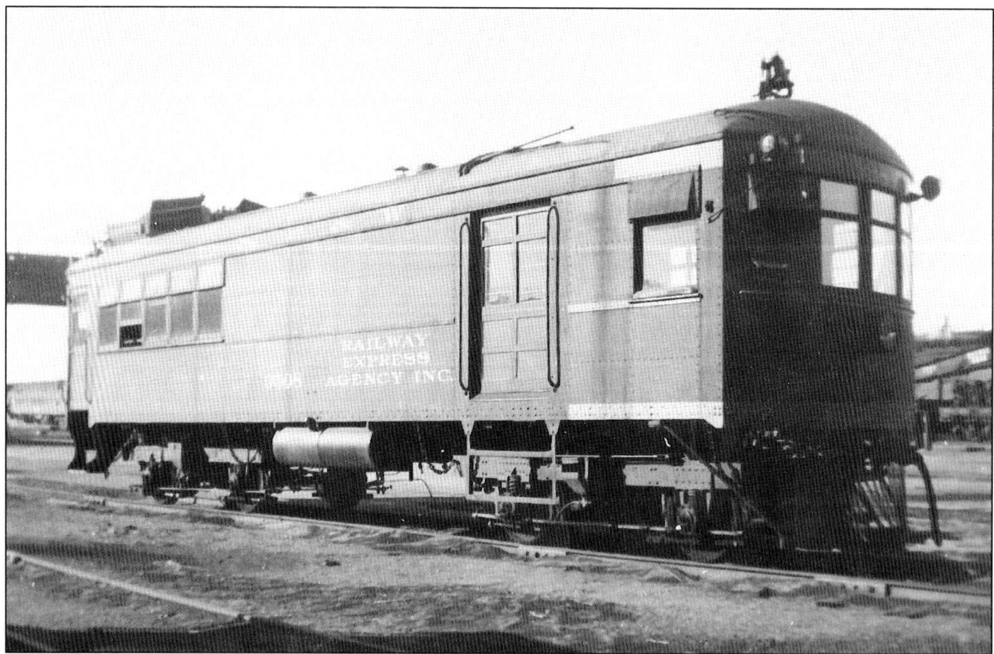

A motor car from the Laramie, North Park & Western line is seen on December 28, 1938. Such cars were primarily used for passenger and less-than-car-load (LCL) travel on branch and short lines. They were also good for hauling small crews and personnel around the line. This was one of two such cars owned by the LNP&W. (JLEC.)

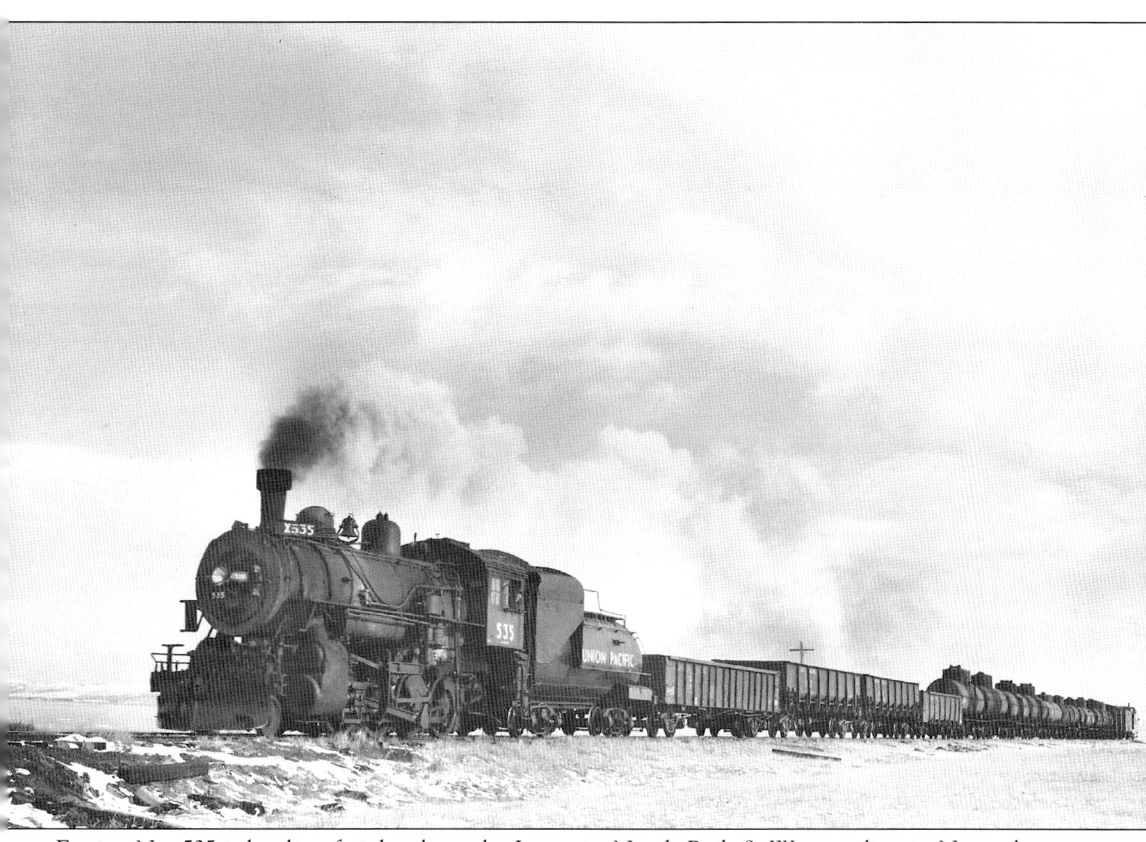

Engine No. 535 is hauling freight along the Laramie, North Park & Western line in November 1948. A dusting of snow can be seen along the train, but those were tame conditions for an engine that spent most of its operational life hauling freight over a mountain range nicknamed "the Snowies." It is a mixed train of different gondola, oil, and boxcars. (Photograph by Donald Duke; JLEC.)

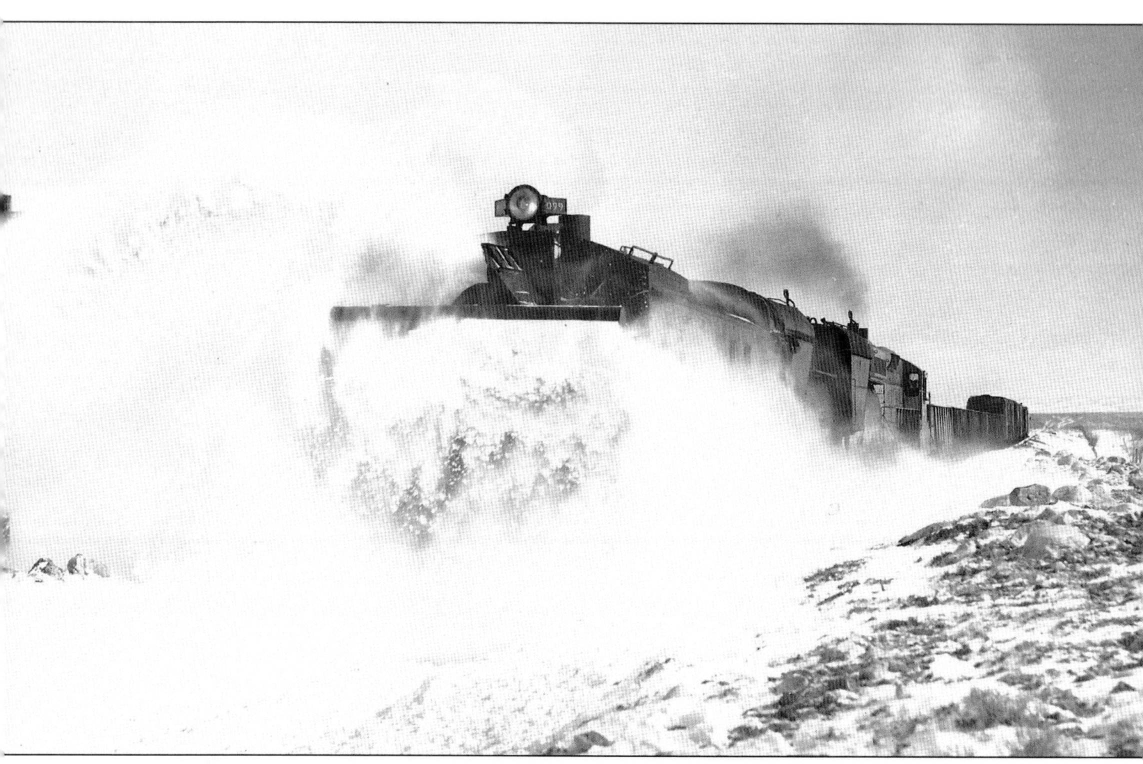

In 1951, the Union Pacific bought the Laramie, North Park & Western line and renamed it the "Coalmont branch." Here, UP engine No. 457 is pushing rotary plow No. 99 about 1957. This was the same plow used in 1909 by the Laramie, Hans Peak & Pacific. It continued to see use until the 1960s. (JLEC.)

Five

1960–Today

Keeping Laramie's Railroading Legacy Alive

By the mid-1960s, Laramie's roundhouse complex, which included the roundhouse, turntable, machine shop, and powerhouse, was finally demolished. All that remains is the large smoke stack that once belonged to the powerhouse. Too dangerous and costly to remove, it stands to this day as a relic of Laramie's industrial past. In the late 1960s, one new railroad industry did arrive in the midst of the destruction of the old. A welding plant, which welded high-speed rail for modern railroads, was constructed where the roundhouse had stood. The small spur lines finally died as well. The Laramie Valley Railway, which held the distinction of operating steam-powered engines well into the 1960s, ceased operation in 1983. The old Coalmont branch ended its life as the WyCo Railroad, but the track and engines were eventually sold for scrap in the late 1990s. By the turn of the 21st century, most of Laramie's railroading past had been all but forgotten.

Recent years have seen a resurgence in interest in the significant role that railroads, and specifically the Union Pacific Railroad, played in the founding of the town of Laramie. Once called the "Pittsburgh of the West," it is now thought of mostly as a sleepy college town. Much of the Coalmont branch has been converted into hiking and biking trails throughout the Snowy Range. People may not be able to ride the trains through the mountains anymore, but they can certainly enjoy much of the beautiful scenery through which the trains once traveled. The Laramie depot was restored and is now used as a reception hall and, soon, as a museum. And four old friends that had once served the local railroads have been restored. A snowplow and engine No. 535, both veterans of the Coalmont line, head a small snow train that also includes a bunk car and a caboose. The Historic Laramie Railroad Depot and the Laramie Railroad Heritage Park now stand as reminders of the town's storied past.

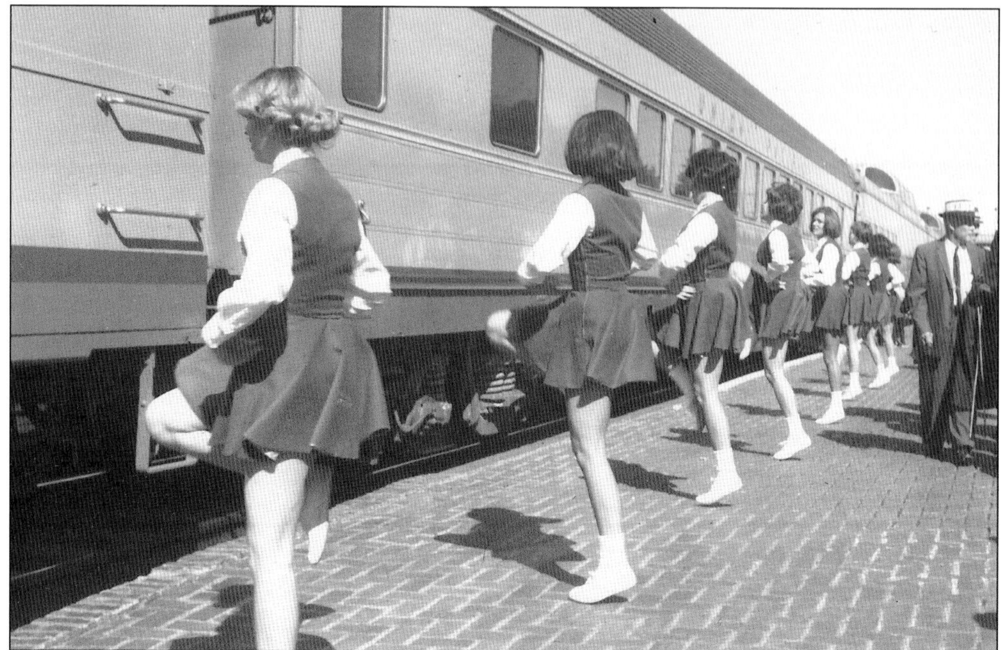

University of Wyoming cheerleaders greet the *Treagle Train* at the Laramie depot on September 28, 1963. The annual football special first ran in 1935 and was last operated in 1979. The name *Treagle* was derived from a combination of the names of Cheyenne's newspapers, *Wyoming State Tribune* and *Wyoming Eagle*. (Photograph by A.J. Wolff; AJWC.)

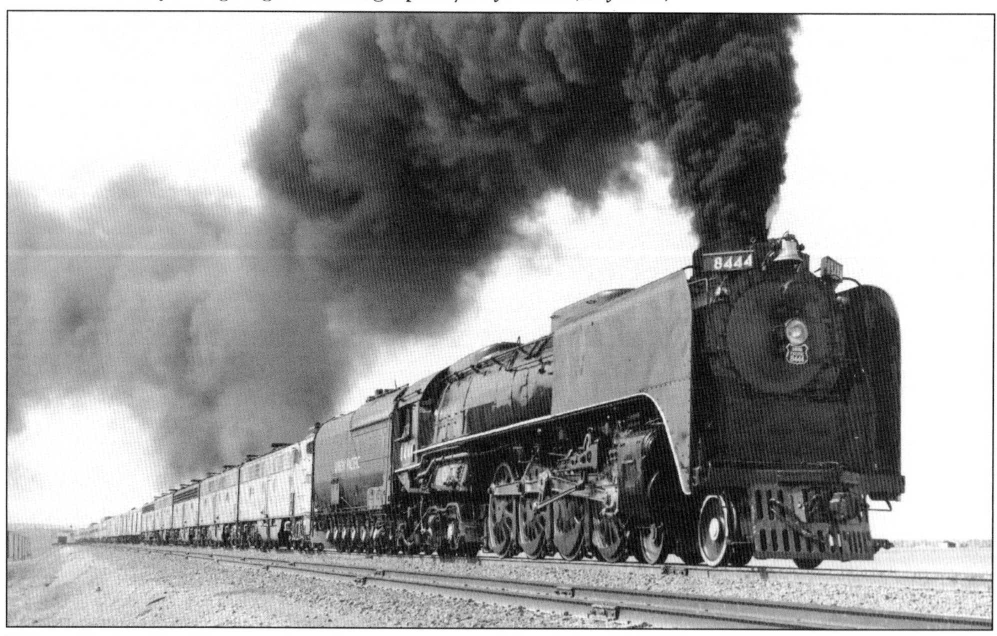

When Union Pacific agreed to the provisions of the federal Rail Passenger Service Act of 1970, effective May 1, 1971, scheduled passenger train service through Laramie came to a close. To mark the event, UP assigned its last operable steam locomotive, No. 8444, to the final westbound and eastbound runs of the *City of Los Angeles*. The train is seen here on May 1 on its last run. (Photograph by A.J. Wolff; AJWC.)

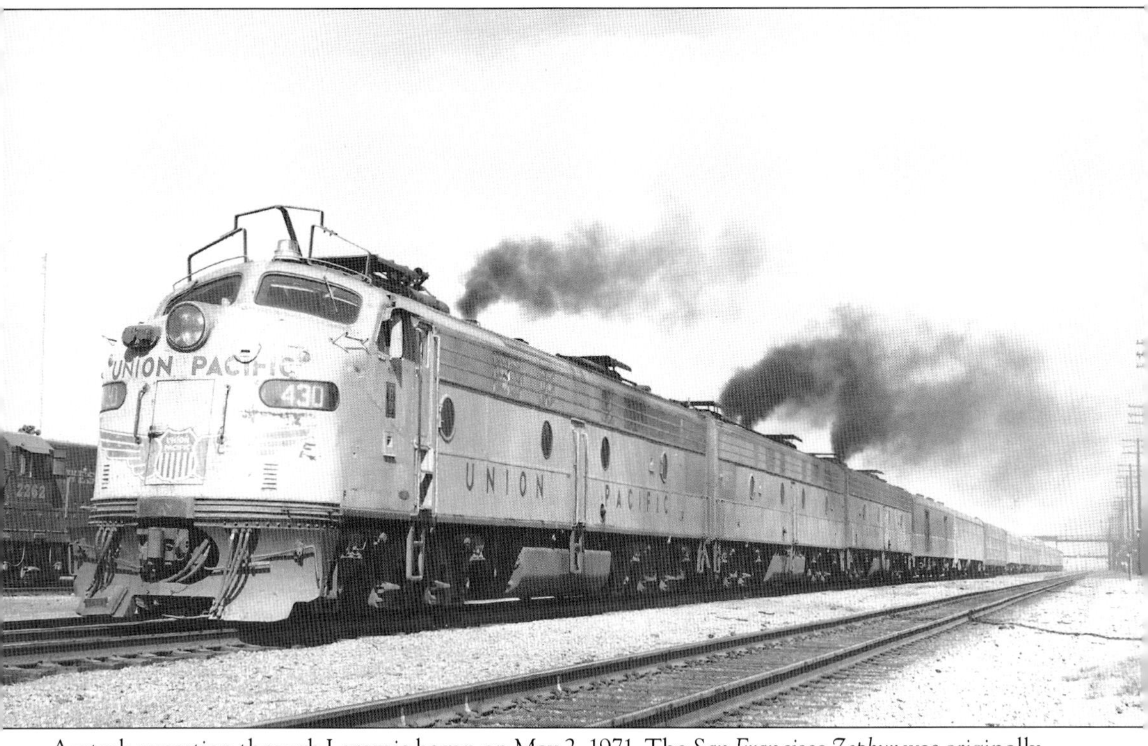

Amtrak operation through Laramie began on May 2, 1971. The *San Francisco Zephyr* was originally scheduled to operate over the Denver & Rio Grande Western, but that railroad opted out of Amtrak. Here, Amtrak E9 430, the former UP No. 957, with two E9Bs, leads the eastbound *San Francisco Zephyr* out of Laramie on October 6, 1973. (Photograph by A.J. Wolff; AJWC.)

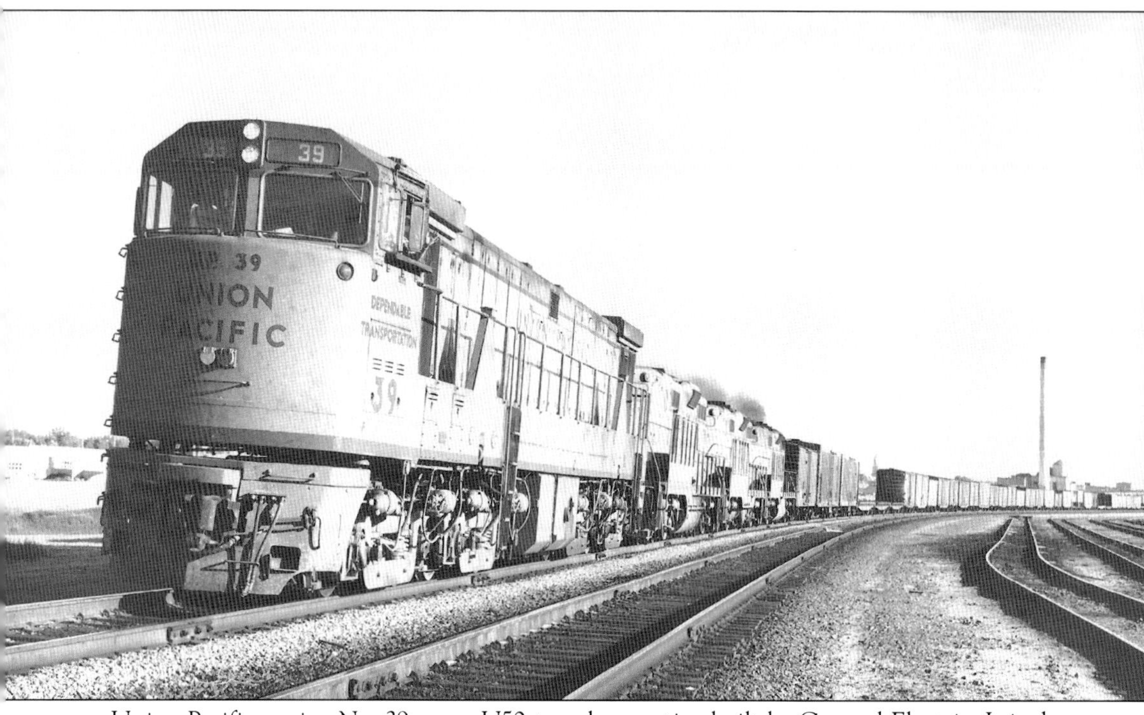

Union Pacific engine No. 39 was a U50-type locomotive built by General Electric. It is shown here on August 18, 1968, with three additional engines, pulling a long mixed freight west from Laramie. The U50 was purchased in 1964, one of 23 such units, and traded back to GE in 1974. (Photograph by A.J. Wolff; AJWC.)

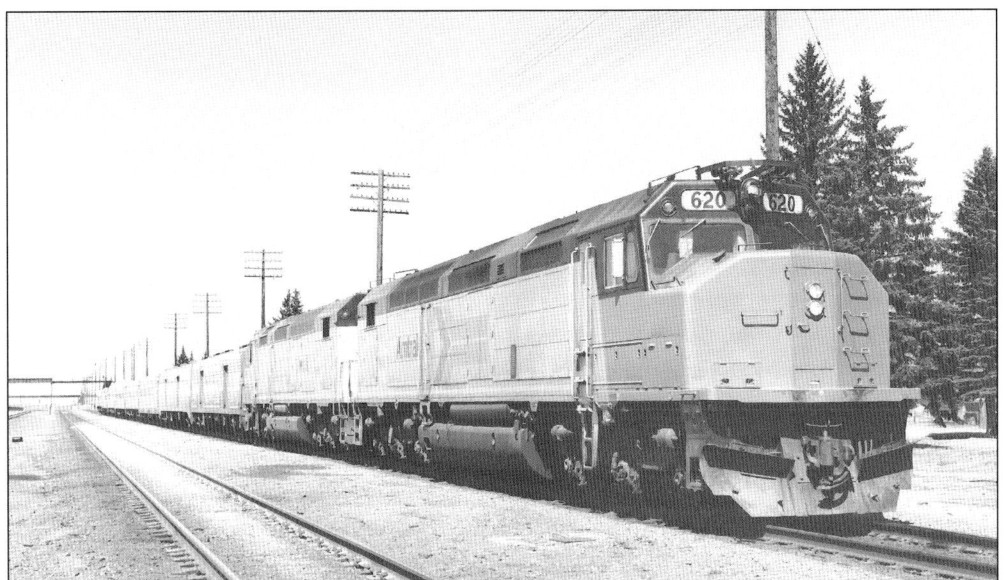

In 1972, the *San Francisco Zephyr* was the Amtrak passenger train between Chicago and San Francisco. Amtrak originally wanted to route the line between Denver and Salt Lake City, but it could not arrange a deal with the Rio Grande Railroad. The route for the *Zephyr* continued along the Union Pacific's lines until Amtrak finally worked a deal with the Rio Grande in 1983. The *Zephyr* is seen here on April 3, 1976. (Photograph by A.J. Wolff; AJWC.)

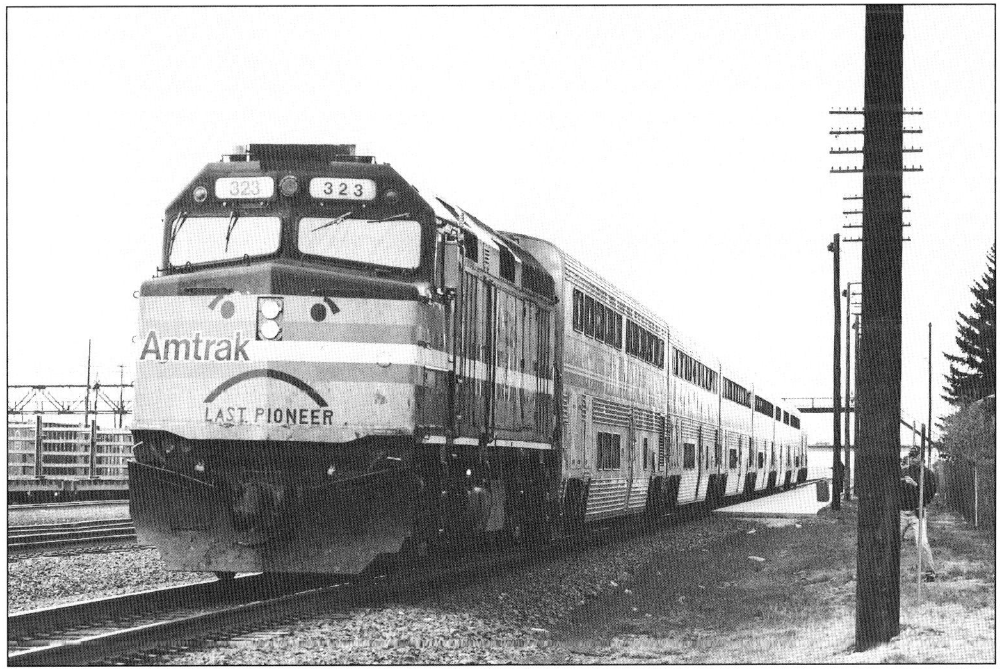

Amtrak service returned to Laramie on June 19, 1991, with the initiation of the Denver-to-Portland *Pioneer*, trains No. 25 and No. 26. After an operational period of six years, the train was dropped due to a shortage of funds for Amtrak at the national level. The last *Pioneer* through Laramie, seen here, occurred on May 11, 1997, a sad event for the train-loving traveling public. (Photograph by A.J. Wolff; AJWC.)

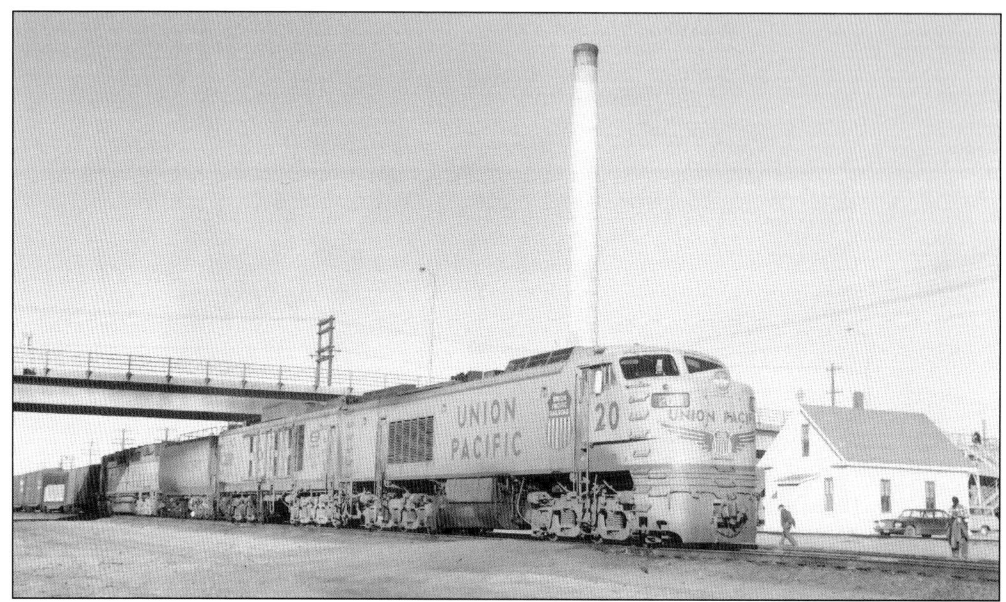

Gas turbine No. 20, with an EMD DD35, has stopped for a crew change at a house-like frame building near the new Clark Street overpass on November 18, 1967. The conductor and rear-end brakeman were transported to the caboose via a UP-provided van. Laramie was eliminated as a crew-change point in 1972. (Photograph by A.J. Wolff; AJWC.)

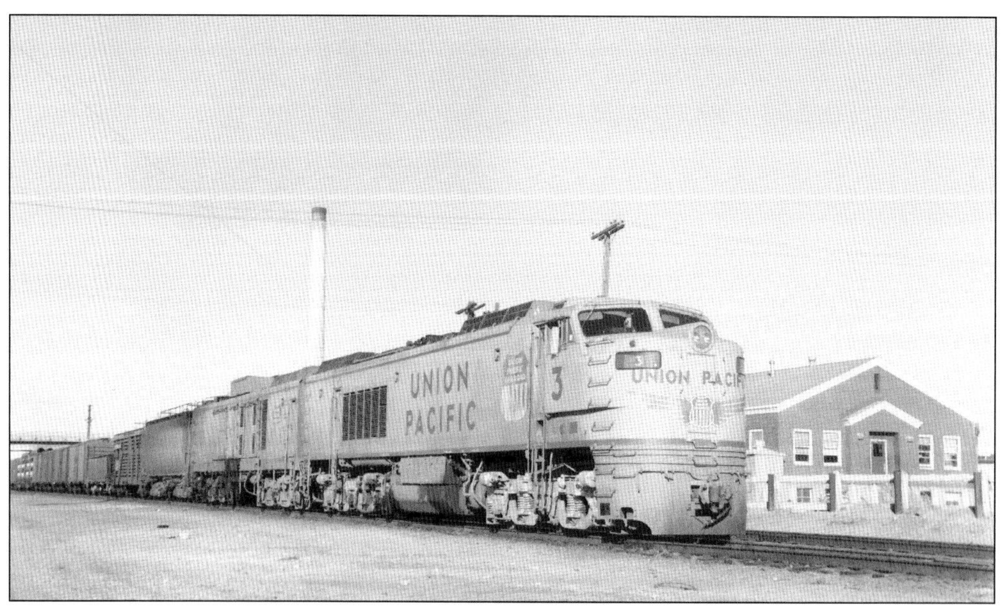

Eastbound turbine No. 3 rolls by the UP yard office/freight depot in November 1967. The substantial brick structure was built in 1945, and it was demolished in 1994. The loud and voluminous roar of the turbines was frequently heard across Laramie proper for a period of some 15 years, from 1954 to 1969. (Photograph by A.J. Wolff; AJWC.)

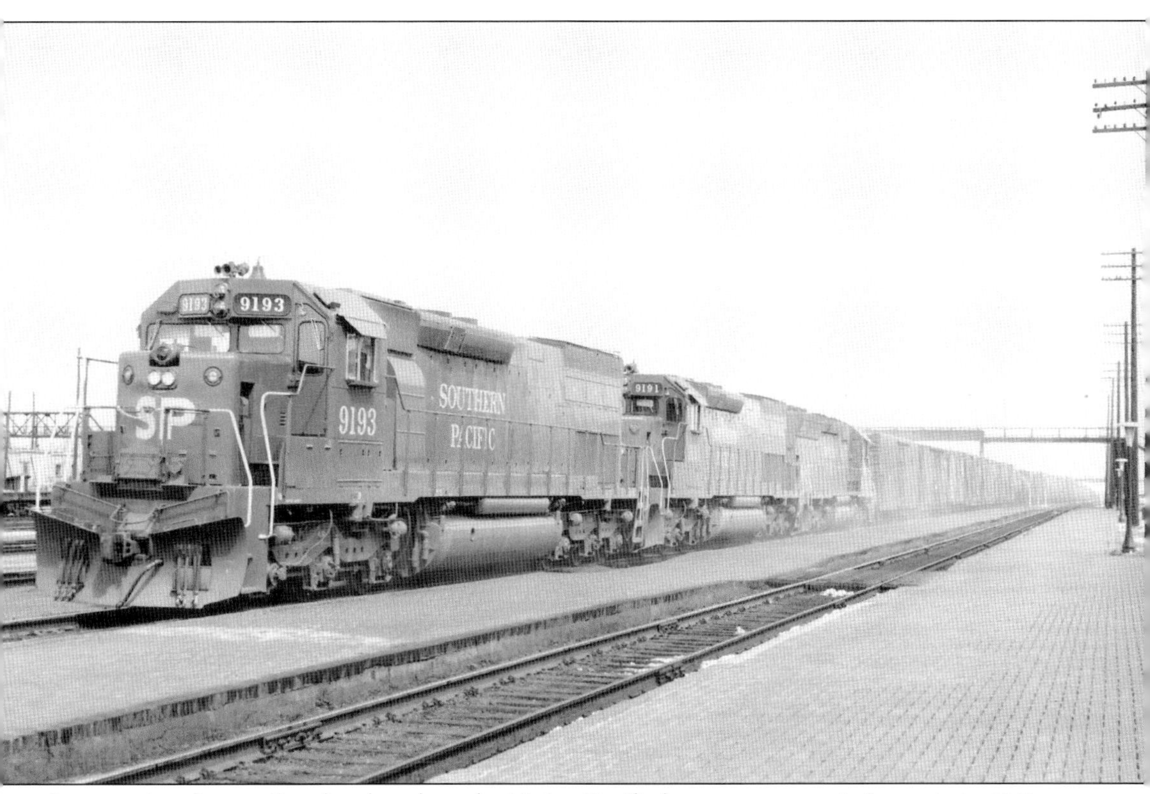

Locomotives from railroads other than the Union Pacific began to appear in Laramie in 1961, when Chicago, Burlington & Quincy units were "pooled" with UP power. These run-through, or pool, arrangements were implemented to reduce terminal layover time. Here, a solid three-unit Southern Pacific set takes an eastbound train past the Laramie depot on April 15, 1972. (Photograph by A.J. Wolff; AJWC.)

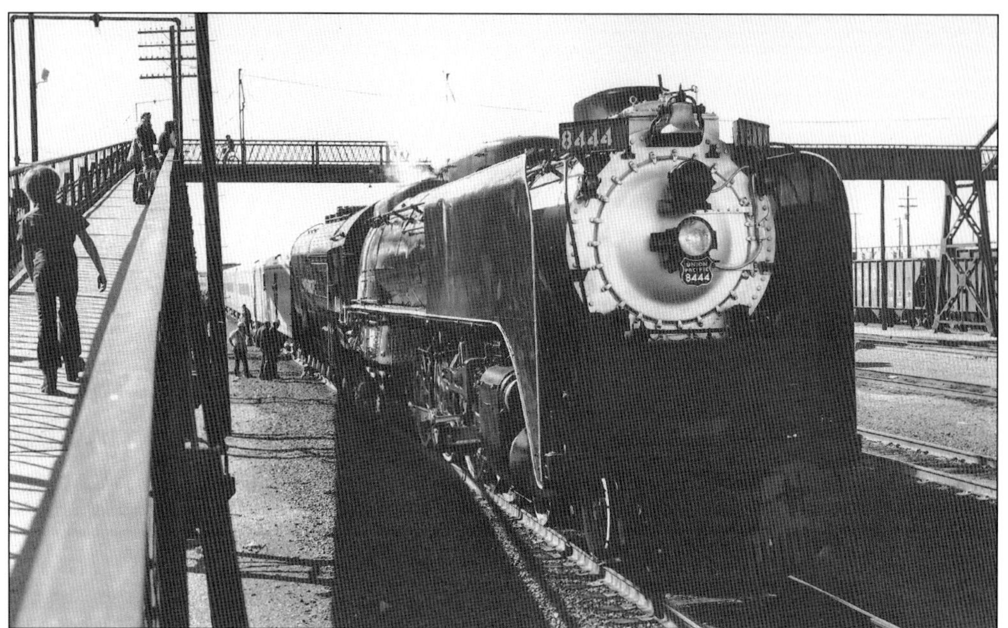

Occasionally, passengers of the *Treagle Train* had a double treat. The No. 8444 would sometimes be coupled at the front of the *Treagle*, as here on September 29, 1979. Originally numbered 844, it was redesignated 8444 for several years because of a numbering conflict with another locomotive. That engine has since retired, and the 844 has reclaimed its number. (Photograph by A.J. Wolff; AJWC.)

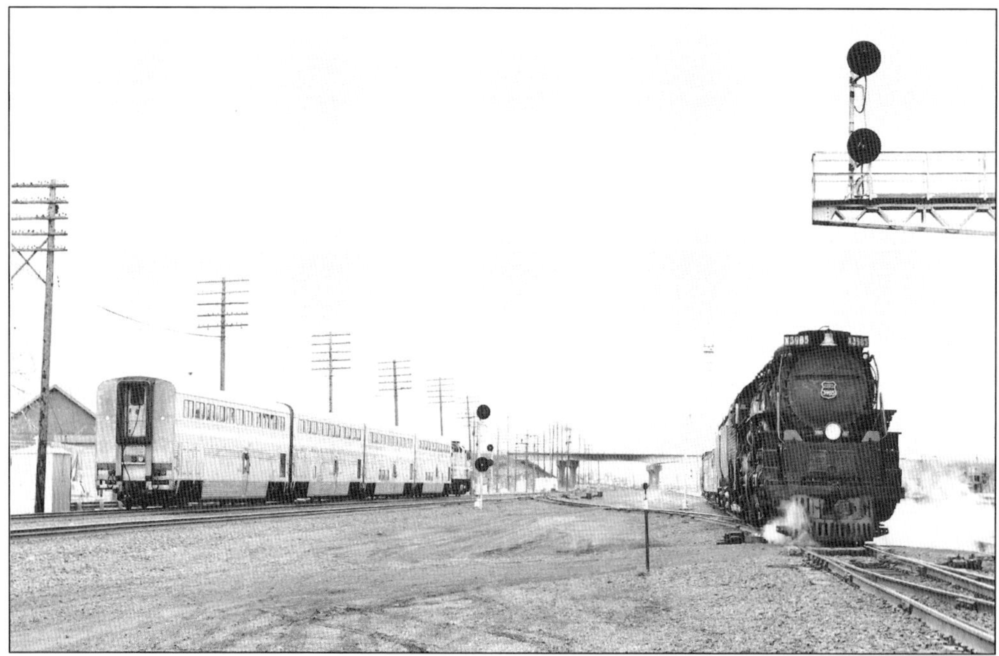

Amtrak train No. 26, the eastbound *Pioneer* (left), leaves Laramie on April 12, 1993, just as the Union Pacific No. 3985 rolls into town. The Challenger was making a "break-in" run between Cheyenne and Laramie for the purpose of checking performance prior to its scheduled 1993 trips. (Photograph by A.J. Wolff; AJWC.)

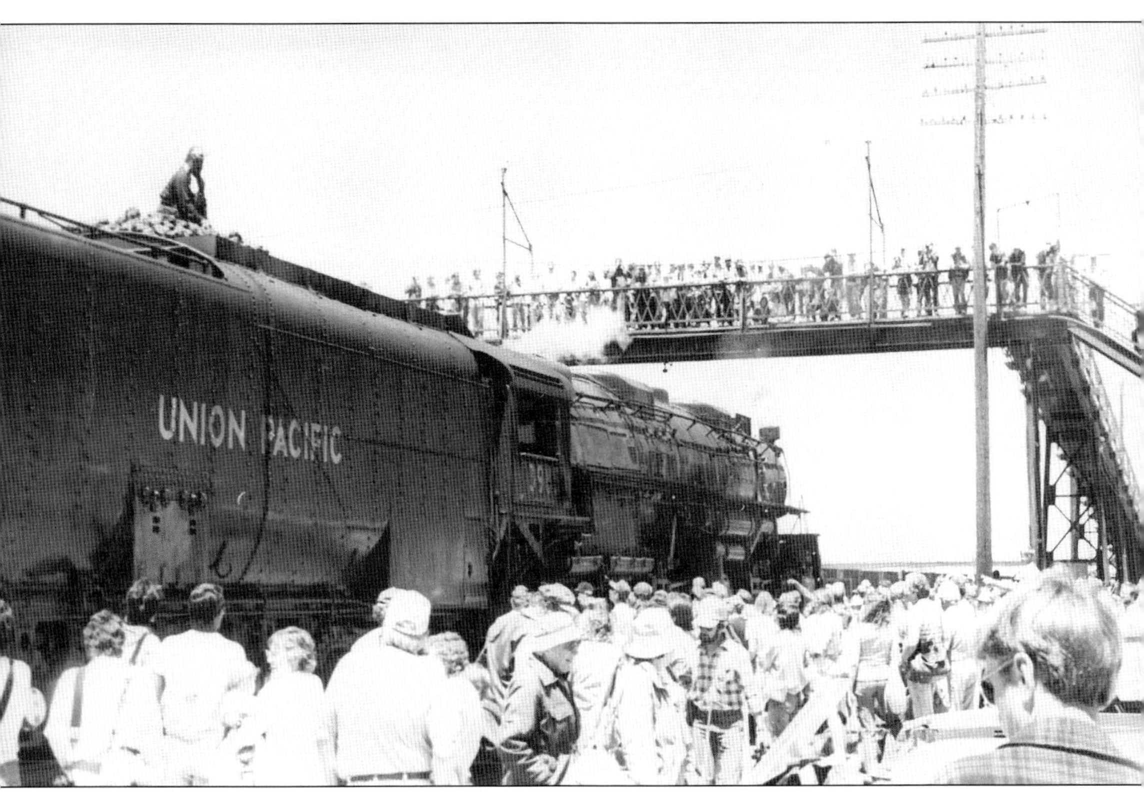

The Union Pacific Railroad never retired the 844 steam locomotive. As the years went on, its survival in continual service began to attract more and more of a following among railfans. Perhaps owing to this, a group of dedicated Union Pacific employees began refurbishing the 3985. This photograph shows the jubilant public response of its return to service on June 16, 1982. (Laramie Plains Museum.)

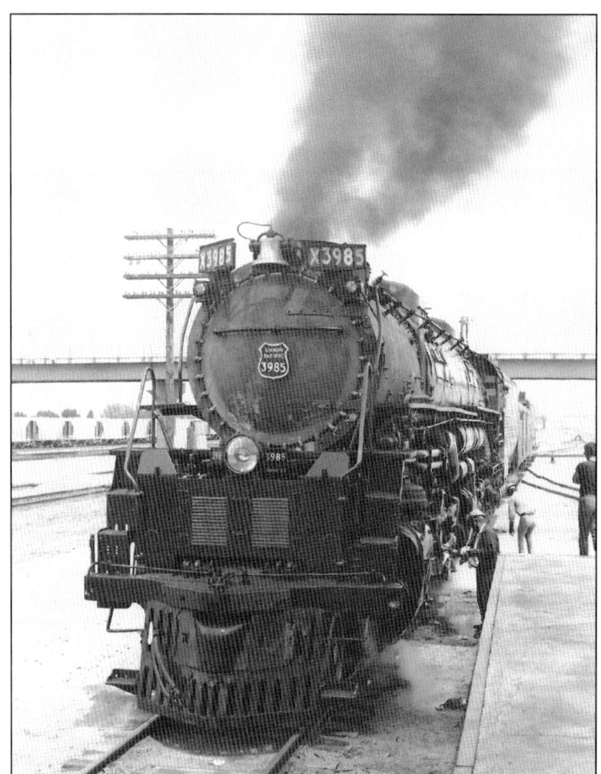

The No. 3985 is a 4-6-6-4 locomotive, which means that it has four leading wheels, followed by two sets of six driving wheels, and four wheels at the rear to support the firebox. When the Challenger last ran, it was the largest operating steam locomotive in the world. It is shown here on July 9, 1982, next to the Laramie yard office for display during UP Family Days. (Photograph by A.J. Wolff; AJWC.)

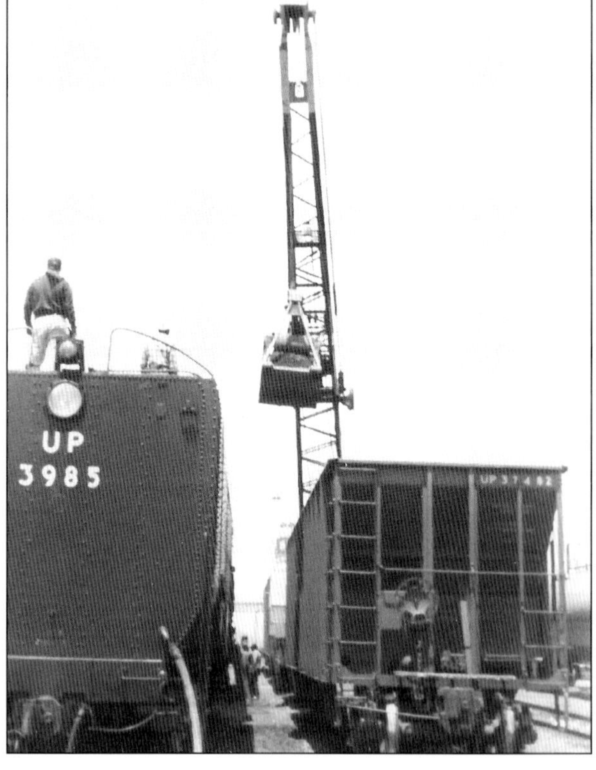

A clamshell bucket loads coal from a hopper into No. 3985's waiting tender in this 1980s photograph. When the engine was restored to service in April 1981, it was a coal burner, and it remained so until July 1990, when it was converted to oil. (JHC.)

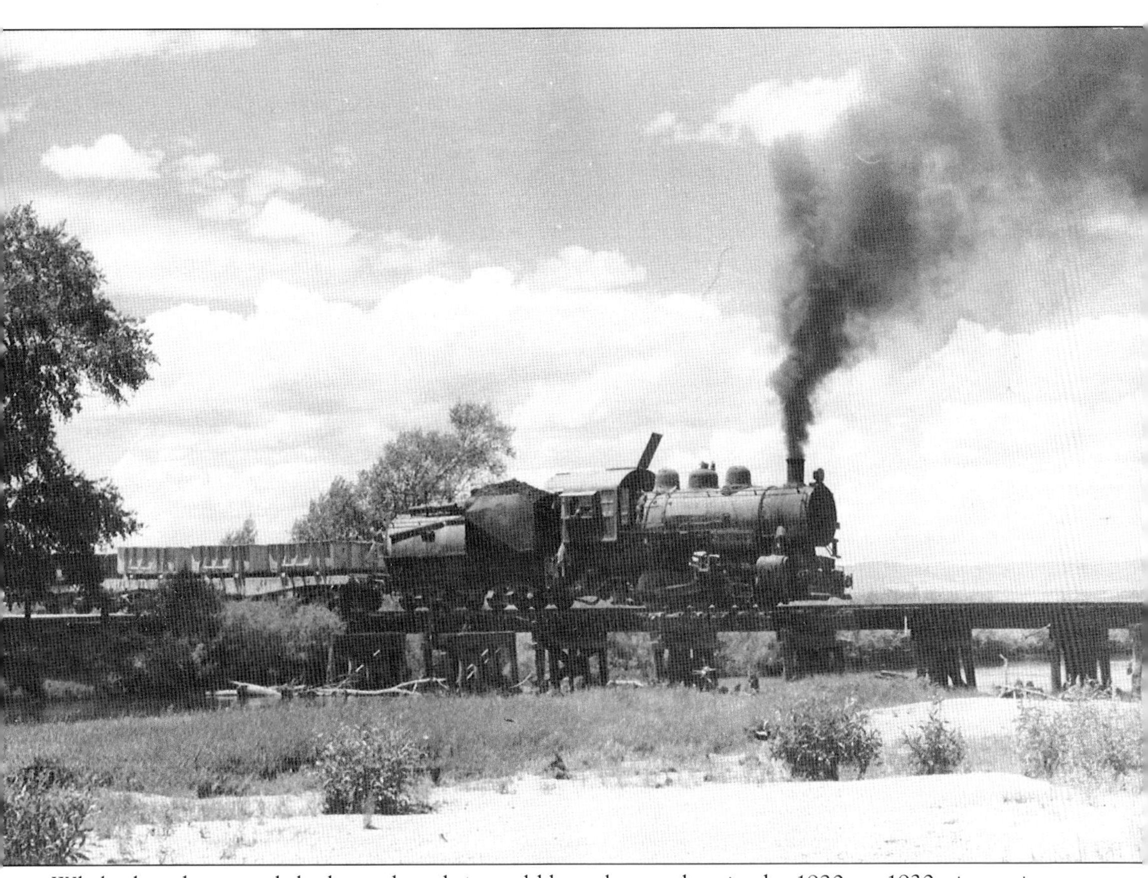

While this photograph looks as though it could have been taken in the 1920s or 1930s, it was in fact taken on July 11, 1970. The Laramie Valley Railway, built in 1928, went from the Monolith Portland Midwest Company cement plant, located south of Laramie, to a limestone quarry nine miles southwest of the facility. (Robert Gonzales Collection, Historic Laramie Railroad Depot.)

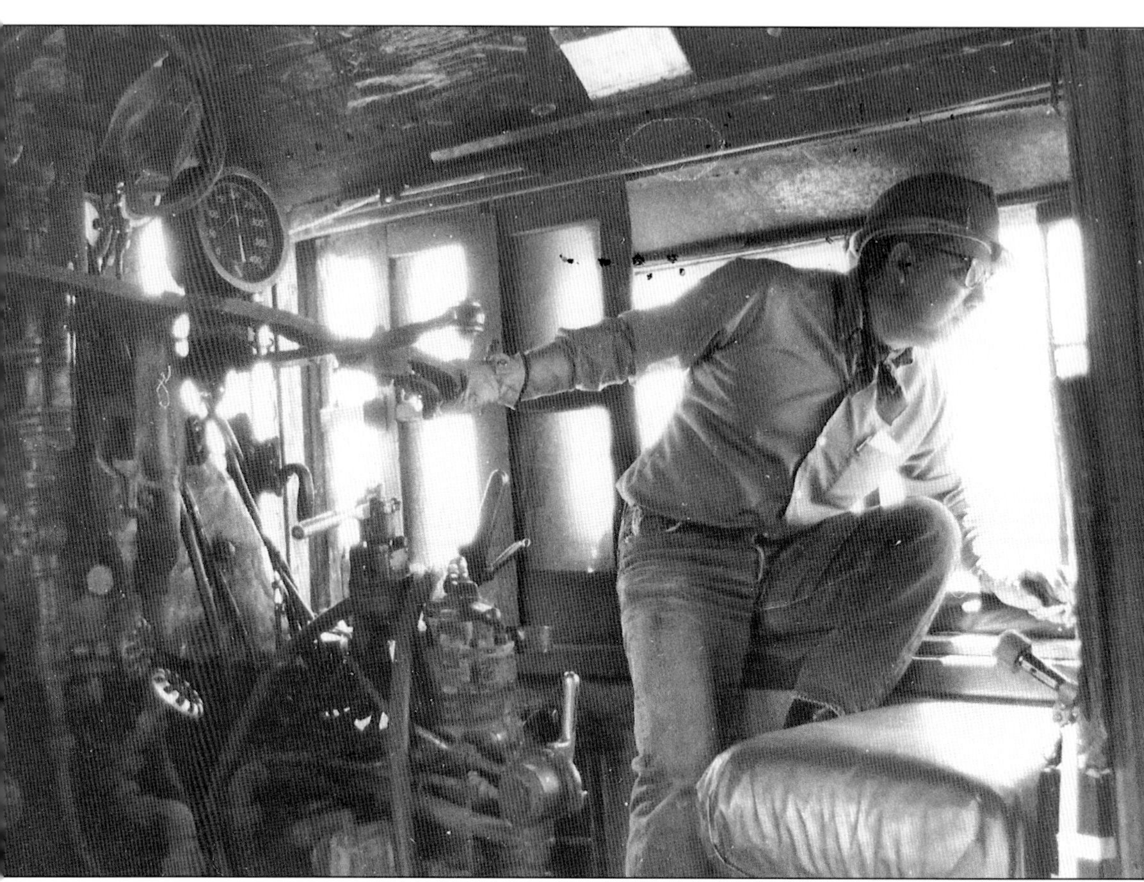

The Laramie Valley Railway maintained steam power for its small railroad line until 1970. It was one of the last railroads in the United States to sport non-tourist-related steam engines. Here, engineer Levi E. Gonzales is at the controls of LVRY engine No. 4455 in September 1970. (Robert Gonzales Collection, Historic Laramie Railroad Depot.)

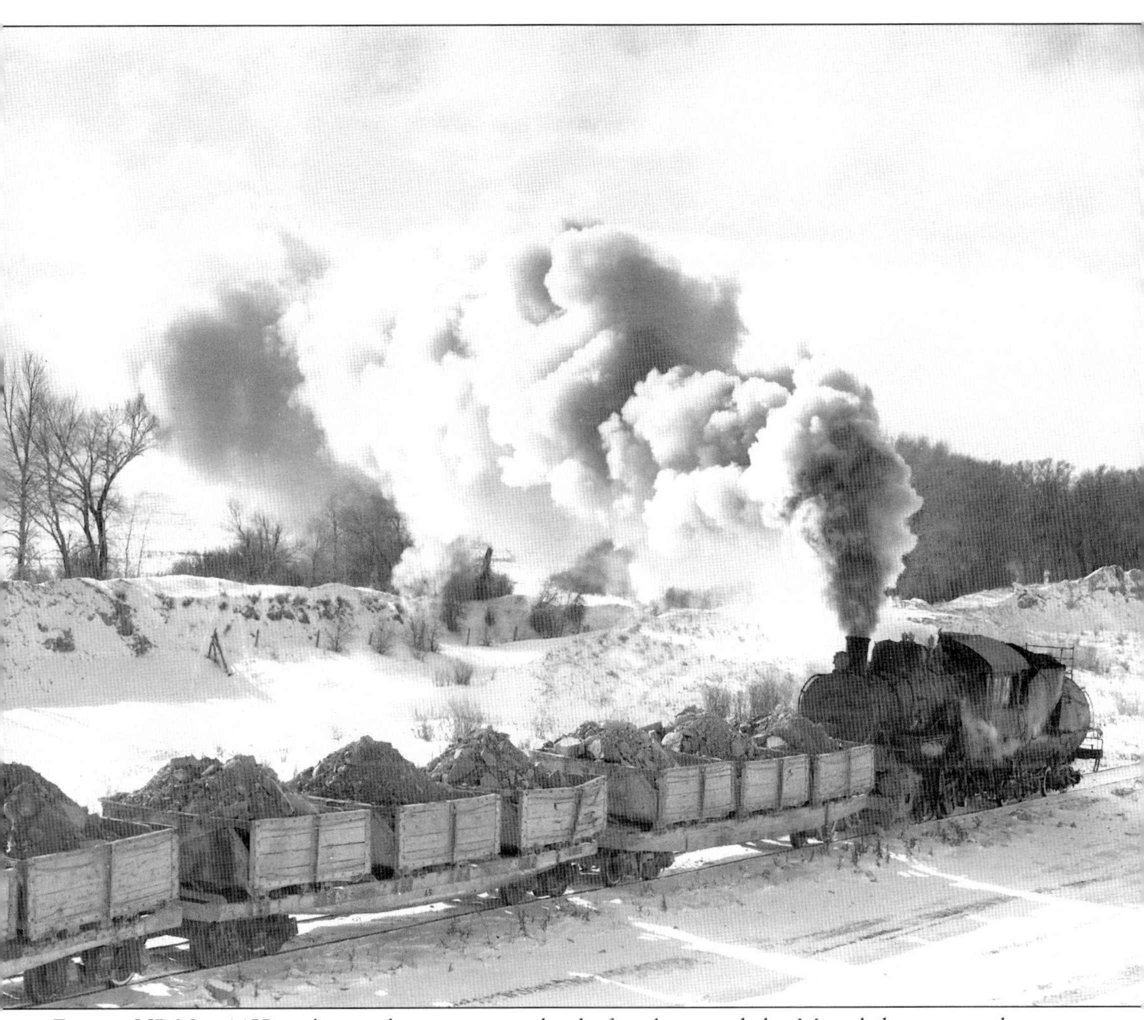

Former UP No. 4455 is shown shoving a trainload of rock toward the Monolith cement plant on December 28, 1967. The 0-6-0 locomotive was built by the Lima Locomotive Works in 1920 and was purchased by the LVRY in January 1949. The Laramie Valley line had another Lima-built 0-6-0 on the roster, former UP No. 4453, which arrived on the property in October 1955. (Photograph by James L. Ehernberger; JLEC.)

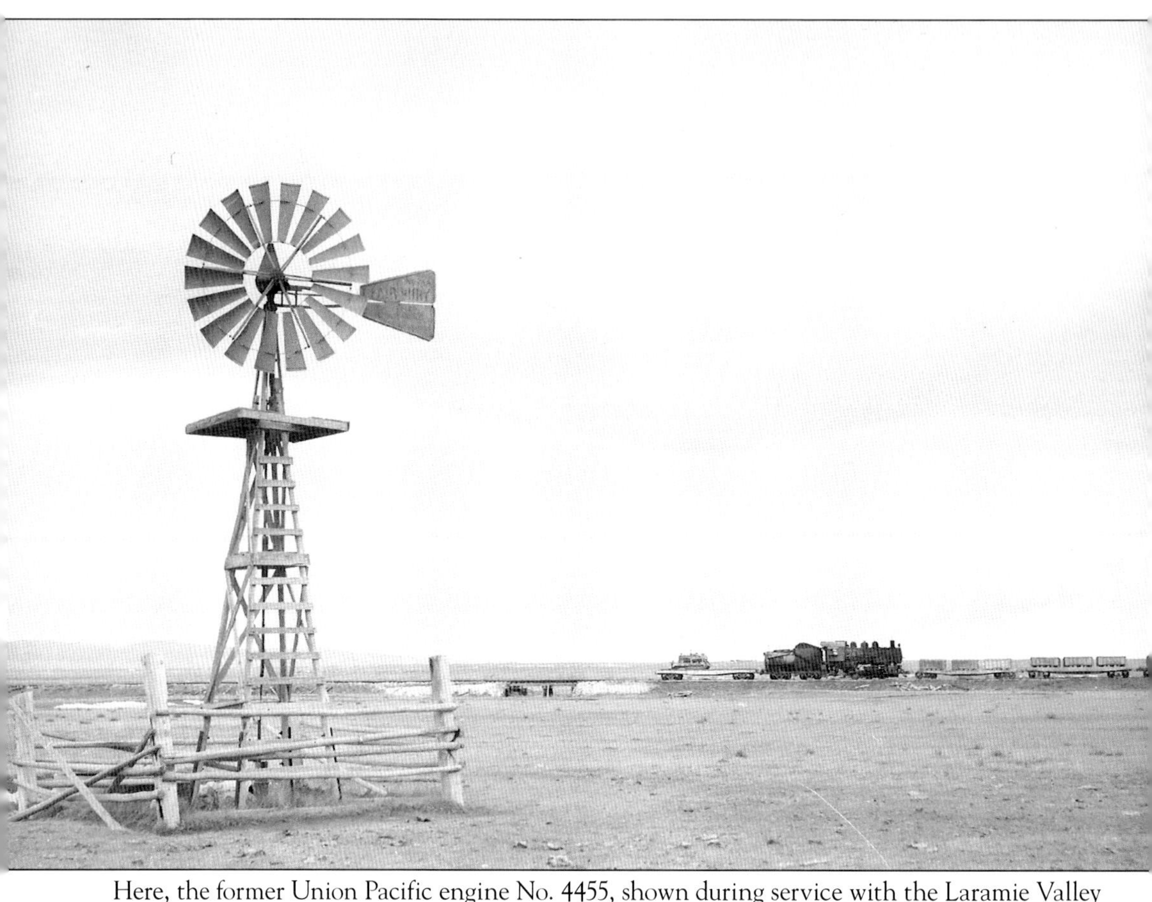

Here, the former Union Pacific engine No. 4455, shown during service with the Laramie Valley Railway, pulls empty rock cars toward the limestone quarry for loading on November 14, 1966. The empty cars and full load of coal in the engine help identify this as an outgoing, not an incoming, train. (Photograph by James L. Ehernberger; JLEC.)

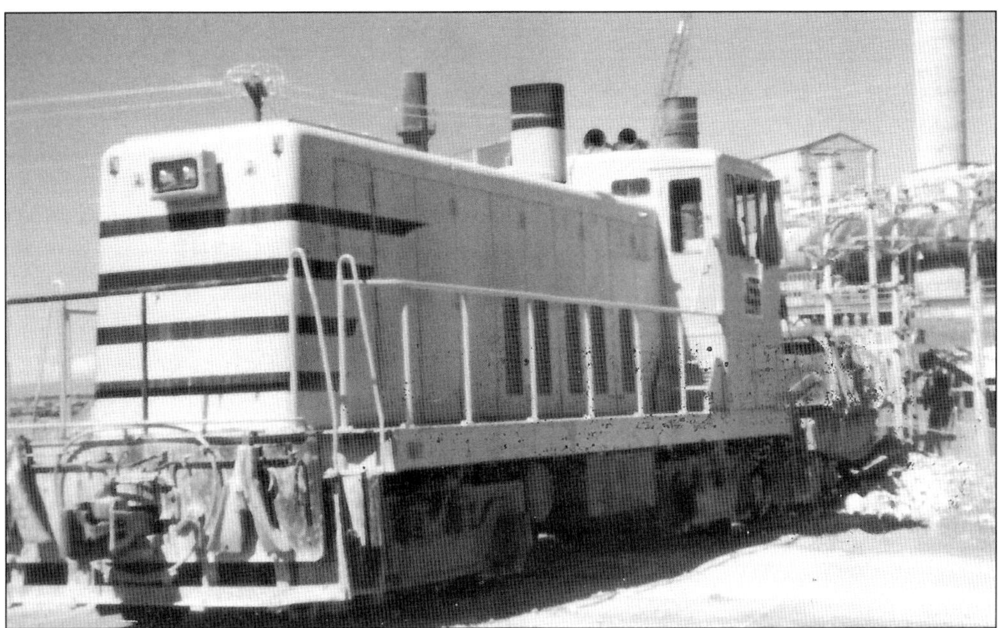

This Laramie Valley Railway 70-ton diesel switcher, built by General Electric, works the yards at the Monolith cement plant just outside Laramie on June 3, 1973. Production of these engines stopped in 1955. The plant, now Mountain Cement, has always sported vintage equipment. As of 2013, it still operated a GP-9 and a highly modified GP-10. (Photograph by Jerry Hansen; JHC.)

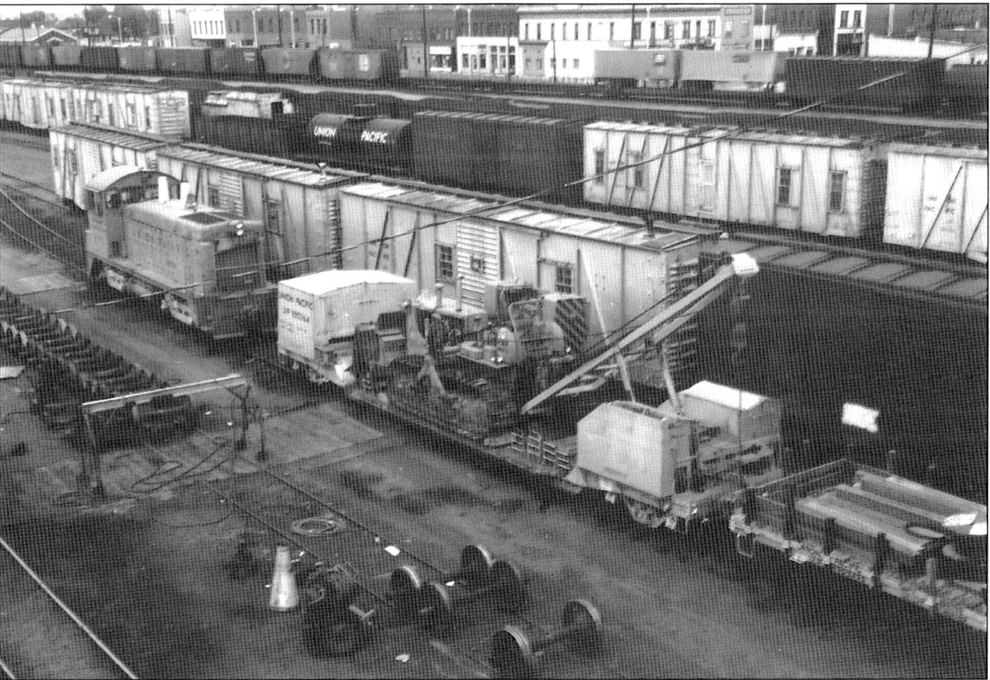

The railroad cars with windows are bunk cars, typically used to house track workers repairing the lines in places were lodging was hard to find. They were essentially a motel on wheels. A bunk car similar to those shown here is part of the snow train in Railroad Heritage Park, south of the Laramie depot. This photograph was taken about 1970. (Photograph by Keith Woolf; JHC.)

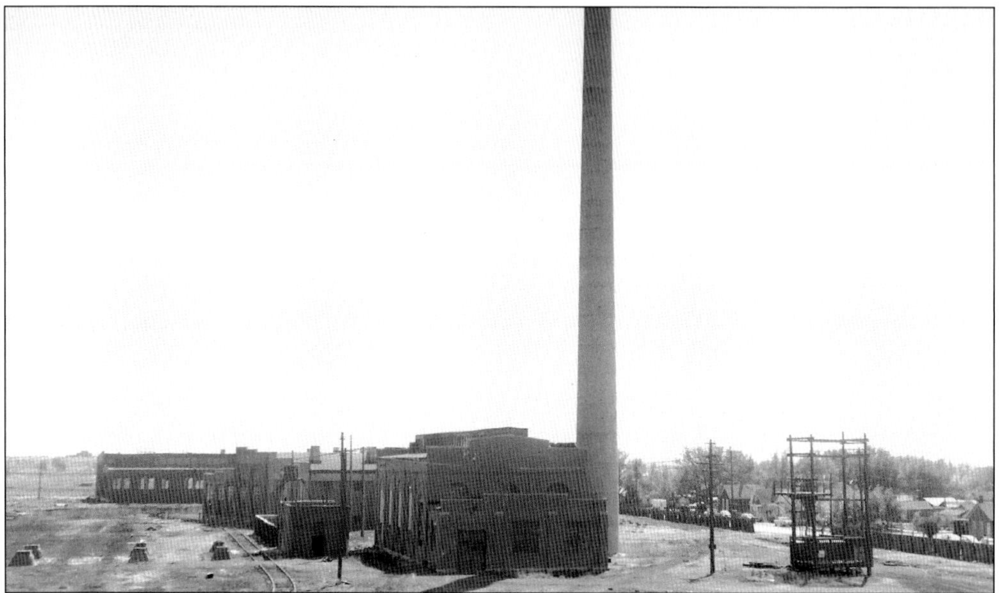

This photograph, taken in August 1964, is one of the last showing the Laramie roundhouse and power plant before they were destroyed. These two buildings had been fixtures of the local economy, but by the 1960s, Laramie's significance to the Union Pacific Railroad had dwindled. The University of Wyoming replaced the railroad as the primary engine of the local economy. (Photograph by A.J. Wolff; AJWC.)

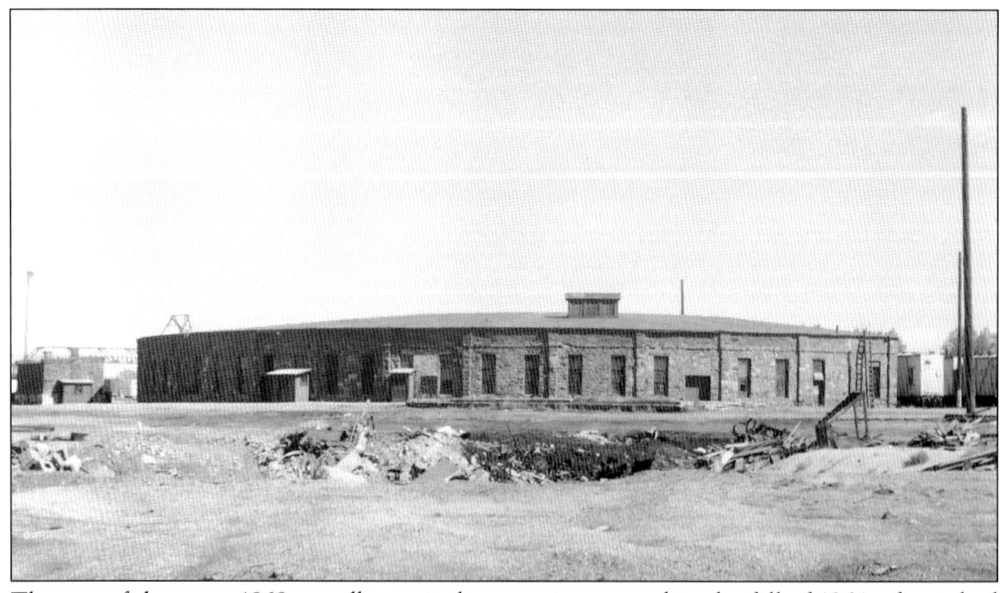

The rear of the stone 1868 roundhouse is shown as it appeared in the fall of 1964, after it had been retired. It shared a design that was common for roundhouses constructed at division points at the time of the building of the Union Pacific. This 20-stall structure lasted almost 100 years, far more than any similar roundhouse along the UP. (Photograph by A.J. Wolff; AJWC.)

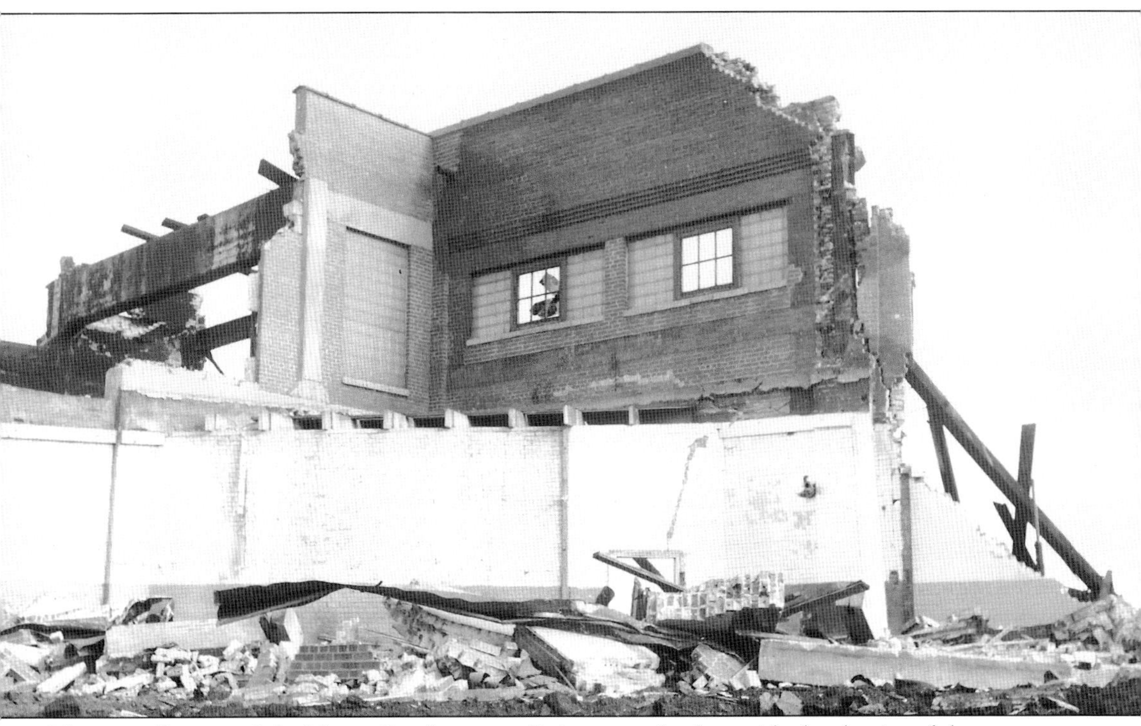

The roundhouses of the Union Pacific generally became obsolete with the demise of the steam locomotive. With the long-haul capability and low maintenance cost of the modern diesel electric locomotive, extensive repair and fueling facilities were no longer necessary at every division point. Demolition of the Laramie roundhouse is well under way in this December 9, 1965, photograph. (Photograph by A.J. Wolff; AJWC.)

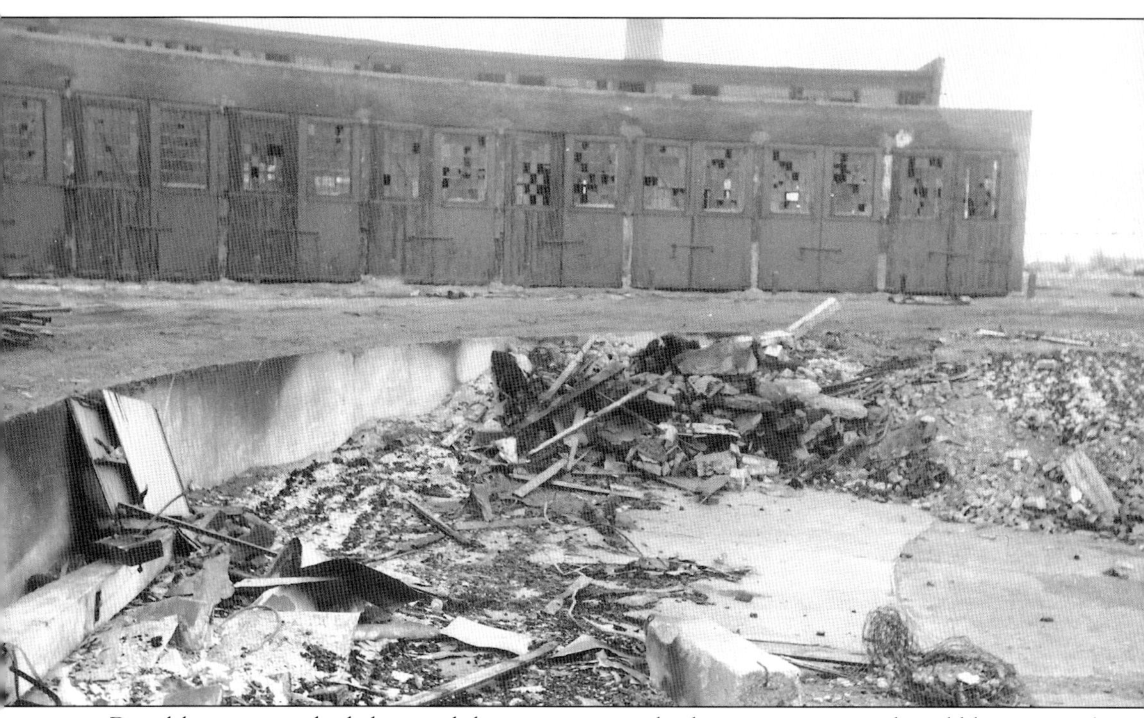

Diesel locomotives had the capability to run in multiple-unit consists and could be operated from either end, depending on the orientation of the trailing unit. This generally negated the need for turntables. In this c. 1965 photograph, the turntable pit at the Laramie roundhouse is being filled with the rubble of demolished structures from the engine yard. (Photograph by A.J. Wolff; AJWC.)

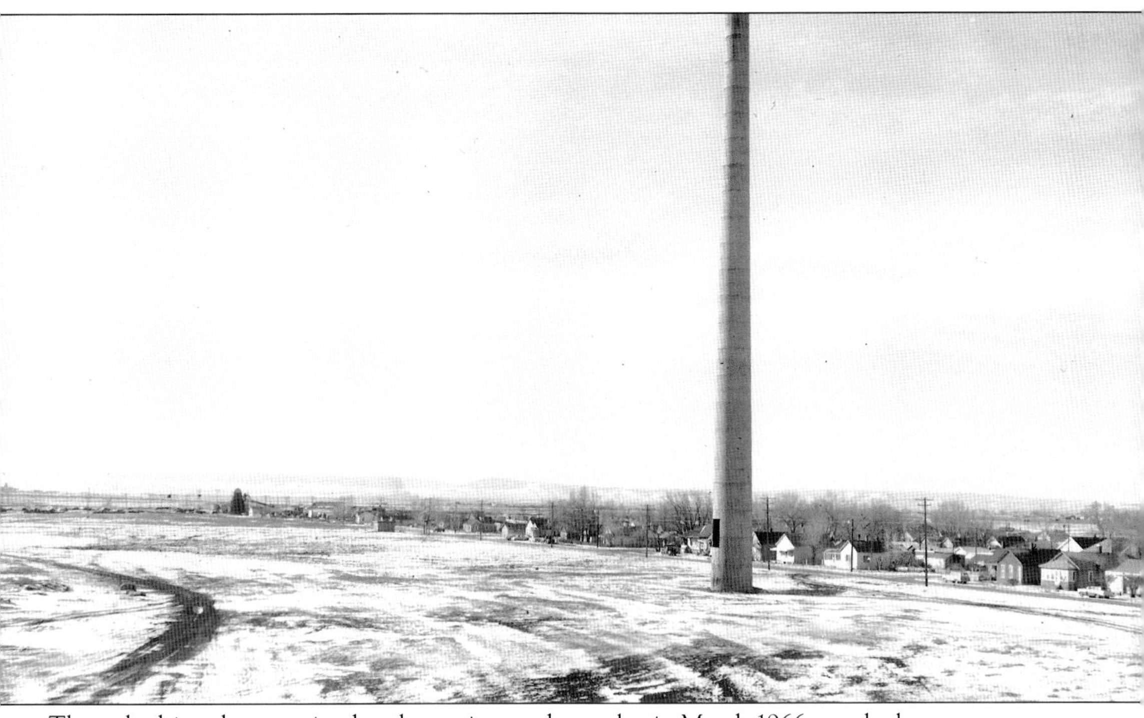

The only thing that remained at the engine-yard complex in March 1966 was the large concrete smokestack, still prominent on the Laramie skyline. Stacks like these were often safer to leave standing than to demolish, due to potential infrastructure damage to water and sewer lines. (Photograph by A.J. Wolff; AJWC.)

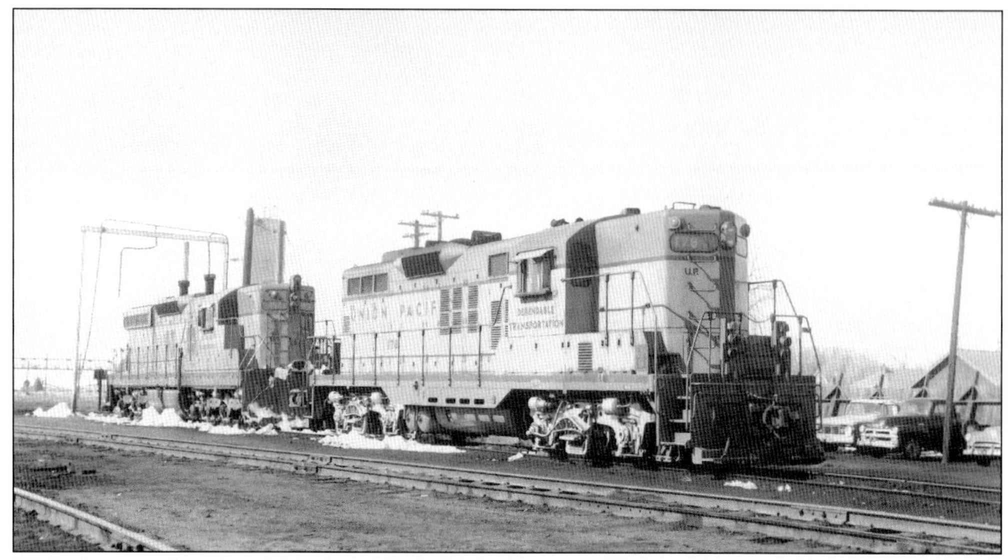

With the introduction of diesel switchers in the Laramie yard, UP built a small two-track service facility near the site of the old University Avenue Bridge in December 1948. It had provisions to fuel and sand units. Here, SD7 457 rests under the sanding stanchion on April 20, 1968. (Photograph by A.J. Wolff; AJWC.)

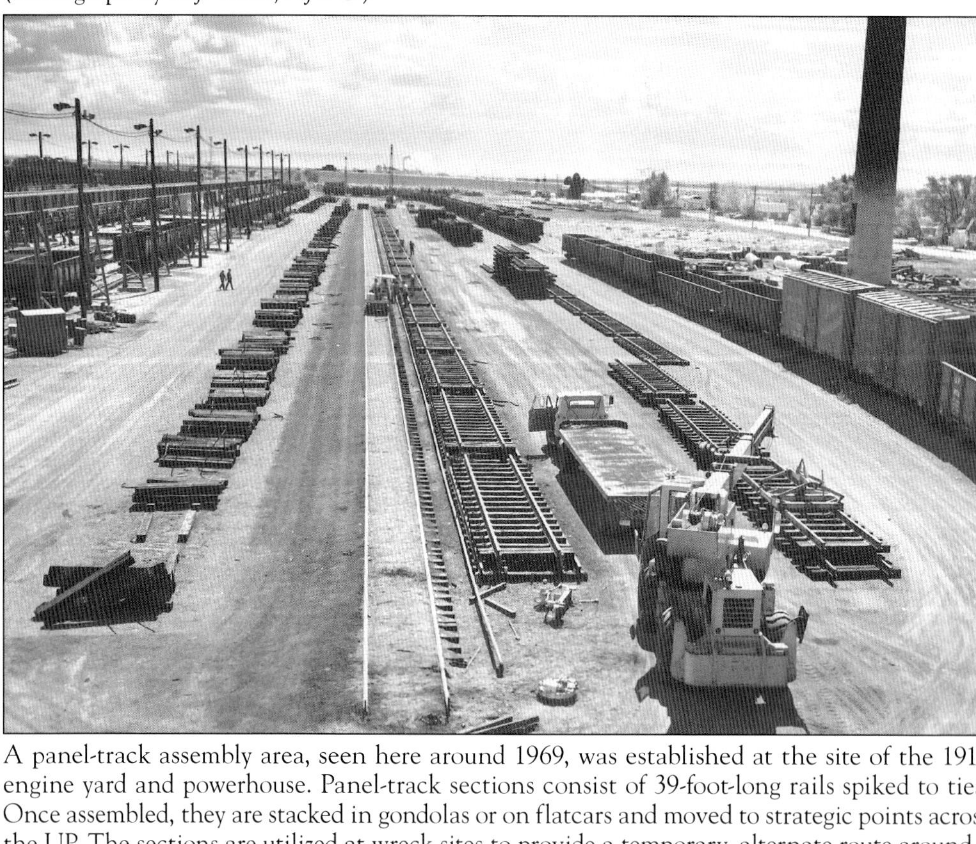

A panel-track assembly area, seen here around 1969, was established at the site of the 1911 engine yard and powerhouse. Panel-track sections consist of 39-foot-long rails spiked to ties. Once assembled, they are stacked in gondolas or on flatcars and moved to strategic points across the UP. The sections are utilized at wreck sites to provide a temporary, alternate route around a pileup. (Photograph by Union Pacific; JLEC.)

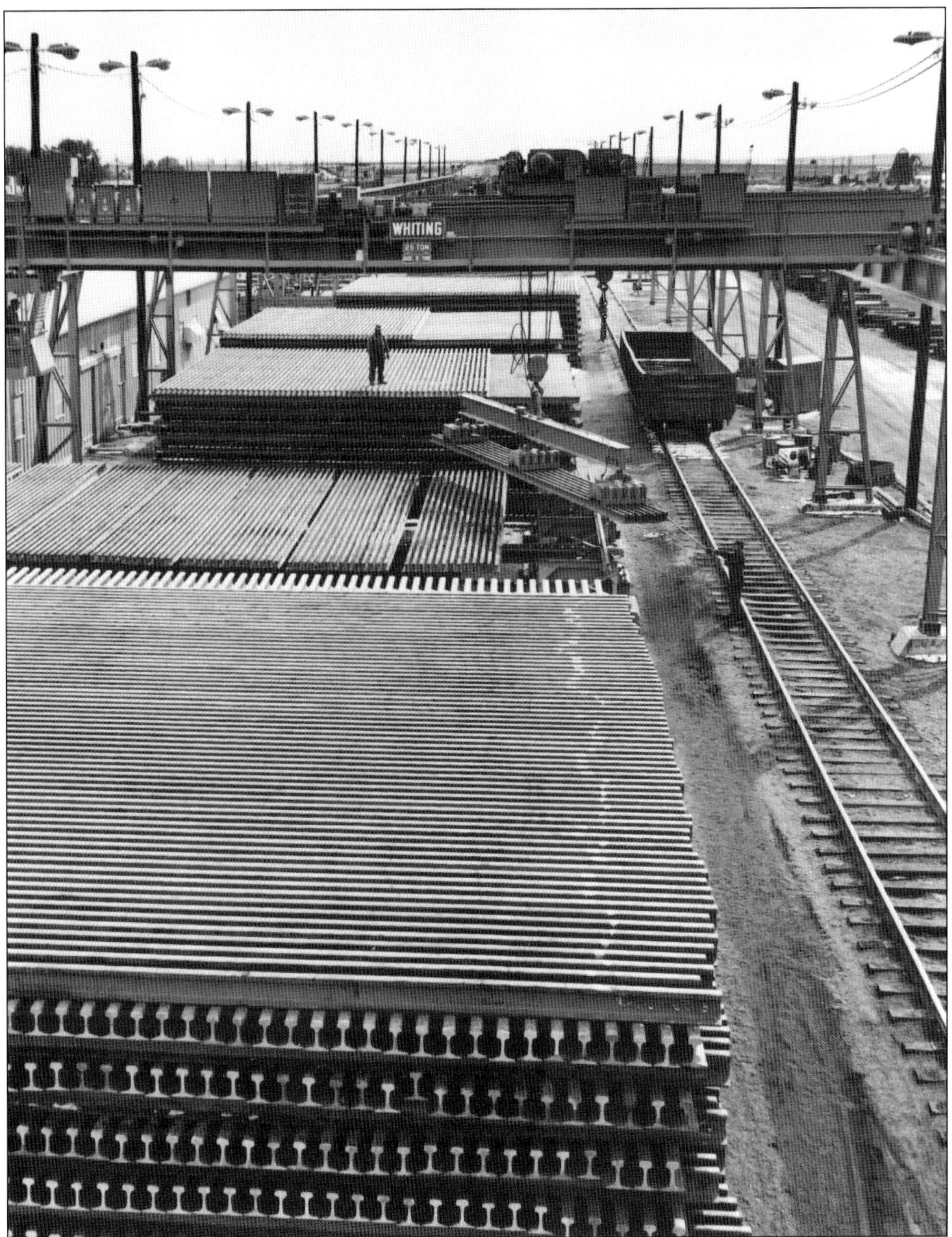

A continuous welded rail plant was operational by 1970, around the time this photograph was taken. It was built where the 1868 roundhouse and shops had stood. Rail welding allowed railroads to eliminate bolted rail joints. The plant welds rails into quarter mile lengths and loads them into specialized cars for transport and unloading. Once in place, mobile welding units finish the job by joining the sections of rail together. (Photograph by Union Pacific; JLEC.)

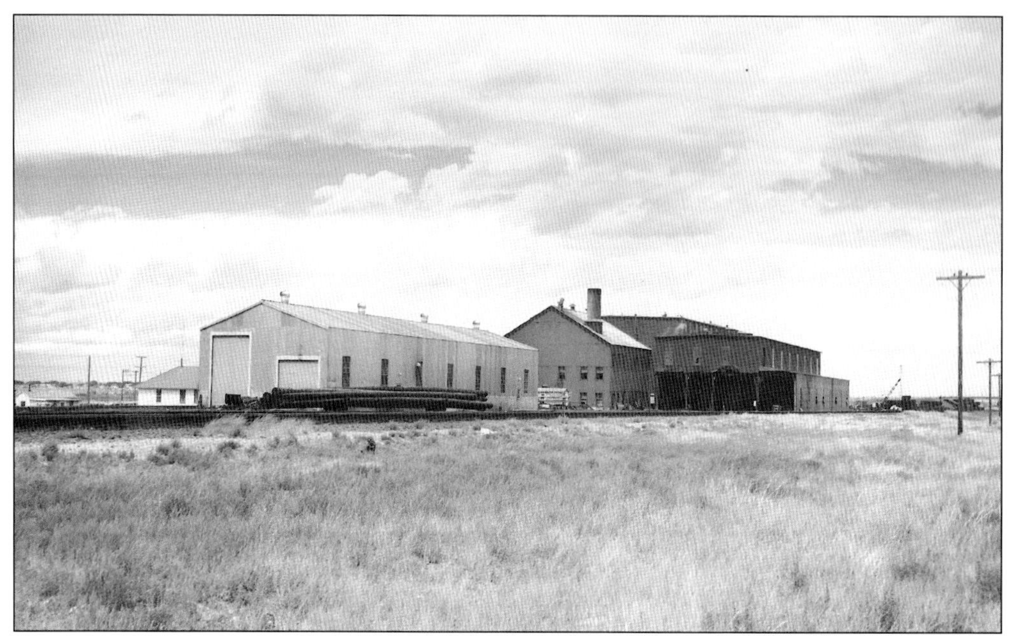

The Union Pacific established a tie-treating plant just southwest of Laramie in 1886 and operated the facility on an intermittent basis until May 1983. The purpose of the facility, seen here about 1957, was to preserve precut ties and other wood products subject to harsh outdoor conditions with creosote injected under pressure and heat. The facility was demolished in 1984. (Photograph by Union Pacific; JLEC.)

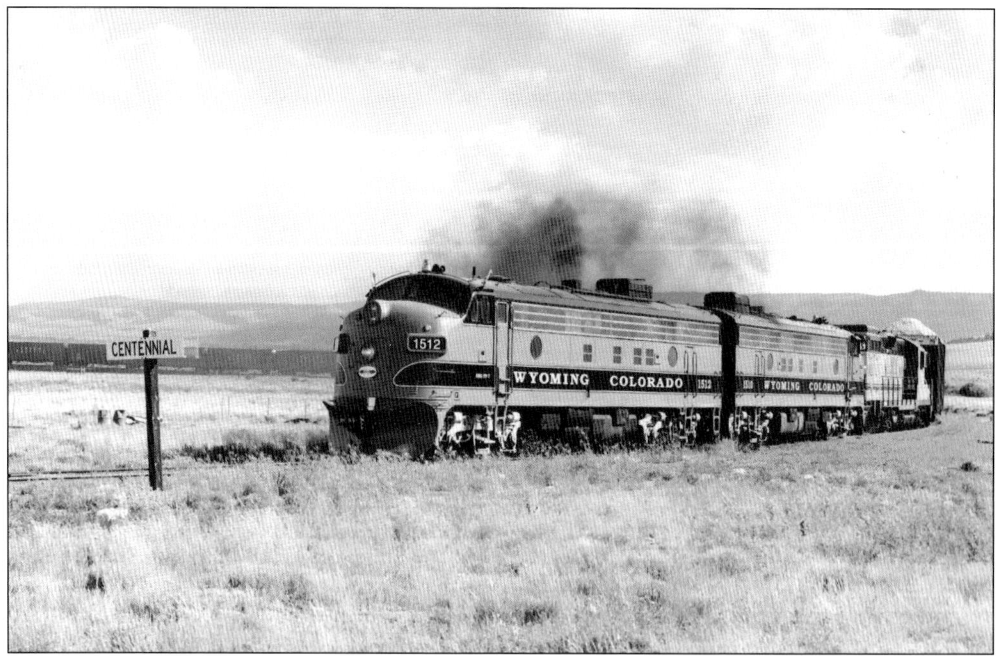

The last railroad to operate on the Coalmont branch through the Medicine Bow Mountains was the Wyoming/Colorado Railroad (WyCo). The final run (seen here), from Walden, Colorado, with a load of wood chips, was made on July 6, 1994. The railroad utilized former Alaska RR FP7 diesel locomotives that were painted a deep red. (Photograph by James L. Ehernberger; JLEC.)

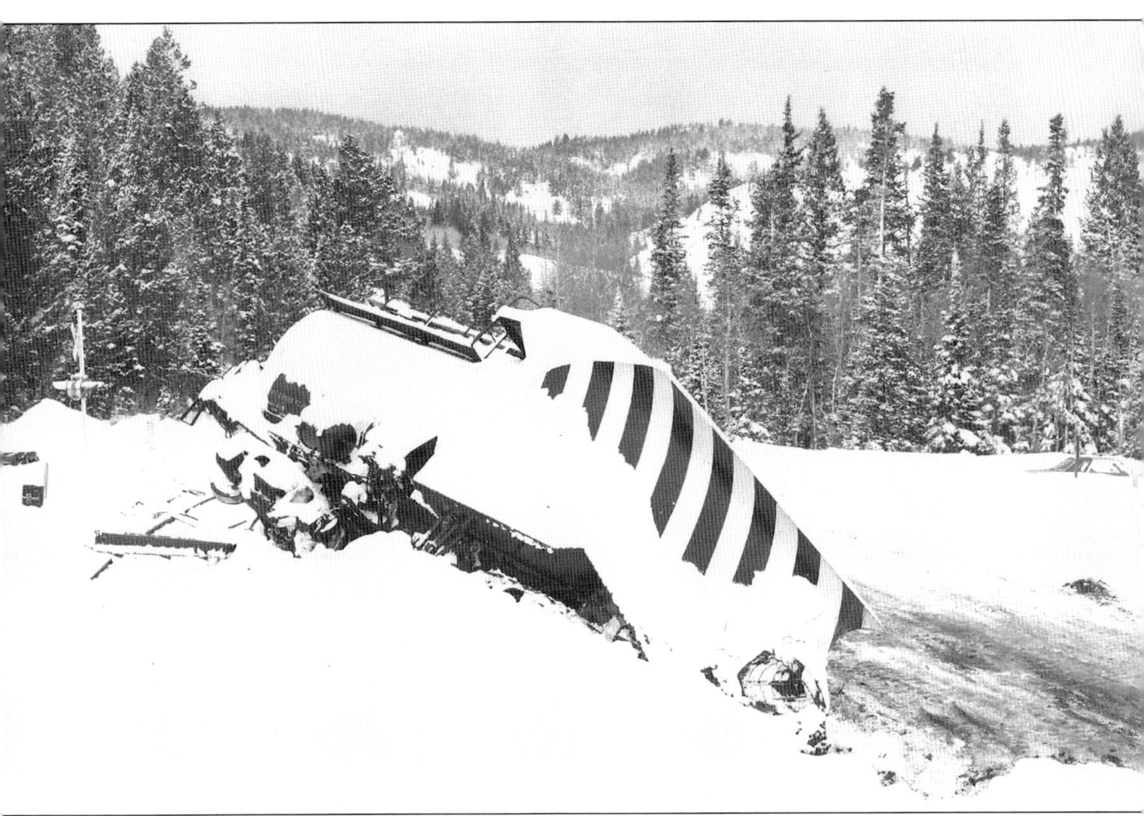

Wedge plows like this one were much preferred over the rotary plows, due to their lower maintenance costs. They were not indestructible, though. The one shown here was being used near Woods Landing in January 1979 when this accident occurred. It was never used again. It is now at the head of the snow train on display at the Laramie Historic Depot. (JLEC.)

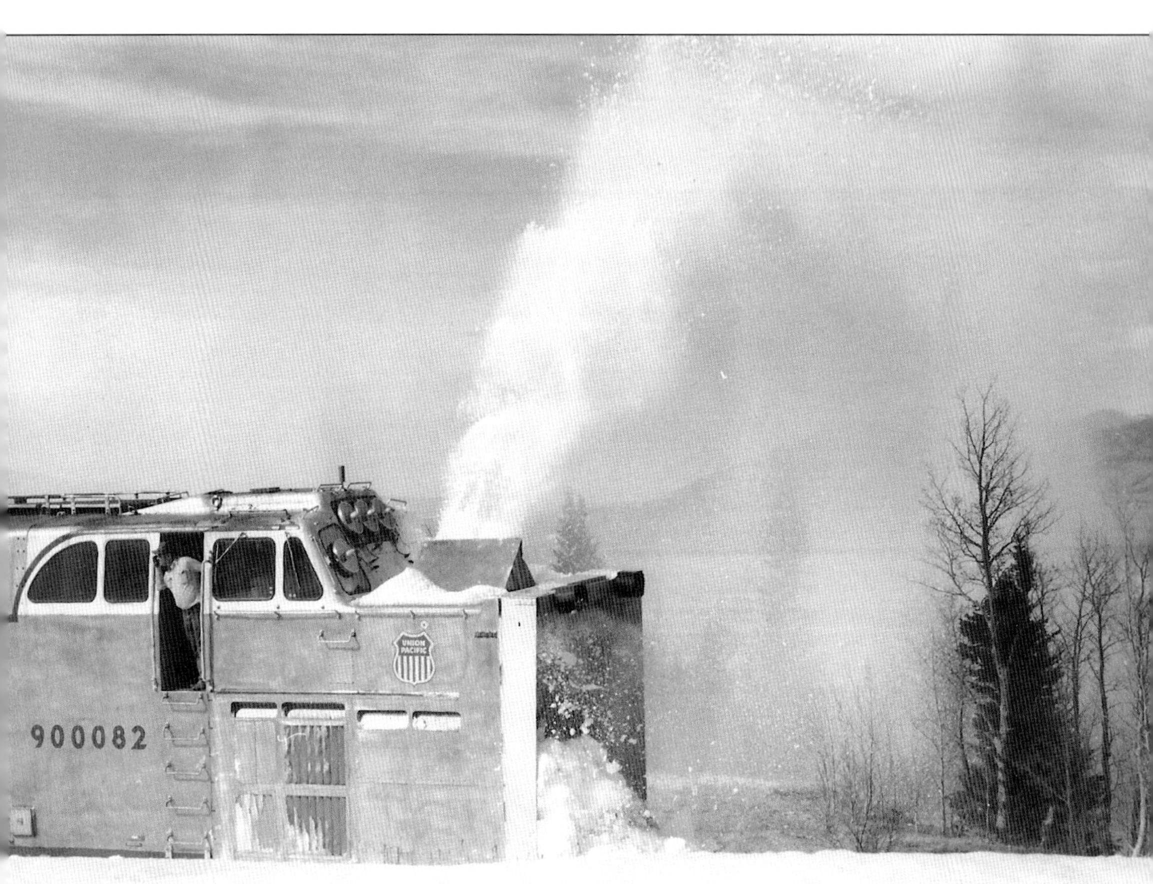

The Union Pacific's rotary plow No. 82 is seen working its way up the Coalmont branch. This May 1996 photograph was taken between Albany, Wyoming, and Lake Owen. With what appears to be only a few feet of snow, this would have been an easy day for a plow that was capable of extricating engines from the 1917 and 1949 blizzards. (Photograph by Tom Klinger; JHC.)

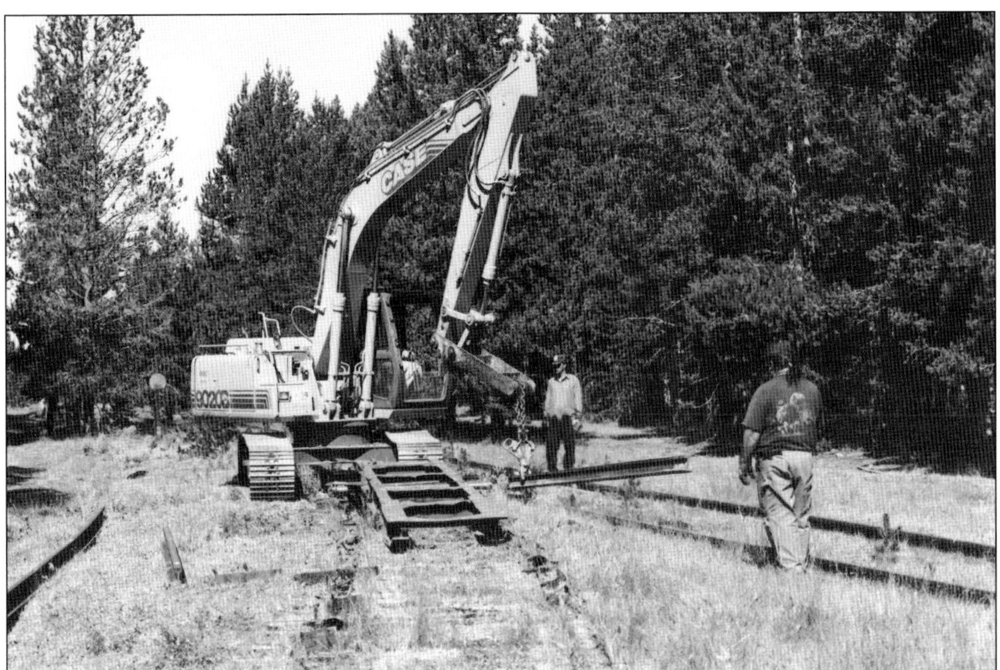

In 1999, the track along the Coalmont branch, the line that tackled the Snowy Mountains head-on, was finally dismantled and sold for scrap, as shown here on August 3, 1999. Roads that utilized the line were the Laramie, Hahns Peak & Pacific (1901–1924), the Laramie, North Park & Western (1924–1951), the Coalmont branch of the UP (1951–1987), and, finally, the Wyoming/Colorado. (Photograph by James L. Ehernberger; JLEC.)

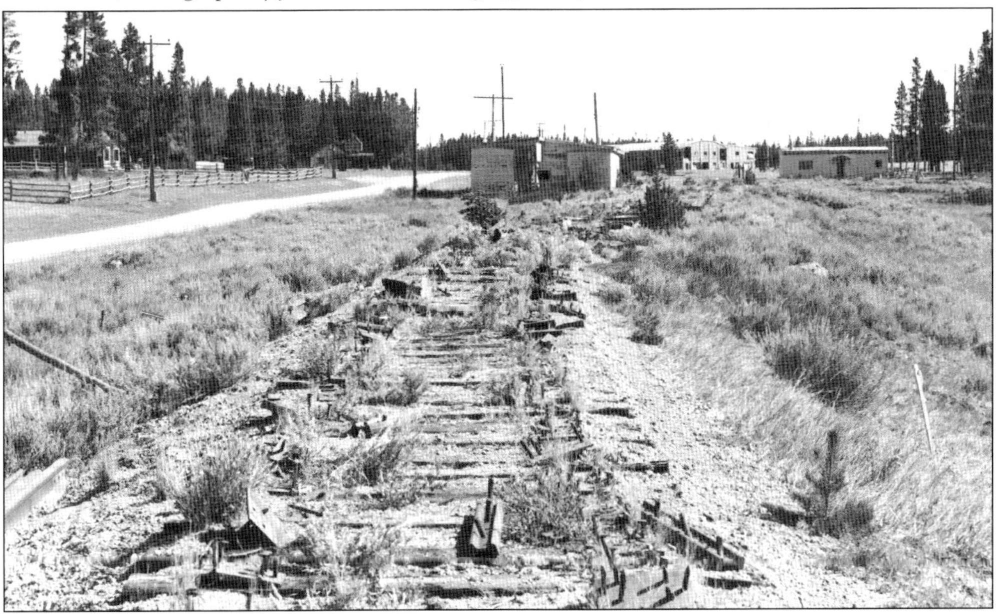

The aftermath of salvaging the line from the Coalmont branch can be seen in this August 1999 photograph, taken just outside of Foxpark, Wyoming. The rail ties and rail joints have yet to be scavenged. In later years, this section of the track was turned into a bike and hiking path through the Rails to Trails program. (Photograph by James L. Ehernberger; JLEC.)

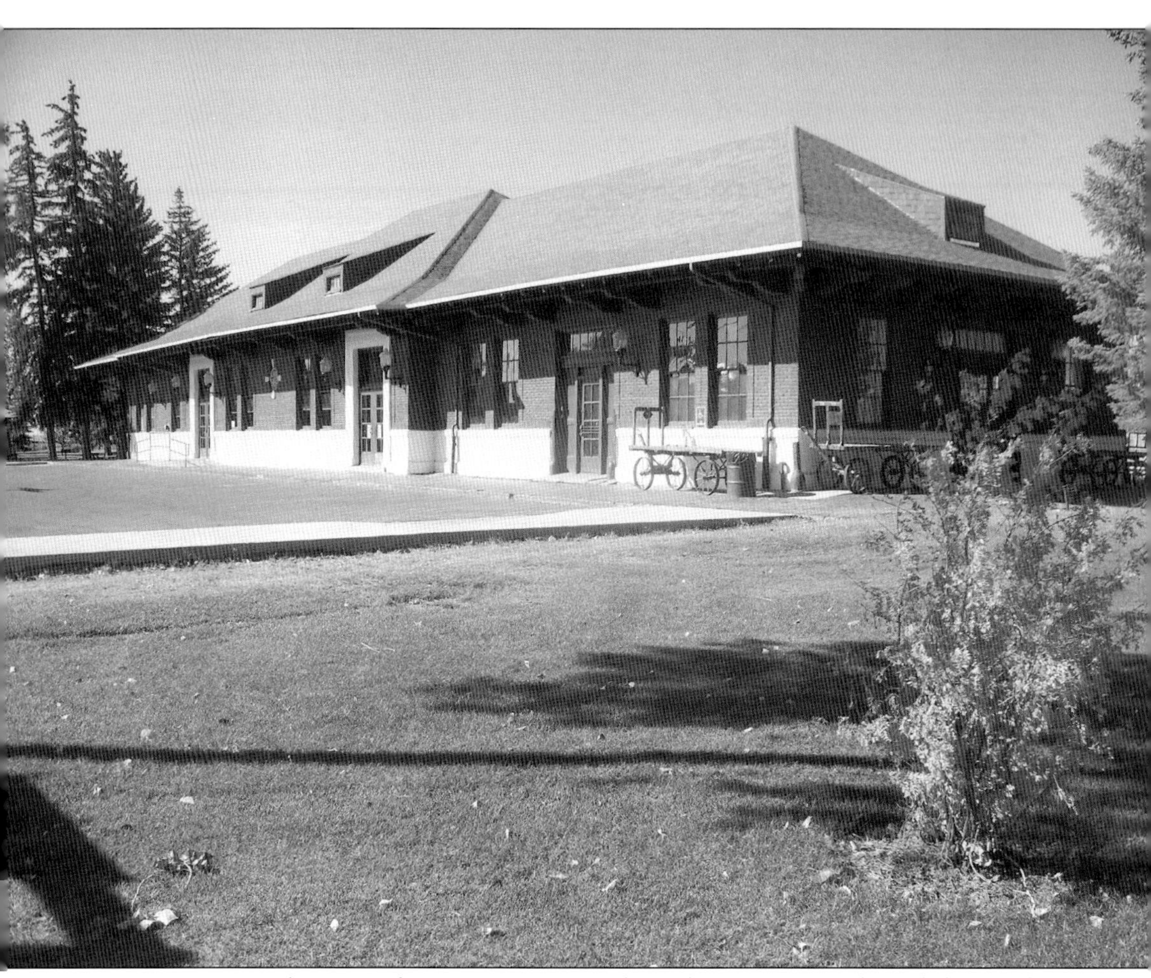

In recent years, the town of Laramie, Wyoming, has taken great steps through local volunteer work, generous donations, and grants to preserve what is left of its railroading past. The Historic Laramie Railroad Depot Association has restored the depot, seen here in 2012, and is in the process of converting the freight room into a railroad museum. (Photograph by Lawrence Ostresh Jr.; Historic Laramie Railroad Depot.)

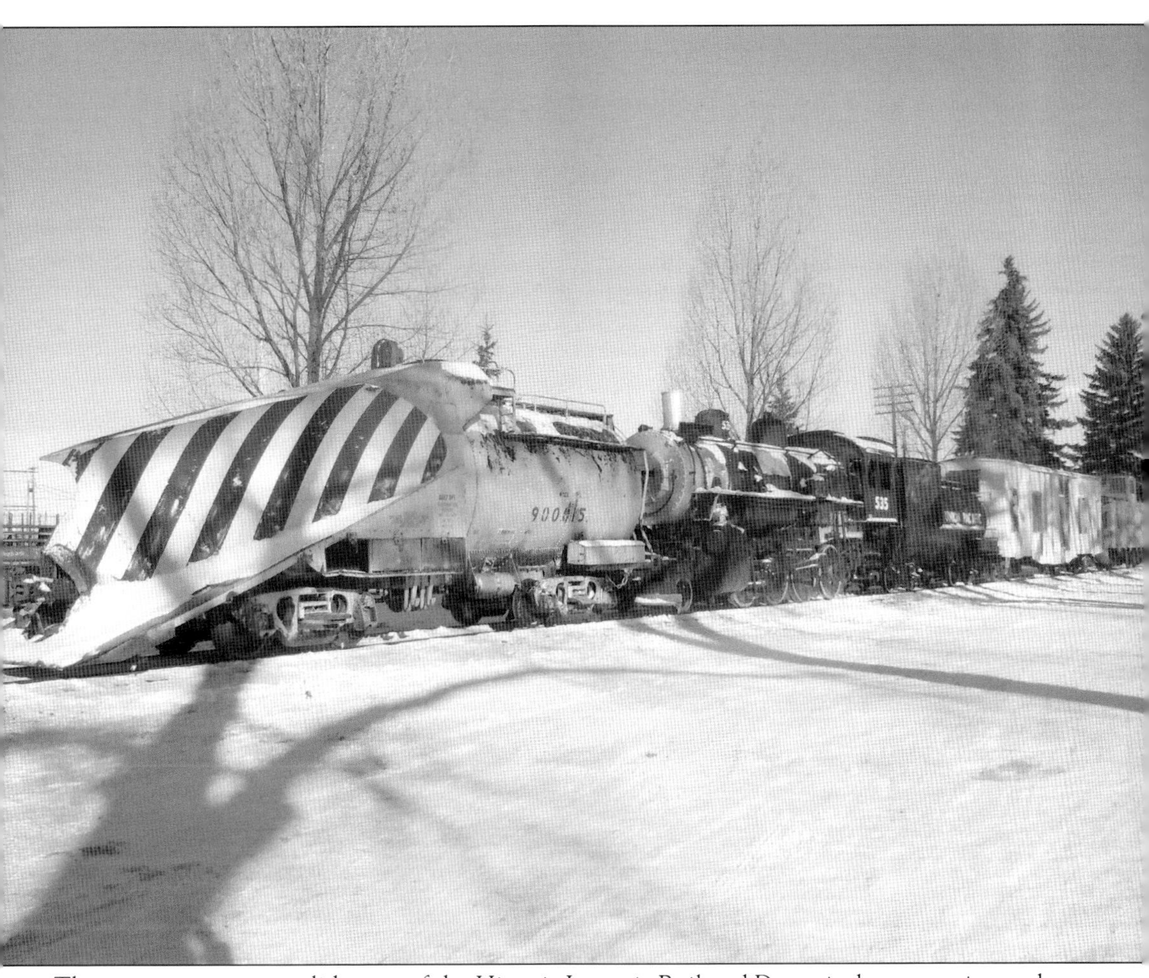

The most recent accomplishment of the Historic Laramie Railroad Depot is the restoration and display of the snow train. A train like this would have been used to clear the snow along the Coalmont branch. On display are a wedge plow, a bunk car, a caboose, and, of course, Laramie's own Engine No. 535. (Photograph by Lawrence Ostresh Jr.; Historic Laramie Railroad Depot.)